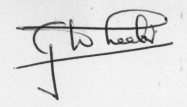

D1436676

EXCAVATIONS AT UR

By the same Author

DIGGING UP THE PAST
UR OF THE CHALDEES
MIDDLE EAST ARCHÆOLOGY
UR: THE FIRST PHASES
A FORGOTTEN KINGDOM
SPADEWORK
DEAD TOWNS AND LIVING MEN

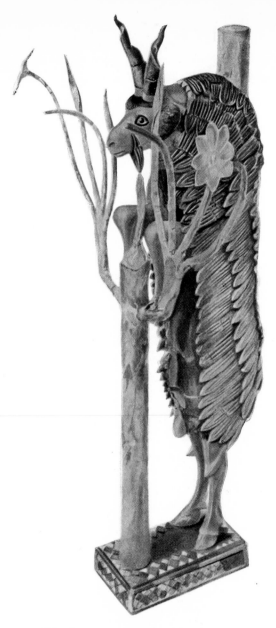

The 'ram in a thicket' from grave PG-1237

EXCAVATIONS AT UR

A Record of Twelve Years' Work by

SIR LEONARD WOOLLEY

*Director of the Joint Expedition of the British Museum
and of the University Museum of Pennsylvania
to Mesopotamia*

ERNEST BENN LIMITED
LONDON

Published by Ernest Benn Limited
Bouverie House. Fleet Street. London. EC4

First published 1954
Second impression 1955
Third (corrected) impression 1955

Printed in Great Britain

CONTENTS

5

PLATES

ILLUSTRATIONS IN TEXT

9

Introduction

U R LIES about half-way between Baghdad and the head of the Persian Gulf, some ten miles west of the present course of the Euphrates. A mile and a half to the east of the ruins runs the single line of railway which joins Basra to the capital of Iraq, and between the rail and the river there is sparse cultivation and little villages of mud huts or reed-mat shelters are dotted here and there; but westwards of the line is desert blank and unredeemed. Out of this waste rise the mounds which were Ur, called by the Arabs after the highest of them all, the Ziggurat hill, 'Tal al Muqayyar', the Mound of Pitch.

Standing on the summit of this mound one can distinguish along the eastern skyline the dark tasselled fringe of the palm-gardens on the river's bank, but to north and west and south as far as the eye can see stretches a waste of unprofitable sand. To the south-west the flat line of the horizon is broken by a grey upstanding pinnacle, the ruins of the staged tower of the sacred city of Eridu which the Sumerians believed to be the oldest city upon earth, and to the north-west a shadow thrown by the low sun may tell the whereabouts of the low mound of al 'Ubaid; but otherwise nothing relieves the monotony of the vast plain over which the shimmering heat-waves dance and the mirage spreads its mockery of placid waters. It seems incredible that such a wilderness should ever have been habitable for man, and yet the weathered hillocks at one's feet cover the temples and houses of a very great city.

As long ago as 1854 Mr. J. E. Taylor, British Consul at Basra, was employed by the British Museum to investigate some of the southern sites of Mesopotamia, and chose for his chief work the Mound of Pitch. Here he unearthed inscriptions which for the first time revealed that the nameless ruin was none other than Ur, so-called 'of the Chaldees', the home of Abraham. Taylor's discoveries were not at the time apprised at their true worth and his excavations closed down after two seasons; but more and more the importance of the site came to be recognized, and though, partly through lack of funds and partly because of the lawless character of the district into which foreigners could penetrate only at their own risk, no further excavations were undertaken, yet the British Museum never gave up hope of carrying on the work which Taylor had begun.

Towards the end of the nineteenth century an expedition sent out by the University of Pennsylvania visited Ur and contrived to do a little excavation of which the results have never been published, and then again the site lay fallow until the Great War brought British troops into Mesopotamia and gave an opportunity for long-cherished hopes to be revived and realized. In 1918 Mr. R. Campbell Thompson, formerly assistant in the British Museum and then on the Intelligence Staff of the Army in Mesopotamia, excavated at Eridu and made soundings at Ur. The British Museum was encouraged to put a regular expedition into the field, and when Mr. Leonard King, who was to have led it, fell ill, Dr. H. R. Hall took his place and during the winter of 1918–19 dug at Ur, Eridu, and al 'Ubaid. Dr. Hall's work at Ur was of an experimental nature, richer in promise than fulfilment, but his expedition was of prime importance in that he discovered and partly excavated the little mound of al 'Ubaid with its remarkable remains of early architectural decoration.

Again the want of pence which vexes public institutions brought matters to a standstill. Then, in 1922, Dr. G. B. Gordon, Director of the University Museum of Pennsylvania, approached the British Museum with the proposal of a joint expedition to Mesopotamia; the offer was accepted, and Ur was chosen as the scene of operations.

The directorship of the Joint Expedition was entrusted to me and I carried on the field work without interruption for the next twelve winters. We could not in that time excavate the whole of Ur, for the site is immense and to reach the earlier levels we often had to dig very deeply so that, although work was always done at high pressure and the number of men employed was the maximum consistent with proper supervision—at one moment it topped the four hundred—only a minute fraction of the city's area was thoroughly explored. None the less, we did secure a reasonably detailed picture of Ur throughout its four thousand years of existence and had made discoveries far surpassing anything we had dared to expect; now there was the danger that more digging would yield results more or less repetitive, and the preparing of our material for publication, an imperative duty, could not be undertaken while field work was still in progress; it was therefore decided, in 1934, to close down the Expedition.

Almost from the outset our work at Ur attracted the interest not only of scholars but of a wide general public and it was to satisfy that interest in what had already been done and to enable people to follow future discoveries with better understanding that in 1929 I published a small book, *Ur of the Chaldees*, dealing with the results of our first seven years. In the present volume I am concerned with the whole of the twelve years of excavation and, since it is meant to be a comprehensive account, a good deal that was written in my former book must be repeated. The facts, of course, remain, and the description of them cannot be radically altered, but the conclusions which we formed about them may have been modified by later discoveries so that there must always be a certain amount of re-writing, even where the finds belong to our early seasons; and all the later discoveries, as numerous and as important as those of the first seven years, have now to be duly recorded.

This is a book about excavation, about the buildings and the objects that we unearthed, and the wealth of our archæological material is so great that I do not propose to deal with anything outside it. So far as is possible I shall treat of things in historical order, but I am not writing a history of Ur; that has been done, and admirably done, by Mr. C. J. Gadd[1] who draws, as I am not qualified to do, upon literary sources, and I shall do no more than try to

[1] C. J. Gadd, *The History and Monuments of Ur*, Chatto & Windus, 1929.

show how our finds illustrate or supplement his historical framework. But the introduction to my book does seem to be the appropriate place in which to describe the positive additions to history afforded by our work in the field.

When the Expedition was being planned I was told that we might expect to recover monuments taking us back so far in time as the reign of King Ur-Nammu, founder of the Third Dynasty of Ur, but should probably find nothing earlier. King Ur-Nammu was indeed almost the first character in the history of Mesopotamia acknowledged by scholars to be historically authentic. It was known that cities went back far beyond Ur-Nammu; there were in museums actual monuments of earlier kings with their names written against them—but there was no means of saying when they reigned; about one great figure, Sargon of Akkad, there were poems and legends—but so late as 1916 Dr. Leonard King[1] found it necessary to argue at length the real identity of one who had been discounted as a mere hero of romance. There was even a list of kings which had been drawn up by Sumerian scribes soon after 2000 B.C., a sort of skeleton of history not unlike the King-list 'William I, 1066, William II, 1087 . . .' of our English school-books, but unfortunately it did not seem to help; the earlier part of the list is printed here on p. 251, and anyone looking at it will understand why scholars could give it little credence. It starts with kings who reigned 'before the Flood' and the reigns of eight kings add up to the total of 241,200 years! In the first dynasty after the Flood the rulers are credited with reigns of a thousand years each, on the average, in the next with an average of about two centuries, and although the dynasty after that, the First Dynasty of Ur, is marked by no such wild exaggeration, it is followed by other dynasties of impossibly long-lived kings. The figures from the Flood to the accession of Sargon of Akkad give a total of 31,917 years, and even though one may assume that dynasties overlap, and were really contemporary, as is known to be the case with those after Sargon's time, the entire chronology is palpably absurd. The natural result was

[1] *A History of Sumer and Akkad*, Chatto & Windus, 1916.

that scholars were led to reject the King-lists altogether and
to maintain that history properly speaking began little if at
all before the time of Ur-Nammu of Ur.

It was therefore most satisfactory to find at Ur contemporary records of Sargon of Akkad, these including a
portrait group of his daughter, who was High Priestess of the
Moon-god, and the personal seals of three officials of her
suite. Much more important was the discovery at al 'Ubaid of
the foundation-tablet of the little temple there which stated
that it was built by A-anni-pad-da King of Ur, son of Mes-
anni-pad-da King of Ur; the latter figures in the King-lists
as the founder of the First Dynasty of Ur, and with the discovery that First Dynasty, which had been regarded as
mythical, emerged into history. It also cleared up a minor
difficulty. Owing to the similarity of the two names that of
A-anni-pad-da had dropped out of the King-lists and Mes-
anni-pad-da was credited with the unlikely reign of eighty
years; as soon as it became evident that the figure had to be
divided between father and son the improbability vanished
and the record could be accepted as authentic. The written
history of the country had been carried back for something
like five hundred years; and although nothing could justify
the swollen chronology of the King-lists one could at least
suspect that behind it all there lurks an element of misunder-
stood truth. At an archæological congress of excavators held
at Baghdad in 1929 it was agreed that the early civilization of
Southern Mesopotamia could be classified in successive
phases which should be called, after the places where the
evidence for each was first discovered, the al 'Ubaid Period,
the Uruk Period (named after Uruk, the Biblical Erech and
the modern Warka), the Jamdat Nasr Period, and then the
Early Dynastic Period within which (but relatively late in it)
comes the First Dynasty of Ur. On this archæological
sequence all of us agree, but for my own part I am inclined
to go farther and to emphasize the extent to which our factual
sequence harmonizes with the divisions of the King-lists; the
al 'Ubaid Period is pre-Flood, properly speaking, and survived the Flood only in a degenerate form and for a short
while; we have two periods corresponding to the two dynas-

ties (of Kish and Erech) given by the Lists, and the next dynasty is proved to have existed. There may, after all, be something in the tradition on which the Sumerian scribes based their scheme of history—but they were hopelessly wrong with their dates.

We too cannot possibly establish a fixed chronology for the early periods, for the simple reason that writing was unknown (it seems to have been invented in the Jamdat Nasr Period) and without written records there can be no exact dating. Even when writing comes in a positive chronology is hard to arrive at, and any system that we may adopt must be regarded as tentative and liable to revision. Thus when we found at al 'Ubaid the tablet of A-anni-pad-da Assyriologists reckoned that the First Dynasty of Ur, now shown to have existed, must have started about 3100 B.C.; naturally I accepted this decision and, further, since I knew that the Royal Cemetery dated to just before the First Dynasty of Ur and, judging by the number of royal burials, must represent a considerable period of time, I suggested that it be put between 3500 and 3200 B.C., and these are the dates given by me in *Ur of the Chaldees*. But very soon after that book was published a revised version of the chronology brought the First Dynasty of Ur down to 2900 B.C., and to-day some Assyriologists at least favour a further reduction and make Mes-anni-pad-da come to the throne about 2700 B.C.—and the dates of Sargon of Akkad, of Ur-Nammu of Ur and of Hammurabi of Babylon have all been subject to reduction. The question has to be settled on literary evidence, and the archæologist must accept that; consequently I adopt here a chronological system quite different from that put forward in 1929; the inconsistency really witnesses to the advance of knowledge. But I would point out that no change in the positive dates can upset or alter the archæological sequence, which is based on observed facts.

When the Joint Expedition began its work at Ur no other digging was being done in Iraq, but later on other archæological missions entered the field, and at one time there were no less than eleven engaged in different parts of the country, and although some of those were shortlived and none of them are functioning at the present time, yet for very many years the Archæological Department of the Iraq Government has worked without interruption and with excellent results. Now no single dig, however successful, can give a complete picture of the history even of its own site, much less of the whole country. Sites may be very large, so that the excavations cannot cover their entire area, or may be very complicated so that digging has to be done down to great depths in order to reach the earlier levels, and the expense of such work may be prohibitive. Part of a site may at one time have been deserted, with the result that excavation in that part will fail to produce any evidence of a cultural phase which elsewhere on the site may be well represented; in preparing the foundations of an important building the old builders may have swept away a whole series of earlier strata and so have made a gap in our archæological series which we have no reason to suspect; or that building may have stood unaltered throughout a period of time that saw many vicissitudes in the town's history—but if our excavation is limited to the building it will tell us nothing of those vicissitudes. Our own excavations therefore do not give us the full story of Ur; what they do give has to be amplified and sometimes modified by the results of the many other digs on other sites; but since the subject of this book is the Ur excavation and not a complete history I shall refer to the other digs only when such reference is necessary for the proper understanding of what we found. If then I say little or nothing about the discoveries made by fellow archæologists working in Iraq it is not because I under-rate their importance but because they do not fall within my province. But I should indeed be doing injustice if I failed to acknowledge the debt that I owe to my own staff. In the course of twelve years I had the help of a large number of assistants; my wife was with me for ten seasons, Professor Mallowan for six, others for four or less; if they are not mentioned individually in the course of this book it is because the work was team-work throughout and each was prone to sink his personality in the common task; looking back now, I am surprised to find how seldom I can say of a particular job 'So-and-so did that';—nearly always it was a joint affair. And perhaps that is the highest praise I can give to a staff which deserves all my praise and gratitude; they did not do this job or that—they were the Expedition, and its success was the measure of their devotion.

I

The Beginnings of Ur, and the Flood

LOWER Mesopotamia, the Sumer of the ancient world, is no more nor less than the river-valley of the Tigris and the Euphrates; it does not include the high-lying Syrian desert to the west, because that is desert— a waterless expanse of gravel barren for most of the year at least—where the wandering Bedouin may pitch their tents for a brief space but no man claiming to be civilized could make his home; and it does not include the Persian mountains that fringe it on the east because always those mountains were held by warlike tribes more ready to raid the cultivated fields of the valley people than to submit to their sway. And it is a land of recent formation. Originally that arm of the sea which we call the Persian Gulf extended far inland, to the north of modern Baghdad, and it was only at a relatively late date in human history that salt water gave place to dry land, a change due not to any sudden cataclysm but to the gradual deposit of river silt filling the great rift between mountain and desert. If the Tigris and the Euphrates alone had been concerned the formation of the delta would have followed the normal pattern; starting in the extreme north it would have pushed southwards very gradually, and man's occupation of the newly-made soil would have been conditioned by that slow progress so that only after centuries or indeed millennia could he have settled in the south country where Ur lies. But as a matter of fact this was not the case at all. The people of Sumer themselves believed that the oldest of their cities was Eridu, which lies about twelve miles south of Ur, and excavation there by an Iraqi Government expedition has gone far towards confirming this belief; nowhere in Lower Mesopotamia proper have there been found traces of a settlement so ancient as that at Eridu. Clearly this requires explanation, and we must look again at the physical geography of our area.

The Tigris and the Euphrates are not the only rivers that empty into the Persian Gulf. Close to the modern town of

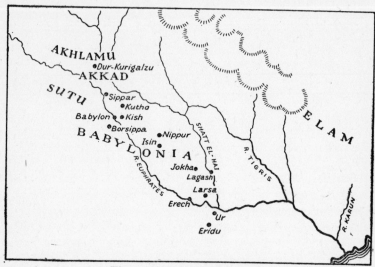

Fig. 1. Lower Mesopotamia

Mohammerah is the mouth of the Karun river which from the Persian mountains brings down almost as much silt as do the two rivers Tigris and Euphrates together; almost opposite to it is the Wadi al Batin, now a dry valley but in ancient times a great river draining the heart of Arabia; not so violent a stream as the Karun, it must yet have carried down in its waters no less heavy a charge of mud collected from the light surface soil through which its long channel was cut. The two rivers, facing each other and flowing at right angles to the Gulf, discharged into it a mass of silt which in time formed a bar across it; this neutralized the scouring action of what little tide the Gulf can boast and also slowed up the current of the lower reaches of the Tigris and Euphrates so that the silt brought by them was heaped

20

against the inner side of the bar; the first dry land to be formed was in fact in the extreme south. The immediate result of this was to turn the upper end of the old gulf into a stagnant lake, whose waters, fed by the great rivers, gradually turned from salt to brackish and from brackish to fresh, and over the whole of it the silt of those same rivers was dropped uniformly, raising the level of the lagoon's bed. Undoubtedly the action would be quickest near the mouths of the streams and dry land would be formed first in the north and in the south with, in the middle, a vast marsh diversified by low islands; but in time this too shrank until where there had been an arm of the sea there stretched a great delta through which ran rivers so flush with their banks that they were for ever changing their courses; every year the spring floods swamped the flat valley, in summer a pitiless sun scorched it, but its light and stoneless soil was as rich as could be found anywhere upon earth. The story of the Creation of the world as man's home which we find in the Book of Genesis was taken over by the Hebrews from the people of Lower Mesopotamia, where it originated, and most faithfully does it record the facts. 'God said "Let the waters under the heaven be gathered together unto one place, and let the dry land appear", and it was so . . . And the earth brought forth grass, and herb yielding seed after his kind, and the tree yielding fruit, whose seed was in itself, after his kind: and God saw that it was good.' It was indeed a good land, inviting settlement, and there were plenty of people ready to accept the invitation; immigrants moved in, land-hungry men snatching at each acre of fertile soil as soon as it emerged from the waters, and with their coming the first chapter in the long history of Sumer began.

This earliest phase was illustrated for us by three distinct sites examined by the Ur expedition, by Ur itself, by Rajeibeh and by Tell al 'Ubaid.

In 1919 Dr. H. R. Hall, who was carrying out an experimental dig at Ur on. behalf of the British Museum, discovered and partly excavated a little mound called by the Arabs Tell al 'Ubaid, which lay some four miles to the north of Ur; the results were so important that the complete

excavation of the site was one of the first items in the programme of the Joint Expedition when it took the field three
years later. The most sensational discovery was that of the
First Dynasty temple which will be described hereafter
(p. 92); what interests us now was something entirely
different and very much older. About sixty yards from the
temple ruins there was a low mound—it rose no more than
six feet above the plain—the surface of which was strewn
with flint implements and fragments of hand-made painted
pottery, of a sort which had already been found at Eridu,
south of Ur, and had been recognized as 'prehistoric',
though little more than that was known about it. We
excavated the mound and were somewhat taken aback to
find how little work it required—everything lay quite close
to the surface. Under a few inches of light dust mixed with
potsherds there came a stratum not more than three feet
thick composed of hard mud in which were quantities of
sherds of painted ware, flint and obsidian tools, and bits of
reed matting plastered with clay mixed with dung or, less
often, with a mixture of earth and bitumen; below this was
clean water-laid soil. This was, in fact, an island of river silt
which originally rose above the marshy plain and had been
seized upon by immigrants who had erected on it their
primitive hut dwellings of reeds plastered with clay. The
village had later been deserted and the dust and potsherds
of the topmost layer represented its ruins; at one point we
found in this layer the foundations of a mud-brick wall contemporary with the First Dynasty temple close by, and since
this lay immediately in and over the older remains from
which it was separated by an unknown length of time, we
could conclude that our village had been definitely abandoned and that its site remained for long uninhabited. The
three feet of hard mud and household rubbish had accumulated during the village's lifetime, as the flimsy huts fell
down and others were erected over them; the lighter soil
above represented the last buildings, but much of it had been
eroded by the desert winds (which accounts for the mass of
potsherds exposed on the surface) and this must have happened during the time when the site lay desolate. But,

scanty as the remains were, they were enough to tell us a great deal about the people who lived there. First and foremost, they belonged to the Late Stone Age; at al 'Ubaid not a trace of metal was found, and if copper was known to them at all it can have been used only for small objects of luxury; all their implements were of stone. The larger tools, such as hoes, were chipped from the flint or chert that can be got from the upper desert; knives and awls might be of rock crystal or obsidian—volcanic glass—both of which had to be imported from abroad; beads were made from rock crystal, carnelian, pink pebble and shell, and these were all chipped into shape and not polished; but one or two ear- or nose-studs of polished obsidian found on the surface may date from this period and if so show that a finer working of stone was not beyond the powers of the al 'Ubaid craftsman. But that in which they excelled was their pottery [*Plate* 1]. The vessels were hand-made without the use of the wheel, but were thinly walled and finely shaped, and the characteristic ware was decorated with designs in black or brown paint on a ground which was intended to be white but often, through over-firing, assumed a curious and rather effective greenish tint. The patterns were all geometrical, built up from the simple elements of triangles, squares, wavy or vandyke lines and chevrons which might be filled in solidly or with hatching, but these were most skilfully combined and in all cases the design was admirably adapted to the shape of the vessel; it can safely be said that this, the earliest pottery of Lower Mesopotamia, is artistically superior to any that was to be produced there until the Arab conquest. At al 'Ubaid the pottery seems to be from the outset fully developed; it is not of local growth. In more recent times excavations at Eridu have brought to light an earlier phase of the same ware, but the difference is one of degree only, not of kind, and the essential characteristics of the al 'Ubaid pottery are already there. It is evident that the first settlers in the river valley brought with them a ceramic style which had been developed in their original home. Now the only thing of the sort known to us at present is the prehistoric painted ware of Elam, discovered in the excavations at Susa; it is by no means the same, but there are certain unmistakable similarities, at least enough to warrant the idea that the two have a common ancestry; if that be the case the al 'Ubaid people must have come down into the valley from the Elamite mountains to the east. It would be natural enough that the attraction of the drying marsh-land with its promise of rich crops should have appealed first to the dwellers on the land's borders; since such nomads as there were in the western desert would have had small interest in agricultural possibilities the invasion must have come either from the east or from the north; what we know of northern pottery makes any connection with al 'Ubaid impossible (the earliest pottery there is un-painted) and even the partial analogy with Elam should settle the question.

Quite definitely the newcomers were agriculturalists; the commonest stone implement is the hoe; many of the small flints seem to come from the sledges used for thrashing grain; stone querns and pounders show that this was used for bread. But the most curious evidence is that given by the sickles, which, or rather the fragments of which, litter the site of the village. These sickles were made of baked clay. Clay would seem to be the very last material that one would use for a cutting instrument, but the shape is indisputable, and the clay is so hard-baked and the jagged edge of the blade so keen that they would cut more or less; and if it be argued that they would certainly break the answer is that they did, only too easily, and that is why we find them in such numbers, and hardly ever one of them intact. The people then tilled the ground, and they kept domestic animals—the cow-dung in the mud plaster of their huts is evidence for that, and we found a clay figurine of a pig; spindle-whorls of baked clay or of bitumen prove that thread was spun, woollen thread presumably, and heavy clay discs pierced with two holes are almost certainly loom-weights. Fish-bones found in the hut ruins show that fish were eaten, as one would expect in a village close to river and marsh; some were so small that the fish must have been taken in nets, and a number of grooved pebbles that we found may have been net-sinkers; we found also a clay model of an open boat with

canoe-like body and curled prow. We have seen that nose-
or ear-studs were worn, and beads; part of a painted clay
figurine shows a woman wearing a very wide necklace and
on the shoulders there are painted lines which may represent
drapery; another figurine fragment, the lower part of the
body, shows either tight-fitting breeches laced down the
front or else tattoo marks on the flesh.

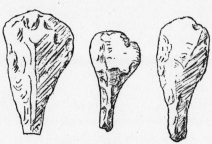

Fig. 2. Flint hoes

One day two Arabs came to the expedition house at Ur
and from a folded handkerchief produced four or five big
flint hoes (Fig. 2) which they had picked up, they said
vaguely, 'in the desert'. They received a good *baksheesh* and,
as I had hoped, returned a day or two later with more hoes,
but again would not specify where they were found. When
they came for the fourth time I refused any reward, protest-
ing that I had hoes enough, but told them that they would
be well paid if they would guide us to the find-spot; which,
seeing that that was the only chance of making any more
money, they agreed to do. The site, called by the Arabs
Rajeibeh, lay some six miles to the North East of Ur; it was
so low a mound as to be hardly noticeable, but as soon as we
came to it the mystery of our visitors' hoe-harvest was explained; one could not walk a step without setting one's foot on
worked flints and painted potsherds lying so thick as to hide
the desert surface. It was a site exactly like al 'Ubaid but
much larger. No excavation would have availed here, for
directly below the stone and pottery refuse was the clean silt
of the island on which the settlers had made their home;

nobody in later times had ever built upon the site[1] so that
there were no upper strata to protect it, and the wind had
carried away everything that wind could carry. Probably
there had been here successive building levels representing a
fairly long period, and the flints, etc. (too numerous to be all
of one date) must have been distributed throughout a deposit
of considerable depth; but as the process of wind erosion
went on the heavier debris of the upper levels had settled
down until all the dust of the decomposed dwellings had
been blown away and the flints and potsherds of many
generations had sunk to one common level which was virtually flush with the surrounding desert and so offered no
challenge to the winds. Rajeibeh did not give us any information beyond what al 'Ubaid had given, but its importance lay in the fact that it repeated exactly the al 'Ubaid
story; in both cases we have a natural island in the marsh-
land inhabited by immigrants of the same stock and culture
and in both, after a period of continuous occupation, the site
is completely and finally deserted. Why this was, we were to
learn from the excavations at Ur itself. And another point
on which we needed evidence was the relative date of these
village settlements; we knew from the stratification at al
'Ubaid that they were older than the First Dynasty of Ur,
and everything pointed to their being of the Late Stone Age,
but we had no means whatsoever of showing how long was
the time-gap between the Stone Age and the First Dynasty,
nor anything to illustrate the development of history during
that time; the al 'Ubaid culture was an isolated phenomenon
which, as one scholar wrote at the time,[2] 'ought to have some
place in the Sumerian historical tradition, and doubtless
had, but the connection is at present missing'.

In the year 1929 the work of excavating the Royal
Cemetery at Ur was drawing towards its end. On the
evidence then to hand I was convinced that the cemetery
came before, but only just before, the First Dynasty of Ur;
the treasures recovered from its graves illustrated a civiliza-

[1] We found ruins of the time of the Third Dynasty of Ur about a mile away,
but the old mound had been left undisturbed.
[2] C. J. Gadd, in *The History and Monuments of Ur*, 1929.

tion of an astonishingly high order and it was therefore all the more important to trace the steps by which man had reached that level of art and culture. That meant, presumably, that we had to dig deeper; but it was just as well to begin by a small-scale test of the lower levels which could be carried out with a minimum of time and cost. Starting then below the level at which the graves had been found we sank a little shaft, not more than five feet square at the outset, into the underlying soil and went down through the mixed rubbish that is characteristic of old inhabited sites—a mixture of decomposed mud brick, ashes and broken pottery, very much like that in which the graves had been dug. This went on for about three feet and then suddenly, it all stopped: there were no more potsherds, no ashes, only clean water-laid mud, and the Arab workman at the bottom of the shaft told me that he had reached virgin soil; there was nothing more to be found, and he had better go elsewhere.

I got down and looked at the evidence and agreed with him; but then I took my levels and discovered that 'virgin soil' was not nearly so deep down as I had expected, for I had assumed that the original Ur was built not on a hill but on a low mound rising only just above the surrounding swampy land; and because I do not like having my theories upset by anything less than proof I told the man to get back and go on digging. Most unwillingly he did so, again turning up nothing but clean soil that yielded no sign of human activity; he dug through eight feet of it in all and then, suddenly, there appeared flint implements and fragments of painted al 'Ubaid pottery vessels. I got into the pit once more, examined the sides, and by the time I had written up my notes was quite convinced of what it all meant; but I wanted to see whether others would come to the same conclusion. So I brought up two of my staff and, after pointing out the facts, asked for their explanation. They did not know what to say. My wife came along and looked and was asked the same question, and she turned away remarking casually, 'Well, of course, it's the Flood.' That was the right answer. But one could scarcely argue for the Deluge on the strength of a pit a yard square; so in the next season I marked out on the low ground where the graves of the Royal Cemetery had been a rectangle some seventy-five feet by sixty and there dug a huge pit which went down, in the end, for sixty-four feet. Now the graves, which had been pretty deep-lying, had been dug down, from a ground-surface much higher than the level at which our pit started, into rubbish-mounds heaped against the flank of the old town; we had cleared away the graves and the rubbish and the level of the pit's mouth there-fore was necessarily older than the graves by the (unknown) length of time required for so much rubbish to accumulate; it was probably quite a long time.

Almost as soon as the new dig started we came upon the ruins of houses. The walls were built of mud bricks of the 'plano-convex' type—rectangular but rounded on the top instead of flat—which we had found alike in the First Dynasty temple at al 'Ubaid and in the Royal Cemetery, and such pottery as lay in the rooms was of the sort common in the graves higher up. Below these ruins (Fig. 3) came a second building stratum, and then a third; in the first twenty feet we dug through no fewer than eight levels of houses, each built above the ruins of the previous age; but in the lowest three the wall-bricks were not plano-convex but flat-topped, and there were types of pottery different from any that the Royal Cemetery had produced. Then, abruptly, the house-ruins stopped and we were digging down through a solid mass of broken pottery which continued for about eighteen feet and in it, at different levels, were the kilns in which the pots had been fired. It was the site of a vase-factory; the sherds represented the pots which went wrong in the firing—were cracked or distorted—and having no commercial value were smashed by the potter and the bits left lying there until they were heaped so high that the kiln was buried and a new kiln had to be built on the top of them; an accumulation of eighteen feet of wasters meant that the factory was in production for a long time, and the changes of fashion during that time could be traced from its discards. The sherds in the upper debris were for the most part similar to the few found in the lower house levels, but amongst them were fragments painted in red and black on a

28

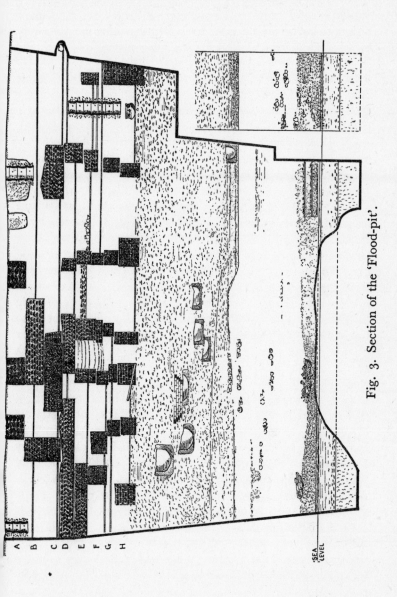

Fig. 3. Section of the 'Flood-pit'.

29

buff ground identical with a ware which on a site called
Jamdat Nasr, a hundred and fifty miles to the north of Ur,
had shortly before been found associated with written clay
tablets of a most primitive sort; but Jamdat Nasr, like al
'Ubaid, was as yet an isolated discovery whose relation to
Sumerian history was a matter of guesswork only. Lower
down in our kiln stratum the character of the potsherds
changed, the polychrome wares disappeared and in their
place all the distinctive fragments showed a monochrome
decoration, plain red produced by a wash of hæmatite or
grey or black resulting from the use of the 'smother-kiln' in
which the smoke is retained to carbonize the clay; this was a
ware which the German excavators at Warka (the ancient
Erech) had been finding in the lowest levels they had yet
reached. Low down in this 'Uruk' stratum we found a
remarkable object, a heavy disc of baked clay about three
feet in diameter with a central pivot-hole and a small hole
near the rim to take a handle; it was a potter's wheel as used
by the maker of the 'Uruk' vases, the earliest known example
of that invention whereby man passed from the age of pure
handicraft into the age of machinery. And only a foot or so
below the point at which the wheel was found the character
of the pottery changed again and we were digging through
sherds of the hand-turned painted ware of al 'Ubaid. But
this was al 'Ubaid with a difference. The hand-made pots
were of the same clay and had the same whitish or greenish
surface, but in most the decoration in black paint was reduced to a minimum—plain horizontal lines or the simplest
patterns perfunctorily and carelessly drawn; clearly they
belonged to the last stages of decadence. Then—it was only
a thin stratum—all the pottery came to an end and we had,
as we expected, the clean silt piled up by the Flood. A few
graves had been dug down into the silt, and in them was
al 'Ubaid pottery of a richer sort than that in the kiln rubbish above; in one of them there was a copper spear-blade,
the earliest example we have found of metal being used for
weapons or tools; the bodies all lay on their backs, rigidly
extended, with the hands crossed below the stomach, a
position not found in Mesopotamian graves of any later date

until the Greek period; such a difference in the ritual of burial is most important in that it implies a difference in the basic religious beliefs of the people. In some of the graves there were terra-cotta figurines of the type also found in the al 'Ubaid house ruins; they were always female and nude [*Plate* 2], sometimes showing a woman suckling a child but more often a single figure with the hands brought in front of the body very much in the attitude of the dead beside whom they lay. These graves, dug into the silt deposit, were of course later than the Flood, but they had been made before the vase factory occupied the area in the last phase of the al 'Ubaid period.

At this point the clean silt measured about eleven feet in thickness and except for one scarcely noticeable stratum of darker mud was absolutely uniform throughout; microscopic analysis proved that it was water-laid, subject to the action of gentle currents, and it was composed of material brought down from the middle reaches of the Euphrates. Below it came the level of human occupation—decayed mud brick, ashes and potsherds, in which we could distinguish three successive floor levels; here was the richly-decorated al 'Ubaid pottery in abundance, flints, clay figurines and flat rectangular bricks (preserved because they had been accidentally burnt) and fragments of clay plaster, also hardened by fire, which on one side were smooth, flat or convex, and on the other side bore the imprint of reed stems, the daub from the walls of the reed huts which, as we saw at al 'Ubaid, were the normal houses of the pre-Flood people, as they are of the Marsh Arab to-day.

The first huts had been set up on the surface of a belt of mud which was clearly formed, for the most part, of decayed vegetable matter; in it were potsherds (thicker at the bottom of the belt) all lying horizontally as if they had been thrown there and had sunk of their own weight through water into soft mud; below this again, three feet below modern sea level, there was stiff green clay pierced by sinuous brown stains which had been the roots of reeds; here all traces of human activity ceased and we were at the bottom of Mesopotamia.

The digging of so great a pit was a long and expensive matter, but it amply repaid us in historical results; it confirmed the sequence which had been tentatively drawn upon the strength of our own and other excavations—particularly those of Warka—and it added a lot of valuable detail.

The green clay at the bottom was the floor of the original marsh bordering the island which was occupied by the first settlers in the part of the valley; it was dense with reeds, and with the decay of their stems and leaves and with the rubbish thrown into the water from the island the bottom rose and gradually dry land was formed; when it was dry enough people set up their huts on it at the foot of what was by now the city mound. All this low-lying quarter was overwhelmed by a great flood and buried beneath its silt. There were survivors, of course, and they carried on the old culture, as we can see from the graves, but they were a disheartened and impoverished remnant and when, some time later, the kilns were established on the site of the old graveyard the traditional arts were in their last decadence.

The appearance in the kiln stratum of the red, black or grey 'Uruk' pottery marks a new chapter in the history of the delta. Into the rich but now sparsely-inhabited valley there poured a new wave of immigrants, coming this time from the north, who brought with them a more advanced culture—they enjoyed a free use of metal and were skilled workers in copper, and they made their pottery not by hand but on the potter's wheel; and though they were content to settle down side by side with the al 'Ubaid survivors they very soon made themselves the masters of the country. Above the 'Uruk' potsherds comes the painted 'Jamdat Nasr' ware, made on the same factory site, and this again means a fresh invasion, probably (though we cannot yet be sure) from the east; the lordship passes to a new stock who developed if they did not actually invent the all-important art of writing, for it is with the Jamdat Nasr pottery that we find tablets with the pictographic writing which was gradually formalized into the cuneiform script of the Sumerians. Then, high up in our pit, with the fourth stratum of house ruins Jamdat Nasr disappears, round-topped bricks replace

32

the old flat type, and the pottery becomes that which we find in the Royal Cemetery—it is the beginning of what we now call the 'Early Dynastic Period'. But the houses were to decay and be rebuilt three times, and thereafter the site of them was to be abandoned and turned into a rubbish-heap before the first grave of the Royal Cemetery was dug; that cemetery therefore, and the First Dynasty of Ur which immediately succeeded it, do not introduce the Period but come relatively late in it.

Such is the outline of history given by the stratification of our great pit. It shows, beyond all question, the order of the historic phases, and until we know that order there is no history at all; but it does not necessarily tell us much about any one phase; the picture has to be completed from the results not of one dig but of many. Thus from the three superimposed floor levels found below the Flood silt it might be argued that the Flood happened when the settlement was still young; but that is far from being the case. At Eridu the Iraq Government expedition unearthed the ruins of fourteen temples, one above the other, and all belonged to the first al 'Ubaid period, prior to the Flood; at Warka the Germans found an al 'Ubaid occupation stratum no less than forty feet thick; evidently the period was very long. We might have found similar evidence if we had been digging into the centre of the prehistoric town, but as it happened our pit was outside its walls, so that our houses represented the town's expansion at a relatively late date. Again it might have been supposed that the people of the al 'Ubaid I phase, before the Flood, being still, apparently, in the Neolithic stage of culture, must have been savages of no concern to the rest of the world. But their peculiar painted pottery spread to the northern limits of Mesopotamia and was thence carried eastwards to the valley of the Orontes river and to the shores of the Mediterranean, witness to a far-flung trade; and actually, in the house ruins under the Flood silt at Ur, we found two beads made of amazonite, a stone of which the nearest known source is the Nilghiri hills of central India; it was a fairly sophisticated community that could import its luxuries from lands so far away. Even the terra-cotta figurines cannot

C

rightly be classed as primitive. The slender bodies, conventional as they are, are skilfully modelled and the queer reptilian faces with the high bitumen-covered head-dress are due not to lack of art but to intention; these are goddesses who must not be represented otherwise. What the religion of the people was we cannot tell, but religion of a sort they certainly had. Whether or not these al 'Ubaid people should properly be called Sumerians is a matter of dispute; but this much at least can safely be said, that the culture which they evolved was not a sterile growth doomed to be obliterated by the disaster of the Deluge, but contributed not a little to the Sumerian civilization which in later times was to flower so richly. And amongst the things which they handed down to their successors was the story of the Flood; that must have been so, for none but they could have been responsible for it.

The familiar Bible story of Noah's Ark is not by origin a Hebrew story at all; it was taken over by the Hebrews from Mesopotamia and incorporated, with suitable emendations, in their own sacred canon; it is exactly the same tale as we find on tablets written before the time of Abraham, and not only the incidents but even much of the phrasing is identical. The Sumerian legend is in the form of a religious poem reflecting the beliefs of a pagan people, and if that were all that we were told about the Flood we might dismiss it as a piece of fantastic mythology. But it does not stand alone. In the King-list which I have already discussed (*see* above, p. 14) we see enumerated at the beginning a series of kings, presumably fabulous, who enjoyed phenomenal reigns of thousands of years each, and then 'The Flood came. After the Flood came, kingship was sent down from on high' and the list gives a dynasty of kings whose capital was at Kish, then a dynasty whose capital was at Erech, and thirdly the First Dynasty of Ur, the historical reality of which has been proved by our excavations. Here there is no picturesque legend, only what the old historians meant to be a plain statement of fact. The statement is indeed so plain that it implies the legend, for otherwise it would have no meaning; 'The Flood' was for the Sumerian reader the only flood that really mattered, what we call Noah's Flood.

34

Both at Ur and on other Mesopotamian sites there has been found evidence of local and temporary water action occurring at various times in history; sometimes this was no more than the effect of rain in an enclosed area, and never is there anything approaching what we found in our 'Flood-pit'. There, it can safely be said, we have proof of an inundation unparalleled in any later period of Mesopotamian history. We were lucky to find it at all because a flood does not, of course, pile up silt everywhere—on the contrary, where the current is strongest it may have a scouring effect; the silt is deposited where the current is held up by some obstacle. To settle this point we dug a whole series of small shafts, covering a large area, in which the depth of the mud differed considerably, and when these were duly plotted it was clear that the mud was heaped up against the north slope of the town mound which, rising above the plain, broke the force of the flood waters; on the plain east or west of the mound we should probably have found nothing. Eleven feet of silt—the maximum—would probably mean a flood not less than twenty-five feet deep; in the flat low-lying land of Mesopotamia[1] a flood of that depth would cover an area about three hundred miles long and a hundred miles across; the whole of the fertile land between the Elamite mountains and the high Syrian desert would disappear, every village would be destroyed, and only a few of the old cities, set high on their built-up mounds, would survive the disaster. We know that Ur did survive; we have seen that villages such as al 'Ubaid and Rajeibeh were suddenly deserted and remained desolate for long or for ever. The compilers of the King-lists regarded the Flood as something that made a breach in the continuity of their country's history; we find that it put an end to the al 'Ubaid culture as such; they dated the Flood as coming two 'dynasties' before the First Dynasty of Ur; if we choose, as I think we may, to correlate with those 'dynasties' our archæological periods of Uruk and Jamdat Nasr and to make the First Dynasty of Ur symbolize

[1] Ur to-day, about two hundred miles from the sea, is only fourteen feet above sea level. Ur Junction, eleven miles from the present course of the Euphrates, lies six feet below the bottom of the river's bed, so that the mere breaching of the artificial banks would put the railway out of action.

our Early Dynastic period of which it is indeed the culmination, then the time of our flood agrees with Sumerian chronology as handed down by tradition. We have proved that there really was a flood, and it is no straining of probabilities to maintain that this is the Flood of the Sumerian King-lists and therefore of the Sumerian legend and therefore of the story in the Old Testament. Of course this does not mean that all the details of the story are true; the background is a historic fact, but both the moralist and the poet have embroidered the account of it to suit their several aims. But the facts remain. The Genesis version says that the waters rose to a height of twenty-six feet, which seems to be true; the Sumerian version describes antediluvian man living in huts made of reeds, which at al 'Ubaid and at Ur we found to be the case; Noah built his ark of light wood waterproofed with bitumen, and just on top of the Flood deposit we found a big lump of bitumen bearing the imprint of the basket in which it had been packed, as I have myself seen the crude bitumen from the pits at Hit on the middle Euphrates being packed in baskets for export down stream. It was not a universal deluge; it was a vast flood in the valley of the Tigris and the Euphrates which drowned the whole of the habitable land between the mountains and the desert; for the people who lived there that was all the world. The great bulk of those people must have perished, and it was but a scanty and dispirited remnant that from the city walls watched the waters recede at last. No wonder that they saw in this disaster the gods' punishment of a sinful generation and described it as such in a religious poem; and if some household had managed to escape by boat from the drowned lowlands the head of it would naturally be chosen as the hero of the saga.

Plate I

Painted pottery of the al 'Ubaid period

Plate 2

Clay figurines of goddesses of the al 'Ubaid period

II

The Uruk and Jamdat Nasr Periods

IN THE 'kiln stratum' of our great Flood-pit the layer of al 'Ubaid potsherds that was spread over the mass of silt was relatively thin and very soon showed an admixture of the monochrome 'Uruk' wares; by the time the broken 'wasters' from the kilns had attained a depth of about two feet al 'Ubaid disappeared and all the recognizable fragments were of the Uruk type. An early culture has therefore been replaced by another; and since the change is not abrupt but gradual it is clear that the two cultures overlapped, existing for a while side by side; that much can safely be deduced from the evidence, but that is all. In view of the complete difference of technique in the manufacture of the two classes of pottery—one is hand-made, the other turned on the wheel, one is painted, the other fired in a well-regulated smother-kiln to produce a monochrome effect—we should suspect the intrusion of a new race rather than a mere process of development on the part of the local stock; but of this we could not be certain. Apart from the Flood-pit we have found nothing at all to witness to the Uruk Period at Ur; had our deep digging been inside the walls of the ancient city we should presumably have found plenty of remains, but as it was we found nothing. Fortunately the Warka excavations have thrown a great deal of light on the period; it introduced the age of metal to the Lower Euphrates valley, it was rich and important and it lasted for a considerable length of time; further, its character makes us fairly sure that the Uruk civilization came into the country from outside, from the north. The fact that the Uruk pottery was used and was made at Ur means that in the course of time the northern invaders came to the place, settled down there alongside the

37

survivors of the pre-Flood population and ended by acquiring such a supremacy over them that the old arts and techniques were superseded by those which they brought with them. All that we have then is proof that Ur lived through an Uruk phase; it is not much, but at least it supplies a link between the al 'Ubaid culture and what was to follow.

The upper layers of potsherds in the kiln stratum of our Flood-pit consisted entirely of Jamdat Nasr ware. Above the kiln stratum lay the ruins of houses, and the three lowest layers of these also belonged to the same period as was proved by the pottery in them and, more particularly, by the occurrence in the third level from the bottom of a curious rough hand-made bowl which has since been found on a number of other sites and is a sort of hall-mark of the Jamdat Nasr potter. The mass of potsherds accumulated on the kiln site and the three building-levels on the top of them together testify to a reasonably long period of Jamdat Nasr occupation; to that occupation, fortunately, the sherds are not the only witness.

Between 1930 and 1933 we were working on the Ziggurat area, trying to trace its history previous to the time when Ur-Nammu, of the Third Dynasty of Ur, built the great structure whose ruins are to-day the outstanding feature of the site. Since we were obliged to respect that monument and its dependent buildings the investigation of the underlying levels was none too easy, and though we were in the end able to work out a good deal of the plans of two successive buildings both belonging to the Early Dynastic Period (these will be described later) it was seldom that we could, in the confined space, dig down to any earlier strata. But a cutting made in the west corner of the Ziggurat terrace gave us just the evidence we wanted. Underneath and partly cut away by the foundations of the earlier walling of the Dynastic Period there was a length of wall whose sharply sloped face proved it to be the retaining-wall of a terrace; it was built of a peculiar small-size type of mud brick which at Warka is characteristic of Uruk construction, but it had been strengthened by the addition of a new facing with bricks of a different type resembling those in the Jamdat Nasr house-walls in our

Flood-pit. Behind the wall stretched a mud-brick floor which was littered with thousands of small cones of baked clay, sharpened at one end and blunt at the other, rather like crayons, most of them about three and a half inches long and half an inch in diameter; they were of a light whitish yellow clay and while some were plain others had the blunt ends covered with red or black paint. Now just a hundred years ago the English traveller and archæologist, Loftus, discovered at Warka a mosaic-covered wall, part of a building which has since been unearthed by the German excavators there. This was a palace[1] with huge mud-brick columns and panelled walls, but that rather prosaic material was entirely disguised by the surface decoration. The walls and columns were thickly plastered with mud and into the mud were pressed little burnt-clay pegs such as we find at Ur; they were driven deeply in, so that only the flat ends showed, touching each other, and the pegs of different colours were so arranged as to produce elaborate patterns, vandykes, lozenges, triangles, etc., in unending variety over the whole building [*Plate* 3]. In the light of this we can safely say that at Ur in the Jamdat Nasr Period there was already a Ziggurat, set high on an artificial platform—of which we found the terrace wall—and richly decorated with a mosaic of coloured cones.

But while we have to look to Warka for examples of the architectural grandeurs of this early time, Ur has given us a cemetery which illustrates very well its domestic crafts. Our deepest digging in the Royal Cemetery area had already brought to light a few graves which seemed to belong to the Jamdat Nasr Period and had also produced quantities of inscribed tablets and seal-impressions of a very early type scattered in a rubbish-stratum into which the Early Dynastic graves had been dug.

We generally connect seals with written documents, and for many historical periods that is natural and correct; but seals as marks of private ownership antedate by many

---

[1] The existence of this astonishing palace at Warka may be an argument for identifying the Jamdat Nasr Period with the First Erech Dynasty of the King-lists.

centuries the invention of the art of writing—indeed, they go back as far as the Stone Age. The impressions found in this rubbish-stratum were on lumps of clay that had secured the tops of jars—a piece of cloth had been tied over the jar's mouth and clay spread over that, and the seal stamped on the wet clay. Some of them bore very simple geometric designs, others had animal figures or human figures, and the designs become more and more elaborate and complicated and there appear what are clearly conventionalized symbols which are repeated in differing connections; this is the beginning of writing, and our seal-impressions give us in graphic detail the evolution of the Sumerian script. In the season of 1932–3, in order to obtain more of these very important objects, we resumed work here and at once found the seal-impressions and the tablets; but the stratum was relatively thin and below it came the ordinary mixed soil of the old rubbish-mounds. In this nothing of great interest could be expected, but there was a possibility of graves lower down, and in any case to carry on the work down to virgin soil would give us a useful check on former results and theories; so we went down. At four feet below the seal-impression stratum we came upon numbers of large clay bowls—the rough hand-made bowls characteristic of the Jamdat Nasr Period—set upside down in the ground, and two feet below those the graves of the Jamdat Nasr Period with which the bowls were associated by some ritual of burial. The graves, most of which were poor, lay thickly together and one above another, and the lowest of them contained pottery vases decorated with red and black paint on a buff ground of the sort found at Jamdat Nasr itself [*Plate* 4]. The discovery was so important that excavation on a larger scale was called for, and therefore in the following season I marked out over what I hoped would be the centre of the graveyard an area of some twelve hundred square yards and started to dig a pit which, since our graves lay fifty-six feet below the modern surface, was almost a rival to the Flood-pit. Close to the surface was the Temenos Wall built by Nebuchadnezzar and part of a contemporary building lying inside it; lower down there were the ruins of Kassite houses, two layers of them, of which the earlier might date to about 1000 B.C. Dug down into their ruins were burials in clay coffins of the Persian period and a few Neo-Babylonian burials with the bodies doubled up inside two large clay jars set mouth to mouth; below the Kassite floors were burials in brick vaults or under inverted clay coffins which had belonged to the dwellers in the houses. Thus far then we had a very satisfactory historic sequence, but below that there were no buildings; the site had been used for dumping builders' rubbish and had lain derelict throughout all the days of Ur's greatness.[1] At about eighteen feet down, on a line following the slope of the rubbish-mound, were hundreds of graves of the time of Sargon of Akkad, an extension of the great cemetery wherein we had dug in former seasons; below these were the outlying graves of the Royal Cemetery, also on the slope, and then, under the tail-end of our "seal-impression stratum", the Jamdat Nasr cemetery, grave above grave so that sometimes they lay eight deep, the lowest dug down to and into the silt of the Flood.

Because the cemetery was in use for a long time and the graves were superimposed more than half, perhaps two-thirds, of them had been destroyed; the diggers of a late grave, happening on an old burial, made off with any objects of value that it contained and smashed the rest without the least compunction; but even so we recorded three hundred and fifty graves in all.

In most cases the body to be buried was wrapped in matting—this may indeed have been general, for where we recorded a 'simple burial' because we could see no trace of matting this may have been due simply to the decay of the fragile material; one only was in a rectangular wickerwork coffin. Most of the graves lay roughly N.N.E. by S.S.W., but the uniformity was probably due only to the need of economizing space in an overcrowded graveyard; inside the grave it was a matter of indifference at which end the dead man's head was placed. What was interesting was the atti-

[1] This may sound improbable, but is really characteristic of the Middle East. Up to 1920 at any rate there was in the centre of Aleppo, facing the Citadel entrance and surrounded by some of the city's finest buildings, a huge empty space which was the regular refuse-dump for the citizens.

tude of the body. Whereas in the al 'Ubaid graves the dead lay extended on their backs, and in the Royal Cemetery lay on one side with the legs slightly bent in the position of sleep, here the body, lying on its side, was tightly flexed, the head bent forward over the breast, the legs brought up so that the knees were at right angles to the body or might even almost touch the chin, while the heels came against the buttocks; the hands were held in front of the face and a little way away from it, usually holding a cup or small vessel; apart from the complication of the cup it was the embryonic attitude—'as a man came out of his mother's womb so shall he return whence he came.' Now the attitude in which a man is buried is part of a solemn ritual dictated by religious beliefs, and any change in it means a change in religion; the difference therefore between the Jamdat Nasr graves and those of the al 'Ubaid Period on the one hand and of the Royal Cemetery on the other implies a serious break in the continuity of the country's history and is probably to be interpreted as evidence for a foreign occupation. A good many other facts support the same conclusion.

Since the graves were often superimposed they could not all be of precisely the same date—the lower were necessarily the older—and it was possible to draw up something like a sequence within the general period represented by the cemetery. The difference in the contents of graves at the successive levels showed a cultural development which required a considerable length of time; a whole range of vase types common in the lowest graves disappears altogether in the higher; there is an intermediate phase in which many of the old types vanish and no new ones are introduced but stone vessels preponderate instead of clay, and a third phase marks the appearance of numerous pottery types not found before. At the beginning we constantly get large clay pots over whose mouths are inverted plain lead tumblers; there are examples of black or smoky grey pottery produced in a 'smother-kiln', and others with a plain red wash highly burnished; with them come simple bowls or cups of white limestone. In the next stage the stone vessels were more numerous and more varied and amongst the pottery vases a good many were of 'reserved slip ware', that is, vessels which after making had been dipped in a bath of watery clay of a different colour from the body-clay of which the pot was made, and then this 'slip' had been wiped off in stripes so as to expose the body clay. The slip, standing out in slight relief and contrasting with the body clay in colour and texture, produces an unambitious but rather pleasing decorative effect. In the topmost graves pottery was almost entirely lacking and its place was taken by an astonishing wealth of cups, bowls and vases in limestone, steatite, diorite or basic diorite, gypsum and alabaster [*Plate* 4]. It will be noticed that all this material had to be imported, much of it from far away—Mosul in the north, the Persian Gulf and the Persian mountains to the east; but the vases were made at Ur. In the rubbish-mounds over the graves we found examples of the stone drill-heads used in vase manufacture; for the hollowing-out of a steatite bowl a start might be made with a narrow-edged metal chisel, steatite being a soft stone, but even in that case the finishing, or in the case of a harder stone the whole of the work, would be done with a bow drill whose head was of diorite. The vase-makers were certainly masters of their craft; many of the shapes are really beautiful, and constantly the shape is modified to suit the character of the material; thus, with a semi-transparent stone like alabaster the wide flat rim may be cut to almost paper-like thinness, while the solidity of the big black diorite vase U.19519 on Plate 4, and the severe strength of its outline, would have done credit to an Athenian artist of the early fifth century B.C. Certainly the vase-maker of Ur could produce a beautiful thing without having recourse to surface decoration, and the great majority of the vessels are plain or at most bear a band of rope moulding in relief; but a few are more elaborately carved, and these show the Sumerian predilection for animal motives. A curious example of this is an alabaster lamp in the form of a *tridacna* shell (we found in the graves several real shells of the sort cut open to make lamps) the five projecting horns serving as troughs to take the wicks; but moved by some whim of fancy the maker has added underneath a bat's head carved in the round, and seen from below the lamp has all the appearance of a flying bat, the horned 'shell' becoming its ribbed extended wings. One alabaster toilet-box is supported by the figure of a ram; two limestone cups have the outside decorated with a procession of oxen carved in low relief; but none of them are very well worked. It has to be remembered that the objects placed in graves would be of the kind normally used by the man in his lifetime, and our graves do not seem to have been those of people of the wealthier class (our pit did *not* hit the centre of the cemetery as I had hoped it would; the better graves lay at the south-west limits of the pit, and presumably the best lay beyond) so that we could not expect to find in them masterpieces of contemporary art such as adorned the temples and palaces of Erech and were found there by the German expedition. Actually the finest example of Jamdat Nasr sculpture that we got came not from the cemetery but from one of the houses in the Flood-pit; this is a steatite figure of a wild boar [*Plate 5a*] made as a support for some object and originally set into a stand—the deep grooves on the sides suggest that the animal was crouched between flat-leafed reeds perhaps of bronze or gold—and as such is truly statuesque; there is a touch of realism in the wrinkling of the upper lip over the tushes, but otherwise all accidentals have been deliberately eliminated in favour of an abstract balance of mass; it is indeed a most successful composition. The bull bowls were crude, as I have already said, but that is because they were cheap 'bazaar' goods not claiming to be works of art and reproducing only the general idea of the real masterpieces; the magnificent steatite bowl shown on [*Plate 5b*] may rank as one of the latter. It is not dated by any external evidence, for it was found in the ruins of a Persian house and certainly does not belong to that period, nor can one guess how it got into such surroundings; it is probably rather later in time than Jamdat Nasr, but it illustrates the artistic tradition which Jamdat Nasr started and may well be a faithful reproduction of the actual products of that age.

The decorated stone vases, indeed the vast bulk of the stone vases in general, came from the later graves in the

Plate 3

Palace wall at Warka decorated with a mosaic
of coloured pegs

Plate 4

Vessels of the Jamdat Nasr period; *above:* two painted
clay pots; *below:* alabaster and diorite vases

upper levels of the cemetery (one of these contained no less than thirty-two stone vessels), but since the three-coloured clay vases which are the hall-mark of Jamdat Nasr occurred throughout the whole series the differences between the early and the late graves denote no more than stages of progress in a single period. One peculiarity they had in common. Whereas most of the graves produced beads, of carnelian, shell, lapis lazuli, hæmatite, glazed frit and gold, which were worn generally as necklaces, sometimes as bracelets or bangles and fairly often as belts round the waist, and beads are, of course, strictly personal belongings, there were no tools or weapons such as are normally found in the graves of other periods. Metal was freely used—we found plenty of copper pots, especially in the lower levels—and therefore metal weapons must have been common enough; we can only conclude that their absence from the graves was due to religious beliefs of which we know nothing.

Something more, though not a great deal, relating to the religion of the Jamdat Nasr age can be got from the seal-impressions found in the rubbish-stratum overlying the graves.[1] Here we have lumps of clay which was plastered over the stoppers of store-jars and then stamped with the owner's seal. Some of them bear pictographic signs—conventionalized pictures which are the beginnings of writing; most are decorative, i.e., have mere patterns, more or less geometrical, patterns distinctive enough to identify ownership, or they are pictorial. The last are very interesting, for side by side with drawings of birds and animals and what are clearly domestic scenes we find primitive versions of religious scenes which were to be revived, or continued, in the art of later times. Thus we have the ritual banquet, with two seated figures facing one another and drinking through tubes; the scene of worship wherein the god is shown in his shrine, the naked priest brings goats for the sacrifice and the traditional jug for libations, and draped worshippers follow with their offerings; the god enthroned on a boat; the milking-scene outside the byre as we have it on the Nin-harsag temple at al 'Ubaid; the ritual dance; all these show that the

[1] Published by L. Legrain, *Ur Excavations*, Vol. III.

religion of classical Sumer has its roots at least in the Jamdat
Nasr age.

And the same must be true of Sumerian civilization as a
whole. Together with the seal-impressions we find in the
rubbish-stratum numerous clay tablets bearing inscriptions.[1]
The stratification shows that they belong to the latter part
of the Jamdat Nasr period, and their character is in agreement with that—the type of writing is less archaic than that
of the tablets found at Jamdat Nasr itself (which presumably
belong to the middle of the period) but more primitive than
that of the Fara tablets which until our discovery had formed
the next known stage in the evolution of the Mesopotamian
script. It is a linear, not a cuneiform writing and still pre-
serves some curvilinear forms, but not nearly to the extent to
which such are found on the contemporary seal-impressions
—evidently the seal-cutter, having an eye to artistic effect,
was far more conservative than the scribe who merely
wanted an easy medium for his records. Just because the
tablets belong to so early a stage in the history of writing the
interest of their contents is strictly limited. Man did not
learn to write with the idea of perpetuating his thoughts and
his actions; that was indeed impossible. The primitive script
is pictographic—each sign represents, directly or by sugges-
tion, a single definite thing, an ox, a house, a man, an ear of
corn, a metal ingot or what-not; you cannot make a picture
of an abstract idea, of a relation or of an action; so the
earliest tablets give us lists of things and numbers, but no
sentences because there is no grammatical construction. Of
about four hundred tablets from Ur the great majority are
lists of cereals and the products of cereals (flour, bread, beer,
etc.) and of live-stock; seventy deal with landed property,
four are lists of men's names and about twenty are school
texts some of which give lists of gods, and numerous temples
are mentioned. This does not sound particularly interesting,
and for the general reader most of it is not; but one curious
point does arise, namely that none of the temples named in
the tablets reappear in Ur of the Dynastic age, and of the

[1] Published by Father Eric Burrows, *Ur Excavations, Texts;* Vol. II, Archaic
Texts.

names of gods very few; if then I am right in thinking that the pictures on the seal-impressions imply a continuity in the religious ritual, none the less in a later age the gods themselves were called by other names than those used by the Jamdat Nasr people—and that is a change which can hardly be explained as the result of evolution.

Our excavations at Ur certainly produced much more material of the Jamdat Nasr Period than of the Uruk Period which preceded it, but admittedly it did not amount to a great deal—in the Flood-pit the piled sherds of the kiln stratum and the ruins of houses which replaced the vase factory, in the Ziggurat area a mere scrap of religious architecture, and finally the cemetery. Does this contribute anything to history?

In the first place the pottery (and pottery is generally our safest guide) does suggest the incoming of a new racial stock; the characteristic three-coloured ware is not developed out of anything made in the Valley before, and its closest analogies are in favour of its having been introduced from the east, i.e., from some part of what is now known as Persia or Iran. There is no need to assume an invasion and a conquest, on the contrary, a gradual infiltration is much more consistent with the facts, for the same factory continued in business, and although it turned out wares of the new type yet, as the mixture of sherds shows, for a time the old industry and the new went on side by side. Moreover, although the newcomers brought in their own arts and their own fashions, to a very large extent they adopted also those of the older inhabitants; we can trace back to the original al 'Ubaid people many elements in the material civilization of classical Sumer and very likely should put with those the language also. But however peaceably they came in, the Jamdat Nasr people in time obtained the mastery over those amongst whom they had settled; State temples are built by rulers, and if at Ur the Ziggurat, the centre of the worship of the city's patron god, was rebuilt in the magnificent style illustrated for us by the mosaic palace at Erech then we can only conclude that the government of the city had passed into the hands of the alien Jamdat Nasr stock. That conclusion is supported by what

47

happened later. The Jamdat Nasr Period ends very abruptly. Because the invaders had absorbed a great deal of the aboriginal culture their suppression did not involve a complete change, and certain things that they had introduced were too obviously valuable to be abandoned—thus, they had been responsible if not for the invention of writing at least for its development, and writing had come to stay; but the arts by which we nowadays can recognize Jamdat Nasr stop suddenly. The three-coloured painted pottery is found in their earliest and their latest graves alike; but not a single sherd of it occurs in the Early Dynastic Period, and their most typical vase-forms also disappear. All their buildings seem to have been violently destroyed, and in those that replaced them there is a remarkable and puzzling change. The Jamdat Nasr builders, like all builders before them, used a rectangular flat brick much like the brick we use to-day—it is the most obvious and practical shape; but the beginning of the Early Dynastic age is signalized by the general and exclusive use of a brick rounded on the top like a loaf of bread, the 'plano-convex brick' of our archæological jargon. Constructionally speaking, this is a thoroughly bad brick. Various suggestions have been put forward to account for its adoption by people who had plenty of experience of the better type, e.g., that it is an imitation of building in stone brought in by people accustomed to using mud and pebbles or rounded boulders; but the Early Dynastic people were not interlopers from abroad but Valley folk who had no such traditions of stone building and no knowledge of it; moreover, the builder in stone has a natural preference for flat stones and would never have been at pains to mould his mud substitutes into so uncongenial a form, nor could so absurd an imitation, if that were all it was, have been imposed uniformly upon every builder in the land and have been employed exclusively, as the plano-convex brick was, for centuries. There must have been a much more compelling reason for it.

It seems to me that the explanation is given by a discovery we made when digging the Ziggurat area. There had been here in the Jamdat Nasr Period a ziggurat with its girdle of

a. Steatite figure of a wild boar, Jamdat Nasr period

b. Steatite bowl in the Jamdat Nasr tradition

Plate 5

Plate 6

a. The grave of Mes-kalam-dug

b. Tomb-chamber of King A-bar-gi; showing the
vaulted roof and arched doorway

walled terraces (we found only a fragment of the latter, but enough to prove that a ziggurat had existed), but this had been razed to the ground and its mosaic decoration torn down and new buildings had been erected on a quite different plan and with a different orientation. Now the underground foundations of the new walls contained a mixture of the flat Jamdat Nasr bricks and of the plano-convex bricks characteristic of the Early Dynasties, but the proportion of the former quickly diminished and by the time the wall rose above ground level it consisted almost entirely, if not entirely, of plano-convex bricks; it was clear that the builders still had some flat bricks in store and did not want to waste them, but could use them only for the underground work whereas for the wall proper the round-topped type was obligatory. And the other outstanding feature was the mud mortar used by the bricklayers. Mortar should be, and in every other building at Ur was, reasonably clean and smooth; but in this case it was mixed with a mass of small sherds of al 'Ubaid pottery—well-nigh as much pottery as mud; and it was not a natural mixture due to the mud having been excavated from an al 'Ubaid level, but artificial and deliberate. I believe that the Jamdat Nasr people, as aliens who had usurped the government of the country, incurred the hatred of the old inhabitants who at last rose in rebellion and put a violent end to the régime. The great buildings, palaces and temples, which had been set up by the tyrants and symbolized their domination had of course to be destroyed—and equally of course had to be replaced. But there had to be a complete change, and even the type of bricks used in those buildings had to be abandoned in favour of one which might perhaps be inconvenient but at any rate broke with the Jamdat Nasr tradition. So everywhere the plano-convex brick came into fashion, and in the first temple to be rebuilt, the central temple of the city's worship, the people of Ur mixed with the mortar the pottery of the old al 'Ubaid days; it was a gesture of ebullient nationalism whereby they linked themselves directly with the original founders of the State, disregarding the Jamdat Nasr interlude.

But for the history of Mesopotamia that interlude was of prime importance; by the time it ended Sumerian civilization was fully developed. The statement involves a question which has often been discussed, 'Who were the Sumerians?' Now the adjective 'Sumerian' has been formed by modern scholars from the place-name 'Sumer' which from the latter part of the third millennium B.C. was the name regularly used for southern Mesopotamia as opposed to 'Akkad', the northern part of the river valley; but the inhabitants did not call themselves 'Sumerians', they were simply 'The people of Sumer'. For the modern historian the invention of the adjective 'Sumerian' was convenient for distinguishing a particular language, a particular people and a particular civilization. The language of the tablets is entirely different from any other ever used in Mesopotamia (but to what family of languages it belongs has not been determined) and thanks to the rich harvest of excavation we know exactly what we mean by 'Sumerian civilization'. But the problem 'Who were the Sumerians?' remains. Ought we to apply the term to the old al 'Ubaid stock? Undoubtedly they contributed much to the civilization which we know as Sumerian, but they were submerged before it had developed very far. To the Uruk people? They introduced metal and so made progress possible; but we know little more about them. To the Jamdat Nasr people? It is tempting to see an allusion to them in the Sumerian legend which tells how a race of monsters, half human and half fish, came from the Persian Gulf, led by one Oannes, and settled in the cities of Sumer and introduced the arts of writing, of agriculture and of working in metal 'and since that time no further inventions have been made'; but that attributes to them too much. It is a fact that the Sumerian civilization was built up from elements derived from all three sources, al 'Ubaid, Uruk and Jamdat Nasr, and only took on its characteristic shape after those three sources had amalgamated; it is safest to assume that only then could the people of the land be termed 'Sumerians'. Just as England can be so called only after wave after wave of invaders had forced their way into Britain and by their joint contributions produced an island culture which was not peculiar to any one of them, so we should, I think, reserve the name 'Sumerians' for the hybrid stock whose disparate forebears had made Sumer but, by the Dynastic Period, had merged their individuality in a civilization common to all.

III

The Royal Cemetery

THE first thing that I did when, in 1922, we started the excavations at Ur, was to dig trial trenches which might give us some idea of the lay-out of the old city. The main purpose was to trace the line of the great wall with which Nebuchadnezzar enclosed the Temenos or Sacred Area of Ur; Dr. Hall had cleared a short stretch of it in 1919, but since within the Temenos would lie the principal temples of the city it was necessary to establish as early as possible its exact limits as a guide to our future work. The trench designed to give us Nebuchadnezzar's south-east wall was laid down by guess-work, since there were no surface indications to help us, the ground here being badly denuded, and for most of its length our trench proved to lie actually inside the Temenos; at its south-west end two or three courses of the brick foundations of the wall were found, all the superstructure having been weathered away, but the rest of it produced no vestige of any building at all. The disappearance of the Late Babylonian structures did not of course mean that there was nothing to be found underneath, so I deepened the trench, and at once things began to happen; there turned up, sometimes singly, sometimes apparently in groups, clay vases (nearly all broken), limestone bowls, small bronze objects and quite a lot of beads made of glazed faience or stone; when the foreman spotted beads coming up and either he or one of the staff took over the task of excavating there might be gold beads as well, but none such were produced by our workmen.

It was easy enough to recover what had been stolen. The men worked in gangs of five, each under a pick-man, each in a defined plot of ground. On pay-day I announced that for every gold bead found by Hamoudi the foreman or by ourselves the gang working on the plot concerned was being paid a *baksheesh*; and the *baksheesh* was about three times what I thought the local goldsmiths would have paid. The announcement was greeted with astonishment and very obvious chagrin. This was a Saturday; on the Monday the trench-diggers produced a surprising harvest of gold beads— all of which had on the Sunday been bought back from the goldsmiths. So far so good; but the real difficulty was something quite different. The trench evidently ran across a cemetery which, judging by our finds, might well be a very rich one. Graves, if they are to produce the proper scientific results, have to be dug with the greatest care; we had been digging graves, but in scarcely a single case could we say that all its furniture had been recovered; most of the objects had been got out without any scientific context, and no one grave had been recorded as it should have been. We had a force of very wild Arab tribesmen, few of whom had ever handled tools before; they were completely ignorant, had no idea of what good workmanship was, were reckless and of course dishonest. Moreover we were ignorant too. The archæology of Mesopotamia was in its infancy and there was no means of dating the small objects that come out of graves; the state of knowledge at that time is shown by the fact that when I asked expert opinion as to the date of the things we had found I was told that since they lay fairly close to the surface they must be late Babylonian, about 700 B.C., whereas in truth they were Sargonid and dated to about 2300 B.C. Our object was to get history, not to fill museum cases with miscellaneous curios, and history could not be got unless both we and our men were duly trained. So I stopped work on 'the gold trench' and, in spite of the workmen's annual petition to return to it, waited until four years' experience had equipped us better for the task. The delay was fortunate, for the excavation of the 'gold trench' area, which was to take us a number of seasons, was not only of immense importance but one of the most difficult that I have ever undertaken; but conditions were now all in our favour, for we had secured an outline at least of Sumerian archæology going back to the First Dynasty of Ur and, beyond that, to the al 'Ubaid Period (though this was still isolated from its context) and we had a gang of thoroughly trained workmen, keen, well disciplined and altogether trustworthy, while Hamoudi's two sons Yahia and Ibrahim, now junior foremen, had developed a technical skill in digging which was to prove invaluable to us.

So, at the beginning of 1927, we started to dig the cemetery. As we soon found out, there were really two cemeteries, one above the other, belonging to different periods. The upper graves were dated by inscriptions on cylinder seals to the time of Sargon of Akkad; those will be described later. Below them, dug down into the rubbish-mounds which lay outside the Sacred Area, was what we came to call 'The Royal Cemetery'.

We had started digging, as I have said, inside Nebuchadnezzar's Temenos, but this, we found, was very much larger than the Temenos of the early city. The Ziggurat and main temples of those days stood on a high walled terrace the core of which must have been formed by the superimposed ruins of buildings going back to the first settlement of the al 'Ubaid people at Ur; south of the terrace there was an open space, free of buildings, and here the people of Ur, with true Oriental *insouciance*, emptied their rubbish; in time this rose to form a rough *talus* sloping gently down from the walls of the Sacred Area. Granted that it was a rubbish-mound, none the less it did lie as near as might be to the holiest place in Ur, and it was an empty space; not unnaturally therefore men got into the way of burying their dead there.

The burials were of two sorts, the graves of the common folk and the tombs of kings; of the former we cleared about two thousand, and of the latter sixteen were more or less preserved.

The ordinary grave consisted of a rectangular shaft, anything from four to twelve feet deep, in which the dead man was laid either wrapped in matting or enclosed in a coffin which might be of basket-work, of wood or of clay; there was no rule regarding orientation and the head might be facing in any direction, but the attitude of the body was invariable;

54

it lay on its side, the back straight or very slightly curved, the legs more or less flexed at hip and knee and the hands brought up in front of the breast almost to the level of the mouth; it is the attitude of a person asleep, and is wholly unlike the rigid straightness of the al 'Ubaid dead or the tightly-contracted 'embryonic' position which marks the Jamdat Nasr graves. That this should be invariable whereas so much else in the ritual of the burials seems casual and capricious must mean that a special significance attached to it and that it reflected some religious belief. With the body there were placed such personal belongings as beads and ear-rings, a knife or dagger, the pin that fastened the dress or the shroud and perhaps the cylinder seal the impression of which on a clay tablet was equivalent to the owner's sig-nature. Outside the matting roll or the coffin were set what were more properly offerings to the dead, food and drink in vessels of clay, copper or stone, weapons and tools, toilet articles, etc.; in most cases the bottom of the pit was lined with matting and mats were spread over the offerings to keep them from immediate contact with the earth which was thrown in to fill the shaft.

This provision made for the dead seems clearly to prove a belief in a future life of some sort, but there is nothing found which expressly defines such belief; in no single grave has there been any figure of a god, any symbol or ornament that strikes one as being of a religious nature; the dead man took with him what he might require for a journey to or for a sojourn in another world, but what he thought about the world to which he was going nothing tells us. The tomb furniture is intended to satisfy purely material needs and its quantity and quality merely reflect the social standing of the dead man and his family in this world. It was essentially a very simple form of burial and so far as we could tell there was nothing in the way of a tombstone. Generally the first sign that a workman had of a grave as he dug down into the mixed soil of the cemetery was a paper-thin wavy line of white powder, the edge of the reed matting that lined the original shaft, or else a few small holes set in a line and running down vertically into the earth, holes left by the decay of the wooden staves which strengthened the sides of a wooden or wickerwork coffin. It is a strange thing that in soil wherein so much that might be thought enduring rots away completely a fragile material such as wood or matting, though it lose all its substance, yet retains its appearance and its texture and can with care be exposed in such condition that a photograph of it looks like the real thing whereas it is but a film which a touch of the finger or even a breath obliterates more easily than it dislodges the plumage from the wing of a butterfly. There was one tragic instance of this. The cemetery site had been squared and poles set up as bench-marks from which measurements could be taken for plotting the position of the graves, and every now and then as work went deeper the poles would be left standing on pillars of earth too high up for convenient measuring and had to be re-set at a lower level. On one such occasion I told a workman to knock down a pillar and he, for fun, simply gave it a hard push. The upper part fell, as he expected, but with a clean diagonal break, and in a moment he was shouting to me to come. On the top of the column-stump, lying aslope, there was what looked like a wooden panel, and it was exquisitely carved with a procession of little figures in relief. Hurriedly I sent for the camera, and in the meantime began to make a measured sketch of the design, when, all of a sudden, down came one of the rare rainstorms of southern Iraq and, though the workmen did their inadequate best to shelter the monument with their cloaks, before I had more than outlined two or three figures the 'panel' had disintegrated into featureless mud.

But the traces of matting and the impression made by wood were of the greatest help to us in the digging of the cemetery because they gave timely warning of things to come, so that we were not taken by surprise, the pick-men striking blindly into the earth only to ruin some delicate treasure; the pick could be dropped in due time and be replaced by the excavator's knife and brush and some member of the staff was always on the spot for the final clearing and recording of the grave. I must admit that with two thousand graves to be duly noted the necessary routine

56

became wearisome at times, for there was a great deal of repetition and only too many of them contained nothing of very obvious interest, either because of their original poverty or because of subsequent plundering. At least two-thirds of the graves in the cemetery had been plundered or completely destroyed. While the cemetery was still in use the men digging a new grave, if they hit upon one of earlier date—and in the overcrowded graveyard that was more likely to happen than not—could not resist the temptation to remove its more valuable contents. At a later date men, induced perhaps by chance discoveries, went in for deliberate tomb-robbing. They must have known—perhaps from the survival of surface monuments—the whereabouts of the old royal tombs, but feared to attack them openly, for we found circular shafts (one of them was dated by potsherds found in it to the time of Sargon of Akkad) driven down vertically to the level of the tombs but at some distance from them and then turning horizontally to tunnel towards the tomb they proposed to plunder; in some cases they succeeded only too well, in one or two they missed their mark and abandoned the attempt in disgust. At Ur, as in Egypt, tomb-robbing is a very ancient profession, and the men who followed it did not work at random but had direct knowledge to guide them to what was most worth while. We found hundreds of untouched private graves whose contents were valuable indeed for scientific archæology but of no interest for seekers after treasure; only by a stroke of unusual luck would we hit upon a grave at once rich and intact.

The finest of all such was the grave of Mes-kalam-dug found in the season 1927–8; it was dug down into the shaft of one of the largest of the royal tombs but was itself an ordinary grave distinguished from countless others in the cemetery only by its wealth. The first indication we had of what was to come was a copper spear-head sticking straight up in the ground; following this down we found that it was attached to a golden haft, and below this was the hole left by the decay of the wooden shaft running down to a corner of the grave. Except for the fact that it was rather larger than usual, the grave was a normal one, a plain earth pit big enough to take a wooden coffin and to leave on three sides of this a free space for offerings. Along the head of the grave were stuck spears in a row, the blades downwards, and between these were vases of alabaster and clay; by the side of the coffin, lying on the remains of what may have been a bossed shield, were two gold-mounted daggers, copper daggers, chisels and other tools, some fifty copper bowls, many of them fluted, and other bowls of silver, copper jugs and plates, and more vessels of stone and clay; at the foot of the grave again spears, and with them a set of arrows having chisel-edged points of chipped flint.

But it was when the earth from the coffin itself was removed that we had our great surprise. The body lay in normal fashion on its right side; round the waist was a broad belt of silver, now decayed, from which hung a gold dagger and a whetstone of lapis lazuli fixed on a gold ring; in front of the waist was a solid mass of lapis and gold beads, hundreds in all; between the hands was placed a bowl of heavy gold, a larger oval gold bowl lay close by, and near the elbow a gold lamp in the form of a shell, while yet another gold bowl stood behind the head. Against the right shoulder was a double axe-head of electrum, and an electrum axe-head of normal type was by the left shoulder; behind the body there were jumbled together in a heap a gold head-dress, bracelets, beads, and amulets, lunate ear-rings, and spiral rings of gold wire [*Plate 6a*].

The bones were so far decayed that there was here none of the grimness of a skeleton, only a few strips of crumbling brown which served to show the attitude of the dead man, and the prevailing note was struck rather by the gold, clean as when it was put into the grave; and most of all was the eye taken by the helmet which still covered the rotten fragments of the skull. It was a helmet of beaten gold made to fit low over the head with cheek-pieces to protect the face, and it was in the form of a wig, the locks of hair hammered up in relief, the individual hairs shown by delicate engraved lines [*Plate 7a*]. Parted down the middle, the hair covers the head in flat wavy tresses and is bound round with a twisted fillet; behind it is tied into a little chignon, and below the fillet hangs in rows of formal curls about the ears, which are rendered in high relief and are pierced so as not to interfere with hearing; similar curls on the cheek-pieces represent whiskers; round the edge of the metal are small holes for the laces which secured inside it a padded cap, of which some traces yet remained.

As an example of goldsmith's work this is the most beautiful thing we have found in the cemetery, finer than the gold daggers or the heads of bulls, and if there were nothing else by which the art of these ancient Sumerians could be judged we should still, on the strength of it alone, accord them high rank in the roll of civilized races.

On two of the golden bowls and on the lamp was repeated the inscription 'Mes-kalam-dug. Hero of the Good Land'. The name is the same as that found on the cylinder seal dedicated with the two gold daggers above the domed stone tomb of a queen, but the owner of the seal is called 'King', and here there is no such title of royalty: the term 'Hero of the Good Land' and the exceptional richness of the grave may justify us in seeing in this Mes-kalam-dug a prince of the royal house, but the omission of any claim to kingly power ought certainly to mean that he never occupied the throne, and this omission is precisely what we should expect if our theory is correct, for the grave is essentially of the commoner's type. Had the royal tombs not been discovered, it would probably have been hailed as a king's grave; as it is, its wealth only emphasizes the difference between it and them.

There were sixteen royal graves found in the cemetery, and although no two of them were exactly alike yet they all shared certain characteristics which set them altogether apart from the ordinary graves. The dead was laid not merely in a coffin but in a builded tomb of stone or of stone and burnt or mud brick—it might be a single chamber or it might be a more elaborate structure with several rooms, an underground palace. The ritual of burial included human sacrifice; the number of victims might vary from a mere half dozen to seventy or eighty, but a certain number had to accompany the owner of the tomb. The re-filling of the tomb shaft was not a simple matter of throwing back the earth; it was a long-drawn ceremony involving elaborate rites.

Owing to the destruction caused by plunderers and, to some extent, by the diggers of later graves, (only two royal tombs were intact), the evidence for the ritual was not complete in every case; it had to be drawn impartially from different graves on the assumption, which cannot always be proved, that what was true of one was true of the rest also; it is a composite picture that I give, but the description of a few graves will justify it.

The first of the royal tombs to be found told us, in effect, very little, partly because it had been hopelessly wrecked by robbers and partly because we had only just begun to excavate it (knowing nothing about what it was to prove) on the last day of the 1926–7 season. Amongst a mass of bronze weapons which did not at the time seem to be associated with any burial we found the famous gold dagger of Ur, whose blade was of gold, its hilt of blue lapis lazuli decorated with gold studs and its sheath of gold beautifully worked with an openwork design derived from plaited grass—the material of which a commoner's dagger-sheath was sometimes made; with it was another object, almost equally remarkable, a cone-shaped reticule of gold ornamented with a spiral pattern containing a set of little toilet instruments, tweezers, lancet and pencil, also of gold. Nothing at all resembling these things had ever yet been unearthed in Mesopotamia; so novel were they that a recognized expert took them to be Arab work of the thirteenth century A.D., and no one could blame him for the error, for no one could have suspected such art in the third millennium before Christ. Returning to the spot at the beginning of the next season we were able to get more evidence as to the dagger's associations, but even so it had to be interpreted in the light of more complete discoveries.

In that season, 1927–8, digging in another part of the cemetery area, we came upon five bodies lying side by side in a sloping trench; except for the copper daggers at their waists and one or two small clay cups they had none of the normal furniture of a grave, and the mere fact of there being a number thus together was unusual. Then, below them, a layer of matting was found, and tracing this along we came to another group of bodies, those of ten women carefully arranged in two rows; they wore head-dresses of gold, lapis lazuli, and carnelian, and elaborate bead necklaces, but they too possessed no regular tomb furnishings. At the end of the row lay the remains of a wonderful harp, the wood of it decayed but its decoration intact, making its reconstruction only a matter of care; the upright wooden beam was capped with gold, and in it were fastened the gold-headed nails which secured the strings; the sounding-box was edged with a mosaic in red stone, lapis lazuli and white shell, and from the front of it projected a splendid head of a bull wrought in gold with eyes and beard of lapis lazuli; across the ruins of the harp lay the bones of the gold-crowned harpist.

By this time we had found the earth sides of the pit in which the women's bodies lay and could see that the bodies of the five men were on the ramp which led down to it. Following the pit along, we came upon more bones which at first puzzled us by being other than human, but the meaning of them soon became clear. A little way inside the entrance to the pit stood a wooden sledge chariot decorated with red, white, and blue mosaic along the edges of the framework and with golden heads of lions having manes of lapis lazuli and shell on its side panels; along the top rail were smaller gold heads of lions and bulls, silver lionesses' heads adorned the front, and the position of the vanished swingle-tree was shown by a band of blue and white inlay and two smaller heads of lionesses in silver. In front of the chariot lay the crushed skeletons of two asses with the bodies of the grooms by their heads, and on the top of the bones was the double ring, once attached to the pole, through which the reins had passed; it was of silver, and standing on it was a gold 'mascot' in the form of a donkey most beautifully and realistically modelled.

Close to the chariot were an inlaid gaming-board[1] and a

[1] A more elaborate example of a gaming-board is figured on Plate 10 (b).

collection of tools and weapons, including a set of chisels and a saw made of gold, big bowls of grey soapstone, copper vessels, a long tube of gold and lapis which was a drinking-tube for sucking up liquor from the bowls, more human bodies, and then the wreckage of a large wooden chest adorned with a figured mosaic in lapis lazuli and shell which was found empty but had perhaps contained such perishable things as clothes. Behind this box were more offerings, masses of vessels in copper, silver, stone (including exquisite examples in volcanic glass, lapis lazuli, alabaster, and marble), and gold (Pl. 9); one set of silver vessels seemed to be in the nature of a communion-service, for there was a shallow tray or platter, a jug with tall neck and long spout such as we know from carved stone reliefs to have been used in religious rites, and tall slender silver tumblers nested one inside another; a similar tumbler in gold, fluted and chased, with a fluted feeding-bowl, a chalice, and a plain oval bowl of gold lay piled together, and two magnificent lions' heads in silver, perhaps the ornaments of a throne, were amongst the treasures in the crowded pit. The perplexing thing was that with all this wealth of objects we had found no body so far distinguished from the rest as to be that of the person to whom all were dedicated; logically our discovery, however great, was incomplete.

The objects were removed and we started to clear away the remains of the wooden box, a chest some 6 feet long and 3 feet across, when under it we found burnt bricks. They were fallen, but at one end some were still in place and formed the ring-vault of a stone chamber. The first and natural supposition was that here we had the tomb to which all the offerings belonged, but further search proved that the chamber was plundered, the roof had not fallen from decay but had been broken through, and the wooden box had been placed over the hole as if deliberately to hide it. Then, digging round the outside of the chamber, we found just such another pit as that 6 feet above (Fig. 4). At the foot of the ramp lay six soldiers, orderly in two ranks, with copper spears by their sides and copper helmets crushed flat on the broken skulls; just inside, having evidently been backed down the

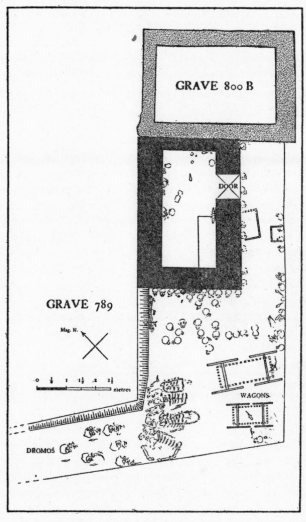

Fig. 4. Plan of the grave of King A-bar-gi

slope, were two wooden four-wheeled wagons each drawn by three oxen—one of the latter so well preserved that we were able to lift the skeleton entire; the wagons were plain, but the reins were decorated with long beads of lapis and silver and passed through silver rings surmounted with mascots in the form of bulls; the grooms lay at the oxen's heads and the drivers in the bodies of the cars; of the cars themselves only the impression of the decayed wood remained in the soil, but so clear was this that a photograph showed the grain of the solid wooden wheel and the grey-white circle which had been the leather tyre.

Against the end wall of the stone chamber lay the bodies of nine women wearing the gala head-dress of lapis and carnelian beads from which hung golden pendants in the form of beech leaves, great lunate ear-rings of gold, silver 'combs' like the palm of a hand with three fingers tipped with flowers whose petals are inlaid with lapis, gold, and shell, and necklaces of lapis and gold; their heads were leaned against the masonry, their bodies extended on to the floor of the pit, and the whole space between them and the wagons was crowded with other dead, women and men, while the passage which led along the side of the chamber to its arched door was lined with soldiers carrying daggers, and with women. Of the soldiers in the central space one had a bundle of four spears with heads of gold, two had sets of four silver spears, and by another there was a remarkable relief in copper with a design of two lions trampling on the bodies of two fallen men which may have been the decoration of a shield.

On the top of the bodies of the 'court ladies' against the chamber wall had been placed a wooden harp, of which there survived only the copper head of a bull and the shell plaques which had adorned the sounding-box; by the side wall of the pit, also set on the top of the bodies, was a second harp with a wonderful bull's head in gold, its eyes, beard, and horn-tips of lapis, and a set of engraved shell plaques [*Plate* 11] not less wonderful; there are four of them with grotesque scenes of animals playing the parts of men, and while the most striking feature about them is that sense of

64

Plate 7

a. The gold helmet of Mes-kalam-dug
b. A gold bowl from Queen Shub-ad's tomb

Plate 8

The head-dress of Queen Shub-ad

humour which is so rare in ancient art, the grace and balance of the design and the fineness of the drawing make of these plaques one of the most instructive documents that we possess for the appreciation of the art of early Sumer.

Inside the tomb the robbers had left enough to show that it had contained bodies of several minor people as well as that of the chief person, whose name, if we can trust the inscription on a cylinder seal, was A-bar-gi; overlooked against the wall we found two model boats, one of copper now hopelessly decayed, the other of silver wonderfully well preserved [*Plate 9b*]; some 2 feet long, it has high stern and prow, five seats, and amidships an arched support for the awning which would protect the passenger, and the leaf-bladed oars are still set in the thwarts; it is a testimony to the conservatism of the East that a boat of identical type is in use to-day on the marshes of the Lower Euphrates, some 50 miles from Ur.

The king's tomb-chamber lay at the far end of his open pit; continuing our search behind it we found a second stone chamber built up against it either at the same time or, more probably, at a later period. This chamber, roofed like the king's with a vault of ring arches in burnt brick, was the tomb of the queen to whom belonged the upper pit with its ass chariot and other offerings: her name, Shub-ad, was given us by a fine cylinder seal of lapis lazuli which was found in the filling of the shaft a little above the roof of the chamber and had probably been thrown into the pit at the moment when the earth was being put back into it. The vault of the chamber had fallen in, but luckily this was due to the weight of earth above, not to the violence of tomb-robbers; the tomb itself was intact.

At one end, on the remains of a wooden bier, lay the body of the queen, a gold cup near her hand; the upper part of the body was entirely hidden by a mass of beads of gold, silver, lapis lazuli, carnelian, agate, and chalcedony, long strings of which, hanging from a collar, had formed a cloak reaching to the waist and bordered below with a broad band of tubular beads of lapis, carnelian, and gold: against the right arm were three long gold pins with lapis heads and three

65   E

amulets in the form of fish, two of gold and one of lapis, and a fourth in the form of two seated gazelles, also of gold.

The head-dress whose remains covered the crushed skull was a more elaborate edition of that worn by the court ladies: its basis was a broad gold ribbon festooned in loops round the hair—and the measurement of the curves showed that this was not the natural hair but a wig padded out to an almost grotesque size; over this came three wreaths, the lowest hanging down over the forehead, of plain gold ring pendants, the second of beech leaves, the third of long willow leaves in sets of three with gold flowers whose petals were of blue and white inlay; all these were strung on triple chains of lapis and carnelian beads. Fixed into the back of the hair was a golden 'Spanish comb' with five points ending in lapis-centred gold flowers. Heavy spiral rings of gold wire were twisted into the side curls of the wig, huge lunate ear-rings of gold hung down to the shoulders, and apparently from the hair also hung on each side a string of large square stone beads with, at the end of each, a lapis amulet, one shaped as a seated bull and the other as a calf. Complicated as the head-dress was, its different parts lay in such good order that it was possible to reconstruct the whole and exhibit the likeness of the queen with all her original finery in place [*Plate* 8].

For the purposes of exhibition a plaster cast was made from a well-preserved female skull of the period (the queen's own skull was too fragmentary to be used), and over this my wife modelled the features in wax, making this as thin as possible so as not to obliterate the bone structure; the face was passed by Sir Arthur Keith, who had made a special study of the Ur and al 'Ubaid skulls, as reproducing faithfully the character of the early Sumerians. On this head was put a wig of the correct dimensions dressed in the fashion illustrated by terra-cotta figures which, though later in date, probably represent an old tradition. The gold hair-ribbon had been lifted from the tomb without disturbing the arrangement of the strands, these having been first fixed in position by strips of glued paper threaded in and out between them and by wires twisted round the gold; when

66

the wig had been fitted on the head, the hair-ribbon was balanced on the top and the wires and paper bands were cut, and the ribbon fell naturally into place and required no further arranging. The wreaths were re-strung and tied on in the order noted at the time of excavation. Though the face is not an actual portrait of the queen, it gives at least the type to which she must have conformed, and the whole reconstructed head presents us with the most accurate picture we are likely ever to possess of what she looked like in her lifetime.

By the side of the body lay a second head-dress of a novel sort. On to a diadem made apparently of a strip of soft white leather had been sewn thousands of minute lapis lazuli beads, and against this background of solid blue was set a row of exquisitely fashioned gold animals, stags, gazelles, bulls, and goats, with between them clusters of pomegranates, three fruits hanging together shielded by their leaves, and branches of some other tree with golden stems and fruit or pods of gold and carnelian, while gold rosettes were sewn on at intervals, and from the lower border of the diadem hung palmettes of twisted gold wire.

The bodies of two women attendants were crouched against the bier, one at its head and one at its foot, and all about the chamber lay strewn offerings of all sorts, another gold bowl, vessels of silver and copper, stone bowls, and clay jars for food, the head of a cow in silver, two silver tables for offerings, silver lamps, and a number of large cockle-shells containing green paint; such shells are nearly always found in women's graves, and the paint in them, presumably used as a cosmetic, may be white, black, or red, but the normal colour is green. Queen Shub-ad's shells were abnormally big, and with them were found two pairs of imitation shells, one in silver and one in gold, each with its green paint.

The discovery was now complete and our earlier difficulty was explained: King A-bar-gi's grave and Queen Shub-ad's were exactly alike, but whereas the former was all on one plane, the queen's tomb-chamber had been sunk below the general level of her grave-pit. Probably they were husband and wife: the king had died first and been buried, and it had been the queen's wish to lie as close to him as might be; for this end the grave-diggers had reopened the king's shaft, going down in it until the top of the chamber vault appeared; then they had stopped work in the main shaft but had dug down at the back of the chamber a pit in which the queen's stone tomb could be built. But the treasures known to lie in the king's grave were too great a temptation for the workmen; the outer pit where the bodies of the court ladies lay was protected by 6 feet of earth which they could not disturb without being detected, but the richer plunder in the royal chamber itself was separated from them only by the bricks of the vault; they broke through the arch, carried off their spoil, and placed the great clothes-chest of the queen over the hole to hide their sacrilege.

No other explanation than this would account for the plundered vault lying immediately below the unplundered grave of the queen. And on this showing we have two almost identical burials, the sole difference being that in the queen's case the tomb chamber is below the level at which the other victims lie, and for this too the sentimental motive is sufficient. What the two graves tell us is quite clear so far as it goes.

To begin with, a more or less rectangular shaft was dug down into the mixed soil of the rubbish-mounds to a depth of some thirty feet; at the top the shaft might measure as much as forty-five feet by thirty; the earth walls were necessarily sloped but were kept as nearly vertical as might be, and on one side there was cut an entrance in the form of a steeply-sloped or stepped passage running down from ground level. On the bottom of the shaft, but occupying only a small part of its area, the tomb chamber was built, with stone walls and brick vaulted roof and a door in one of the longer sides. The royal body was carried down the sloping passage and laid in the chamber, sometimes, perhaps generally, inside a wooden coffin, though Queen Shub-ad lay upon an open wooden bier and another queen in the only other undisturbed burial was apparently stretched upon the floor of the tomb. Three or four of the personal attendants of the dead had their place with him or her in the tomb chamber; thus, two were crouched by Shub-ad's bier and one lay a little apart and four shared the tomb of the other (nameless) queen; in the plundered tombs scattered bones betrayed the presence of more than one body. These attendants must have been killed, or drugged into insensibility, before the door of the tomb chamber was walled up. The owner of the tomb was decked with all the finery befitting his station and with him in the chamber were set all such objects as we find in the graves of commoners, the only difference being that they are more numerous and of more precious material—the vessels for food and drink may be of gold and silver instead of clay—the attendants, on the other hand, while they wear what we may call their court dresses, are not laid out properly as for burial but are in the attitudes of those who serve, and they are unprovided with any grave equipment of their own; they are part of the tomb furniture.

When the door had been blocked with stone and brick and smoothly plastered over, the first phase of the burial ceremony was complete. The second phase, as best illustrated by the tombs of Shub-ad and her husband, was more dramatic. Down into the open pit, with its mat-covered floor and mat-lined walls, empty and unfurnished, there comes a procession of people, the members of the dead ruler's court, soldiers, men-servants and women, the latter in all their finery of brightly-coloured garments and head-dresses of carnelian and lapis lazuli, silver and gold, officers with the insignia of their rank, musicians bearing harps or lyres, and then, driven or backed down the slope, the chariots drawn by oxen or by asses, the drivers in the cars, the grooms holding the heads of the draught animals, and all take up their allotted places at the bottom of the shaft and finally a guard of soldiers forms up at the entrance. Each man and woman brought a little cup of clay or stone or metal, the only equipment needed for the rite that was to follow. There would seem to have been some kind of service down there, at least it is certain that the musicians played up to the last; then each of them drank from their cups a potion which they had brought with them or found prepared for them on the spot—in one case we found in the middle of the pit a great copper pot into which they could have dipped—and they lay down and composed themselves for death. Somebody came down and killed the animals (we found their bones on the top of those of the grooms, so they must have died later) and perhaps saw to it that all was decently in order—thus, in the king's grave the lyres had been placed on the top of the bodies of the women players, leant against the tomb wall—and when that was done earth was flung in from above, over the unconscious victims, and the filling-in of the grave-shaft was begun.

This account is based for the most part on the two tombs, of Shub-ad and of A-bar-gi, which have been described in detail; the royal tombs, as I have said, differed a good deal one from another, but not to the extent that the account would not apply broadly to them all. Where the single built chamber was elaborated into a building containing several rooms and occupying the whole area of the shaft, one of these was clearly the monarch's actual burial-chamber and the others were for the members of his court, taking the place of the open 'death-pit' which is invariably associated with the single-chamber tombs; in one case the sacrifice of the human victims took place before even the tomb was prepared for the great dead, for the stone chamber was built on the earth which covered the bodies lying at the bottom of the mat-lined shaft, but normally the rite must have followed the order described above. The best example of the 'death-pit' was that of our royal grave PG/1237; the tomb chamber had been completely destroyed by robbers, only one bit of ruined wall and a number of loose limestone blocks remaining from it, but the 'death-pit' was intact, as indeed was always the case, for whereas it was a simple matter to tunnel down and enter a built chamber only such wholesale excavation as we practised could get at individual bodies shrouded in the earth, and the old robbers dared not work thus openly. The pit measured, at the bottom, twenty-seven feet by twenty-four, and had the usual sloped approach and its sides had been mud-plastered and hung with matting. Six menservants carrying knives or axes lay near the entrance, lined up against the wall; in front of them stood a great copper basin, and by it were the bodies of four women harpists, one with her hands still on the strings of her instrument. Over the rest of the pit's area there lay in ordered rows the bodies of sixty-four ladies of the court. All of them wore some sort of ceremonial dress; a few threads and patches preserved by being in contact with stone or metal showed that this had included a short sleeved coat of scarlet, the cuffs enriched with beadwork in lapis lazuli, carnelian and gold, with sometimes a belt of white shell rings; it may have been fastened in front with a long pin of silver or copper; round the neck was worn a 'dog-collar' of lapis lazuli and gold together with other looser necklaces of gold, silver, lapis lazuli and carnelian beads; in the ears were very large crescent-shaped ear-rings of gold or silver and twisted spirals of gold or silver wire kept in order the curls above the ears. The head-dress was much like that of Queen Shub-ad; a long ribbon of gold or silver was looped several times round the hair and, at any rate with those of higher rank, a triple band of gold, lapis lazuli and carnelian beads was fastened below the ribbon with gold beech-leaf pendants hanging across the forehead. Twenty-eight of these court ladies wore golden hair-ribbons, the rest silver. Unfortunately silver is a metal which ill resists the action of the acids in the soil, and where it was but a thin strip and, being worn on the head, was directly affected by the corruption of the flesh, it generally disappears altogether, and at most there may be detected on the bone of the skull slight traces of a purplish colour which is silver chloride in a minutely powdered state: we could be certain that the ribbons were worn, but we could not produce material evidence of them.

But in one case we had better luck. The great gold ear-rings were in place, but not a sign of discoloration betrayed the existence of any silver head-dress, and this negative evidence was duly noted: then, as the body was cleared, there was found against it, about on the level of the waist, a flat disc a little more than 3 inches across of a grey substance which was certainly silver; it might have been a small circular box. Only when I was cleaning it in the house that evening, hoping to find something which would enable me to catalogue it more in detail, did its real nature come to light: it was the silver hair-ribbon, but it had never been worn—carried apparently in the woman's pocket, it was just as she had taken it from her room, done up in a tight coil with the ends brought over to prevent its coming undone; and since it formed thus a comparatively solid mass of metal and had been protected by the cloth of her dress, it was very well preserved and even the delicate edges of the ribbon were sharply distinct. Why the owner had not put it on one could not say; perhaps she was late for the ceremony and had not time to dress properly, but her haste has in any case afforded us the only example of a silver hair-ribbon which we were able to preserve.

Another thing that perishes utterly in the earth is cloth, but occasionally on lifting a stone bowl which has lain inverted over a bit of stuff and has protected it from the soil one sees traces which, although only of fine dust, keep the texture of the material, or a copper vessel may by its corrosion preserve some fragment which was in contact with it. By such evidence we were able to prove that the women in the death-pit wore garments of bright red woollen stuff; and as many of them had at the wrists one or two cuffs made of beads which had been sewn on to cloth, it was tolerably certain that these were sleeved coats rather than cloaks. It must have been a very gaily dressed crowd that assembled in the open mat-lined pit for the royal obsequies, a blaze of colour with the crimson coats, the silver, and the gold; clearly these people were not wretched slaves killed as oxen might be killed, but persons held in honour, wearing their robes of office, and coming, one hopes, voluntarily to a rite which would in their belief be but a passing from one world to another, from the service of a god on earth to that of the same god in another sphere.

Obviously a great pit so crowded with objects could be cleared only a little at a time. The soil was removed until the bodies were almost exposed, covered only by the few inches of broken brick which had been the first of the filling thrown over the dead; here and there a pick driven too deep might bring to view a piece of gold ribbon or a golden beech leaf,

72

showing that everywhere there were bodies richly adorned, but these would be quickly covered up again and left until more methodical work should reveal them in due course. Starting in one corner of the pit, we marked out squares such as might contain from five to six bodies, and all these were cleared, noted, and the objects belonging to them collected and removed before the next square was taken in hand.

It was slow work, and especially so in those cases where we decided to remove the entire skull with all its ornaments in position on it. The wreaths and chains and necklaces restrung and arranged in a glass case may look very well, but it is more interesting to see them as they were actually found, and therefore a few heads on which the original order of the beads and gold work was best preserved were laboriously cleaned with small knives and brushes, the dirt being removed without disturbing any of the ornaments—a difficult matter as they are loose in the soil—and then boiling paraffin wax was poured over them, solidifying them in one mass. The lump of wax, earth, bone, and gold was then strengthened by waxed cloth pressed carefully over it, so that it could be lifted from the ground by undercutting. Mounted in plaster, with the superfluous wax cleaned off, these heads form an exhibit which is not only of interest in itself but proves the accuracy of the restorations which we have made of others.

In the furnishing of the royal graves one constant feature is the harp or lyre; in this great death-pit there were no less than four lyres. One of these was the most magnificent that we have yet found; its sounding-box was bordered with a broad edging of mosaic in red and white and blue, the two uprights were encrusted with shell and lapis lazuli and red stone arranged in zones separated by wide gold bands, the cross-bar was half of plain wood, half plated with silver, shell plaques engraved with animal scenes adorned the front, and above these projected a splendid head of a bearded bull wrought in heavy gold [*Plate* 10*a*]. A second lyre was all of silver with a silver cow's head in front of the sounding-box, which was decorated with a narrow blue and white border and with shell plaques; a third, also of silver, was in the form of a high-prowed boat on which stood a statue of a stag sculptured in the round; the fourth, of wood but with two copper statues of stags, was almost entirely decayed, so much so that we cannot even be certain that it was a harp at all, but the first three instruments were in good condition and are among the finest objects found in the cemetery.

The commonest decoration of a harp or lyre is the head of an animal, and we now have the bearded bull, the cow, and, in an instrument of different form, the stag, though in this case the complete beast is shown; the difference is not, however, so great as might appear, because in the other cases the sounding-box itself represents, though in a highly conventional, not to say 'cubist', form, the body of the animal, resolved almost entirely into straight lines, but still recognisable as such.

Now, there is an inscription by a governor Gudea (it is true that he lived a thousand years later, but tradition also is long-lived) in which he describes a harp he had presented to a temple; it was decorated with the head of a bull, and the sound of the instrument is compared to the bellowing of the beast. If there exists such a connection between the tone of the harp and the figure represented on it, might we not assume that our instruments are of three different sorts, the bull denoting the bass, the cow the tenor, and the stag perhaps the alto? Then the finding of four lyres together in one grave might imply a system of harmony which, at this early date, would be of a very great interest for the history of music.

In a corner of the same pit there were lying two statues made of gold, lapis lazuli, and white shell; slightly different in size, they were otherwise a pair, the subject being the same in each case. On a small oblong base decorated with silver plate and mosaic in pink and white stands a goat, 'a ram of the goats', erect on its hind legs in front of a tree or bush to whose branches its front legs were bound with silver chains; the leaves and flowers of the golden tree stand out high on either side, and the beast's golden head with its horns and hair of lapis lazuli peers out between them [*Frontispiece*]. Irresistibly we are reminded of the biblical story of the 'ram caught in the thicket', but the statues were made fifteen hundred years before Abraham was born and the parallel is therefore difficult to explain. Undoubtedly the subject of the Sumerian sculpture had some religious significance; this and similar scenes are common in the artistic repertoire of the early period and probably illustrate some well-known legend, and there is no reason to suppose that legend and illustration did not survive into a later time: the writer in Genesis may well have taken advantage of a familiar reference to point the moral of his own story; in any case, we have here a striking anticipation of his phrase.

When the earth was thrown back into the death-pit and the tomb-chamber of the king and the bodies of the victims around it had been buried out of sight, the ritual of burial was far from being complete. Generally the upper soil of the cemetery has been so disturbed by later interments and by tomb-robbers that for a long time we failed to find any evidence of the subsequent stages of the ceremony, but in the season 1928–9 we were more fortunate.

We had been digging a patch of ground where, near the surface, the graves of commoners lay unusually thick, and were surprised to find that the shaft of one of them, containing a clay coffin, had been cut into a stout mud-brick wall. Working against the face of this, we came upon a number of clay jars, an alabaster vase, and a rectangle of faint grey lines which represented a wooden box. Scraping away the surface soil, we discovered in the box, lying side by side, two daggers of which the blades were of gold and the hilts decorated with gold studs, and between them a white shell cylinder seal inscribed with the name 'Mes-kalam-dug the King'. Next to the box was a wooden coffin containing the body of a man, but the furniture with it was by no means of the type which one would expect with a royal person, and the wall not only went further down into the soil, but as we followed it out developed into a large square of which the coffin occupied only a humble corner; we felt sure that we had not yet found the king's grave.

Under the floor of beaten clay on which the coffin rested more clay vessels appeared forming a consistent layer over the whole area of the brick enclosure, and with these, but in another corner than that occupied by the coffin, was a second burial of a man with his weapons and vases of copper and stone. This clay floor was removed, and a fresh layer of pots and another burial came to light, and below this more layers of offerings alternating with layers of clay. Then came clean filling extending to the base of the brick walls, and at this level a single great clay bowl put upside-down in the earth sheltering two or three little food-bowls set out on a piece of matting—the meal spread for the god of the underworld.

We dug deeper down, and suddenly limestone blocks appeared bedded in green clay and forming a curve; we took it to be the end of a stone vault, and when the stones quickly dipped again feared that the roof had been broken through by robbers; but another half-hour's work proved to our delight that the masonry continued and that what we had was a small dome absolutely intact. It was particularly exciting because the top of the dome had been built over a centring supported by stout beams which ran right through the stone-work, and the decay of these had left half a dozen holes in the roof through which one could glimpse parts of the dim interior and by the light of electric torches could even see on the floor below the shapes of green copper vessels and catch an occasional glint of gold.

We cleared down to the level of the tops of the walls of the tomb-chamber, and at each corner, resting on the heavy clay which filled the space between the walls and the sides of the pit, found the ashes of fires and broken clay pots and animal bones. In front of the chamber door were laid the carcases of three sheep. The stone blocking of the door was pulled away, and inside, beneath the remains of rotten wood fallen from the ceiling, lay five bodies, four of them were those of men—servants, judging from their poor equipment, and the fifth was that of a woman; she had the golden head-dress of one of high rank, a long curved golden pin such as we had not seen before fastened her cloak, in her hands was a fluted and engraved tumbler of gold, and by her side a golden cylinder seal, the first we have ever found: this clearly was the queen.

Now the ritual of the interment could be understood. The royal body with its attendants, many or few, was laid in the tomb, and the door was sealed and sacrifice was made in the little court before the entrance, and then this was filled in until only the crown of the dome was left above ground. Round it fires were lit and a funeral feast was held, and libations to the dead were poured into a clay drain which ran down into the soil beside the tomb, and then more earth was thrown into the shaft. Next an offering to the under-gods was set out and covered with a clay bowl to shield it from the fresh earth which buried it; and then, in the half-filled pit, there was constructed in mud brick what was to be a subterranean building.

The filling-up of this building was done by degrees; clay was brought and trampled hard to make a floor over which offerings were spread and on which was laid the body of a human victim sacrificed in these later rites; earth buried these, and another floor was made and more offerings placed in order and another victim did honour to the dead below, and this went on till the top of the walls was nearly reached; then half of the building was roofed in with a vault of mud brick, and in this subsidiary tomb was put the coffin of one whom we may suppose to have been the chief sacrifice, and here King Mes-kalam-dug dedicated to the un-named queen his golden daggers and the seal bearing his title. Then this chamber too was buried under the filling of the shaft, and probably on the top of it all there was erected on the ground-surface some kind of funerary chapel which should per-petuate the sanctity of the spot.

Each stage of this elaborate procedure must have been marked by some religious service, and the whole ceremony must have taken a long time; the details of it very likely varied in different cases, but the discovery of a second royal tomb (unfortunately plundered) with layers of offerings above it exactly corresponding to that just described proves that this is no isolated case but illustrates the normal ritual for the burial of a king.

Now there had never before been found in Mesopotamia anything like these tombs; there was no archæological parallel to the age, the wealth, the architecture and, above all, to the ritual which they displayed. Moreover in Sumerian literature there was no hint of human sacrifice forming part of a royal funeral, and such a practice seemed alien to all known Sumerian traditions. When we dug the cemetery I assumed that tombs differing so much from the common run must be those of kings and in the preliminary publication of our results I put that view forward without hesitation, not imagining that it would be called in question. In fact, it was challenged immediately, and scholars are still not in agreement. The alternative theory is that the tombs are those of victims of the Fertility Sacrifice. In historic times in Sumer the chief religious ceremony of the year was that which aimed at assuring the fertility of the fields, of the cattle and of human kind; the great god who was patron of the city-state was brought down from his temple to celebrate his marriage with the goddess; in theory at least the king played the part of the god. Now in the mythology of many lands the chance of harvest is bound up with the story of the god who dies in the winter and is reborn in the spring—Tammuz or Adonis is a case in point—and so the Fertility Sacrifice involves the death of the principal actors; obviously if one of them be the king, the king himself is not prepared to die and therefore there must be a substitute for him, someone who for a brief while enjoys the title and state of king and then must disappear. The tombs at Ur then are the tombs of these festival 'kings' sacrificed together with their mock courts for the sake of the land. That they were not real kings is shown first, by the absence from all our Sumerian texts of any mention of human sacrifice in honour of earthly kings, second, by the fact that where names do occur in these tombs (as names do occur on cylinder seals) no such names are found in the Sumerian King-lists.

To the theory of the Fertility Sacrifice there are, I think, convincing objections.

It is perfectly true that no Sumerian text describes human sacrifice in connection with a king's funeral, but since there is not a single text describing a king's funeral at all there are no grounds for argument. On the other hand, there are texts describing the annual Fertility rites, and those say nothing whatsoever about human sacrifice, from which silence one can fairly conclude that no sacrifice took place. Since, according to the theory, the occupants of the tombs should be the couple chosen to represent the deities in the 'sacred marriage' we should expect to find in each tomb a man and a woman buried together, but this is never the case—each tomb has only one principal occupant, a man or a woman. The bride chosen for the god would surely be a virgin, probably good-looking, certainly young; Shub-ad however was a woman of about forty years of age. The Fertility rite was, naturally, an annual affair; our cemetery, with its thousands of graves, superimposed sometimes five or six deep, must represent a considerable length of time, but there are only sixteen tombs of the kind in dispute; did then the ancient people of Ur celebrate only occasionally the rite that was to assure a good harvest and in most years leave the whole thing to mere chance? That is hard to believe.

For human sacrifice at a king's grave plenty of analogies can be quoted from other lands, most apposite being that of the kings of the early dynasties of Egypt which are more or less contemporary with the Ur tombs; what is even more important is that something of the sort seems to have persisted in Sumer itself right down to the historic days of the Third Dynasty of Ur, for, as I shall describe later, the huge tombs of those late kings were intended for multiple burials. The silence of the literary texts is therefore countered by the evidence of archæology.

But discoveries that were made after the 'Fertility rite' theory had been first mooted go far towards settling the question. Because only two of the tomb-chambers had escaped the notice of the grave-robbers the personal possessions of the principal occupants, which might have told us all that we wanted to know, had disappeared; but a few scattered seal-cylinders found in the ruins were invaluable for they gave us actual names. It had been admitted that Shub-ad's title, *Nin*, the Lady, was perfectly correct for a queen; but now there turned up a seal whose owner, Mes-kalam-dug (not the same as the 'prince' buried with so much splendour in a private grave) definitely called himself *Lugal*, 'King', and in another 'royal tomb' one belonging to A-kalam-dug who claims the more explicit title 'King of Ur'. It would be difficult indeed to maintain that A-kalam-dug would have handed over to his temporary substitute, the destined victim of sacrifice, anything so personal and so important as the royal seal! Here we have the names of kings, and the fact that they do not appear in the Sumerian King-lists is only to be expected. The King-lists enumerate only those rulers whose authority was believed to have extended over the whole country; this was the case with the kings of the First Dynasty of Ur. Our great cemetery is proved by archæological stratification to be just older than the First Dynasty; the kings therefore who were buried there were kings not of Sumer but, as A-kalam-dug says, of Ur; they were local city-kings, vassals of whatever State was at that time suzerain,[1] and as such they would naturally not appear in the dynastic lists.

The real difficulty that has made scholars unwilling to recognize our royal tombs as those of kings accompanied to the grave by the court which attended them in their lifetime is that such recognition implies a view of the after-world which neither the surviving texts nor the evidence of later burial customs would warrant our attributing to the Sumerians. Now as regards the texts this is true; as regards later burial customs it is true also, with however the significant exception of the royal tombs of the Third Dynasty of Ur which I have cited already; and I would add that it is equally true of all the other graves in our contemporary cemetery; the kings' tombs form a striking exception from the general rule. Is there anything in kingship which would justify this?

We know that the kings of the Third Dynasty of Ur were deified after their death and even in their lifetime. How far that was in accord with ancient tradition we do not know for certain, but since the King-lists state that after the Flood 'kingship was again sent down from on high' it looks as if the tradition was very old indeed and that there was always

[1] On this see later, p. 99 and the footnote.

Plate 9

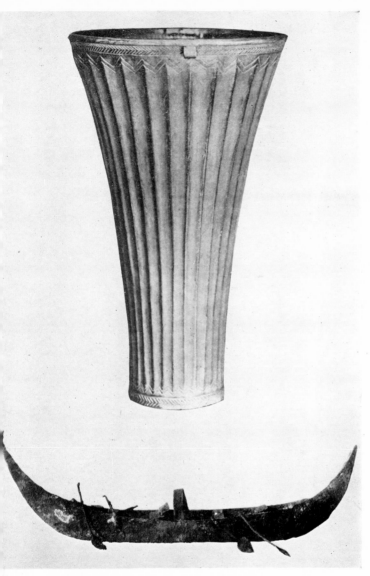

a. A gold tumbler from Queen Shub-ad's tomb
b. A silver model of a rowing-boat from the tomb of
King A-bar-gi

Plate 10

a. A decorated lyre from grave PG/1237
b. An inlaid gaming-board with its 'men'

inherent in kingship an element of divinity. And if rulers such as A-kalam-dug and Mes-kalam-dug were at the same time kings and gods the difficulty regarding their tombs ceases to exist. God does not die, and the 'death' of a god-king is merely his translation to another sphere; he is to continue his life and preserve his state, and therefore he takes with him his court, his chariot and his guards. Probably the word 'sacrifice' is in this connection misleading. I have pointed out that there seems to have been no violence done to the men and women attendants in the tomb-chambers and death-pits, but that they drank of the drug provided and went quietly to sleep; and also that they were not provided with even that minimum of tomb furniture—vessels of food and drink—which judging from the private graves was essential to the dead. They were not the victims of a brutal and savage massacre; it would seem that they were not even regarded as dying; they were going to continue their service to their royal master under new conditions, quite likely assuring themselves thereby of a less nebulous and miserable existence in the next world than Sumerian belief allotted to men dying in the ordinary way. The degree of faith which would make death the gateway of life has not been unknown in primitive ages.

We are always tempted to argue from the better-known periods back to the unknown past, but it is not always safe to do so. The Sumerian texts which give us the Sumerian ideas about the other world do indeed paint the gloomiest picture of it—

> 'Earth is their food, their nourishment clay,
> Ghosts, like bats, flutter their wings there;
> On the gate and the gateposts the dust lies
> undisturbed.'

but none of those texts is earlier in date than 2000 B.C. Now in the time of the Third Dynasty (c. 2100 B.C.) the burial customs of the people of Ur underwent a profound change, and amongst other things the grave furniture was reduced to a minimum; the graves of the well-to-do folk of that age and of the Larsa age which followed it are beggarly compared with those of our Early Dynastic cemetery. The change in custom should reflect a change in religious belief; certainly in the old days the individual was well advised to take with him to the other world all that he required or could afford for his use and his amusement in this. One piece of 'tomb furniture' does undoubtedly point to beliefs existing in the early period for which there is no evidence in after days; in two of the royal tombs and in many private graves both of the Early Dynastic and of the Sargonid cemeteries we find model boats made as a rule of bitumen—that in A-bar-gi's tomb was of silver—and loaded with a cargo of vessels for food and drink. It has been suggested that this is bait to entice away from the dead a demon who might do harm, but more probably it is intended for the use of the dead, a boat to ferry the soul to the other world; in either case the custom is one for which we have no parallel in the thousands of graves at Ur dating from 2000 B.C. to the last days of the city's existence. We are dealing with a period about which nothing was known prior to the Ur excavations and we must judge of it in the light of the evidence which those excavations give us; if we do that, we can only conclude that the builded tombs are those of kings and queens who had died and as dead people were buried just as were their subjects, so much so that in their tomb furniture there is nothing which could not conceivably have been found in a private grave—thus, in an ordinary grave we get a woman wearing the golden head-dress familiar to us from the court ladies of the royal tombs and having alongside her coffin the equally familiar lyre; or again, the body of a little girl only six or seven years old was adorned with a head-dress almost as elaborate as Shub-ad's own, but on a miniature scale, tiny gold rings across the forehead, tiny gold beech-leaves hanging from the strings of lapis lazuli and carnelian beads in her hair; she grasped a gold cup only about two inches high and by her side were two silver bowls and a fluted tumbler reproducing in little those from the queen's tomb. But the kings and queens were also semi-divine and their death is but the passing to another life, so that they unlike the commonalty sleep in walled and roofed houses and are accompanied by the men and women of their court.

As we worked towards the limits of the cemetery we came upon a group of graves which seemed to stand apart from the rest. They were all the graves of men, and they were poor graves, containing the bare minimum of tomb furniture, a cup or bowl and a clay pot was generally all that they could boast. But always there was a weapon with the body, a bronze dagger or spear-blade, and so striking was this uniformity that we concluded that this was the military quarter of the graveyard. And there was another thing. Every one of the bodies had a cylinder seal, but a seal of a special sort; carved in white shell, unusually large (about one and three-quarters of an inch long and an inch and a quarter in diameter, which is nearly double the size of the normal cylinder) and with the same subject repeated in each case with only minor differences of treatment—the heroic hunter and the lion overthrowing the bex or the bull [*Plate* 15.1]. The figures on the seal certainly symbolize victory in battle, and I thing it likely that these very splendid cylinders were in the nature of military medals distributed to the troops for service in the field—but instead of a medal you had something which would testify to your merits every time you put your name to a document. I can think of no other explanation that would account for the distinctiveness and the uniformity of seals found in what seem to be the graves of poor soldiers.

One of these graves, however, simple as its furniture was, contained something that made it unique in the whole cemetery; by the man's body there lay the statuette of a woman carved in white limestone [*Plate* 12]. It was not the figure of a goddess (as has been remarked above, one of the curious features of the cemetery as a whole was the almost total lack of religious symbolism); she was an ordinary woman standing upright with her hands clasped in the attitude of prayer; however much we might value her, for she was the only human statue of the period that we found at Ur, we could not say that she was very beautiful, nor could we explain why one man of all the thousands buried in the cemetery should take a woman's image with him to the

83

grave. Perhaps the sentimental explanation is the simplest and the most probable.

While trying to give some idea of what the graves are like and describing some of the treasures they contain, I have said very little about the condition of the objects at the time of finding. It is true that no imagination was required to grasp the splendour of Mes-kalam-dug's grave, because the objects in that were for the most part of gold, and gold is imperishable; a gold bowl may be crushed or dinted, but its colour and its surface remain and every detail of its workmanship and decoration is as clear as when it was newly wrought; but other materials are less enduring—I have spoken of the way in which silver corrodes and even vanishes —and suffer both from internal decay and from the crushing weight of the 30 or 40 feet of earth below which they have lain buried for five thousand years. Often it is difficult to remove from the soil without further damage an object which it is essential to preserve; sometimes it is hard even to judge of the object's nature and importance; nearly always some measure of repair or restoration is required before the thing is fit for exhibition, and the restoration may be the most laborious task of all.

As an illustration of this I would take one of the two statues of rams found in the great death-pit. The figure was made as follows. The head and legs were carved in wood, the horns of lapis and the inlaid eyes being fixed in position by copper rivets driven through the head, and then gold, little thicker than gold leaf, was laid over them, a thin wash of bitumen acting as glue to fix the metal on to the wood. The head and legs were mortised into a rudimentary wooden body which was next rounded off into proper shape with plaster of paris and given a thick coat of bitumen; a thin silver plate was fixed over the belly, and into the bitumen covering back and sides were pressed the locks of hair, each carved separately from a piece of white shell, or, for the shoulders, in lapis lazuli; the tree was also of wood overlaid with gold leaf, the leaves and flowers made of double gold and fixed on after the trunk and branches were complete.

When we found them, both statues were in very sorry

plight. The wood had decayed to nothing, the bitumen was dry powder, the plaster of paris reduced to irregular lumps and pellets; one figure was lying on its side, crushed absolutely flat so that the shell curls of the two flanks touched each other and the animal was a mere silhouette distorted by pressure, the other, standing upright, preserved some of its roundness but had been telescoped together and the legs had been broken off from the body, flattened and twisted. Nothing except the earth around them kept the fragments of lapis and shell inlay in position, and if that position were once lost, there would have been no guide at all for the restoration of the figure; the whole thing was therefore solidified with hot wax poured liberally on, and then bands of waxed muslin were applied to every exposed part until the ram was as securely wrapped up as a mummy and could be lifted from the earth.

For restoration, the waxed wrappings were softened with heat sufficiently for the sides of the beast to be pressed apart and the dirt removed from inside its body; then wax and bandages were applied to the interior, the outer bandages removed, and with gentle heating the body could be pushed out into its original shape, and that without dislodging the inlaid locks of the fleece now adhering to the inner coating of wax. The complete decay of the silver over the belly really facilitated the task, because it gave a chance to work at the body from the inside through a comparatively large opening. The legs were straightened, and with slender tools inserted down the tubes of them the dinted gold was pressed out again as much as possible, then copper wires were put down them and a boiling mixture of wax and bitumen was poured in to make all solid. The head presented greater difficulties, because the thin gold leaf was broken into eighteen small fragments and these were badly crushed and bent; each had to be unfolded, worked out to its original curve and strengthened from the back, and then the joints had to be found and the various morsels brought together and fixed with due regard to the curves of their outer face. It was a jigsaw puzzle in three dimensions, but in time the head took shape and character. Plastic wood was used to fill the body and to

85

secure the wires of the legs, the belly was painted with silver paint to replace the perished metal, and the statue was complete [*Frontispiece*].

Of course, methods of this kind cannot reproduce all the *finesse* of the original; to do that one would have to take the whole thing to pieces and re-create; but in so doing one loses something which is of sentimental if not always of scientific importance—the object as exhibited is really a copy, new throughout, of the old work, and no one can be quite certain of its faithfulness. In dealing with the antiquities from Ur we have preferred a restoration which implies the least possible interference with the object to a reconstruction which may give a better appearance but depends more on the modern hand.

Another instance will make the point clearer. In the largest of all the stone-built royal tombs, which had been entered by robbers and most thoroughly plundered, there remained only one corner of the last chamber to be cleared, and we had given up expectation of any 'finds' when suddenly a loose bit of shell inlay turned up, and the next minute the foreman's hand, carefully brushing away the earth, laid bare the corner of a mosaic in lapis lazuli and shell. This was the famous 'Standard' of Ur, but at the time we had very little idea of what it might be: the wooden background had perished entirely, and the tiny pieces of inlay, though they kept their relative positions in the soil, were all quite loose; falling stones had bent and twisted the once flat panel, while as the wood decayed and the fragments sank back into the empty space behind, their different thickness made the surface of them rough and uneven. So delicate was the task of removing the dirt without further disturbing the mosaic that only about a square inch could be dealt with at a time—each section was waxed as soon as cleared, but so much of the surrounding dirt mingled with the hot wax that the face of the panel became invisible. When at last it could be lifted from the earth, I knew that we had found a very fine thing, but should have been hard put to it to say exactly what it was.

Now, it would have been perfectly feasible to take the

Plate 11

Shell plaques engraved with mythological scenes
(the background of the design filled in with niello)
from the lyre in King A-bar-gi's tomb

Plate 12

Limestone statuette of a woman from a soldier's
grave in the Royal Cemetery

mosaic to pieces, bit by bit, and re-make it on a new background, and the task might have been done as well by the
modern craftsman as by the old, but the panels would have
been the work of a modern craftsman.

What was done was this. The two sides of the panel were
separated, and waxed cloth was fixed to the back of the inlay
and the face of it was roughly cleaned; it was then laid face
downwards on glass and warmed until the wax was soft, and
it was pressed with the fingers from behind until by looking
underneath one could be sure that each fragment of the inlay
was in direct contact with the glass. The panel was now flat,
but the pattern was much distorted; the edges of the mosaic
fragments had lost contact in the ground and earth and
powdered bitumen had filtered between them, and now wax
as well, so that while some overlapped, others were widely
apart. The next stage was to remove the cloth from the back,
leaving the mosaic virtually loose on the glass, and to pick out
all foreign matter, and then by sideways pressure with the
fingers coax the pieces together. When this was done, fresh
wax and cloth were applied behind and a proper backing
fixed on.

The result of this is that the mosaic is not nearly so regular
or smooth as the Sumerian artist made it, but what we
possess is the work of that artist uninterfered with except by
the accidents of time; the pieces of shell and lapis which he
put together no one else has taken apart and re-set [*Plate* 13].

In the case of the 'Standard' the labour of restoration was
at the same time a process of discovery; the work in the field
had really been done in the dark, and it was only when the
panels were cleaned and had begun to take shape in the
laboratory that their importance could be recognized. There
are two main panels, rectangular and measuring 22 inches
long by 9 inches high, and two triangular pieces which
formed the ends; these were fixed together so that the larger
sides sloped inwards and the whole thing was fastened on to
the end of a pole, and would seem to have been carried in
processions; we actually found it lying against the shoulder
of a man who may have been the king's standard-bearer.

The mosaic is composed of figures, silhouetted in shell

with details engraved, which are set in a background of lapis lazuli relieved here and there with red. The triangular ends have mythological scenes of animals; the main panels illustrate respectively Peace and War. On one side the king and the royal family are seen at feast. They sit in chairs, their costume consists of the old-fashioned sheep-skin kilt or petticoat and the upper part of the body is bare; servants wait on them, and at one end of the scene is a musician playing on a small harp, while by him a woman singer with her hands to her breast sings to the accompaniment of the instrument.

These figures form the top row of the design; in two lower rows attendants are shown bringing in spoils captured from the enemy and food-supplies for the banquet—one is driving a goat, another carries two fish, another is bent under the weight of a corded bale, and so on, several of the figures being repeated. On the other side, in the centre of the top row, stands the king, distinguished by his greater height, with behind him three attendants or members of his house, and a dwarf-like groom who holds the heads of the two asses which draw the monarch's empty chariot while the driver of it walks behind holding the reins; in front of the king soldiers are bringing up prisoners, naked and with their arms bound behind their backs, for him to decide their fate.

In the second row, at the back, comes the phalanx of the royal army, heavy-armed infantry in close order with copper helmets exactly like those found by us in the king's grave, and long cloaks of some stiff material which I take to be felt, just such cloaks as are worn by the shepherds of Anatolia to-day, holding axes in their hands; in front of them are the light-armed infantry without cloaks, wielding axes or short spears, already engaged with an enemy whose naked warriors are either fleeing or being struck down.

In the lowest row we have the chariotry of Sumer, each car drawn by two asses and carrying two men, of whom one is the driver and the other a warrior who flings light javelins, of which four are kept in a quiver tied to the front of the car. The chariots advance over the battlefield, and by a naturalistic touch the artist of the 'Standard' makes the asses at the rear walk sedately, while those drawing the other cars become more and more excited as they encounter the corpses strewn on the ground, until those in front have broken into a gallop which threatens the balance of the riders.

The 'Standard' is a remarkable work of art, but it has yet greater value as an historical document, for here we have figured the earliest detailed picture of that army which carried the civilization of the Sumerians from their early settlements on the fringe of the Persian Gulf to the mountains of Anatolia and to the shores of the Mediterranean Sea. We know from actual examples found in their graves that their weapons were, both in design and in manufacture, far superior to anything that their contemporaries possessed or any other nation was to adopt for two thousand years; from this representation we can learn enough about the organization of the army to know that it must have been more than a match for anything that could be brought against it at that time. The chariotry which was to inspire an almost superstitious terror in the Hebrews of the time of the Judges had been used by the Sumerians more than two thousand years before, and the phalanx which won Alexander his victories had been anticipated by them: it is not surprising that until they had taught their neighbours to profit by their example they found no opponent to withstand their advance.

Not the least surprising aspect of the civilization which the tombs illustrate is the advance it had made in architecture. The doorway of A-bar-gi's tomb was capped with a properly-constructed brick arch, and its roof was formed by a brick barrel vault with apsidal ends; Shub-ad's tomb was similarly vaulted, others had vaults of limestone rubble masonry; we find a complete rubble dome built over a timber centring and supported by pendentives after the modern fashion. In these underground buildings no columns were required, but since the column was, as we shall see, freely used in the immediately succeeding period it must have been known in the cemetery age also. Summing this up, we can say that all the basic forms of architecture used to-day were familiar to the people of Ur in the early part of the third millennium before Christ.

Our royal cemetery dates, as I have said, to the latter part

of the Early Dynastic period with which Sumerian civilization properly so called begins. It was an urban civilization
of a highly developed type; its artists, capable at times of a
very vivid realism (as in the case of the donkey 'mascot' from
Queen Shub-ad's chariot) followed for the most part stan-
dards and conventions whose excellence had been approved
by many generations working before them; its craftsmen in
metal possessed a knowledge of metallurgy and a technical
skill which few ancient peoples have ever rivalled and which
it must have taken long years to perfect; its merchants
carried on a far-flung trade, its agriculture prospered, its
armed forces were scientifically organized and men practised freely the art of writing. In all these things Sumer was
ahead of Egypt, which at the beginning of the Early Dynastic
period in Sumer was only just emerging from a state of
barbarism, and when Egypt does make a real start under
Menes, the first king of the Nile valley, the new age is marked
by the introduction of models and ideas which derive from
the older civilization flourishing in the valley of the Lower
Euphrates. Sumer was the pioneer of the western world and
to it we can trace much of the art and thought of the
Egyptians and Babylonians, of the Assyrians, Phœnicians
and Hebrews, and ultimately of the Greeks also; the things
that we found in the royal cemetery were not merely fine in
themselves, not merely of interest as illustrating the achievements of a particular unknown race at a time whereof
nothing had been known; they were documents enabling us
to write a new chapter in the history of our modern world.

IV

Al 'Ubaid and the First Dynasty of Ur

IN 1919 Dr. Hall, working for the British Museum, visited about four miles to the north-west of the ruins of Ur proper a little mound where the surface indications promised remains of an unusual character; he therefore started excavations, and at once came upon a construction in plano-convex brick. He traced round three sides of a small rectangular building and against the south-east face found a hoard of objects lying under a mass of mud brick.

There was a small stone statue of a man carved in the primitive and summary style already familiar to us from stray examples procured elsewhere, but with this were other monuments of a more novel sort. There was a great copper relief 7 ft. 9 ins. long and 3 ft. 6 ins. high, representing in heraldic fashion an eagle grasping two stags; there were the fore-parts of lions, nearly life-size, made of copper hammered over bitumen and wood with inlaid eyes and white shell teeth through which protruded tongues of red stone; there were fragments of wooden columns incrusted with mother-of-pearl, red stone, and black shale; clay flowers with inlaid petals of white, black, and red, and more heads of animals in copper but on a smaller scale. Altogether it was a most important discovery, and since the excavation was left unfinished by Dr. Hall, it was the obvious duty of the Joint Expedition to complete it as soon as possible. In the season 1923-4, therefore, a branch camp was set up at al 'Ubaid (such is the name of the little mound), and the work was re-started with the hope that more light would be thrown on the nature of the building and that there might yet be objects awaiting discovery.

Dr. Hall's work had given us a warning. The copper

statues found by him had suffered terribly through corrosion and breakage, and, important as they were, were but ghosts of the originals; of the lions' heads little more remained than the bitumen cores with the inlay of eyes and mouth, of the columns only the loose fragments of the incrustation could be collected and brought home, and the great copper relief, of which only one stag's head was recovered intact, had to be reconstructed from fragments, and in several respects the reconstruction was open to doubt. If, then, we should encounter any further objects of the kind we had to be sure that our resources would be adequate to the delicate task of their removal and transport.

The work of excavation which had produced the original hoard of statuary had begun at one corner of the building and had been carried on not quite to its central point, when the diggers had encountered and partly cut into a particularly solid mass of mud brick. We started at this point and, following up the brickwork—with some difficulty, for it showed no true face—found that it was one side of a staircase projecting at right angles from the main building; the treads, of which a number were preserved at the stairs' foot, were great slabs of white limestone, the first example of the use of stone for building that had been noted in the south of Mesopotamia except for a similar flight of stairs leading up to the staged tower of Abu Shahrein, a ruin about 12 miles south of Ur. Further examination proved that the building itself was a solid mass of brick, a platform approached by the flight of steps, and only the substructure of a building which itself had completely disappeared [*Plate* 14*b*].

Working round the stairway and following the wall between it and the far corner of the platform we found, under a mass of mud brick of a later period (a new platform laid down over the ruins of the old), a second hoard of objects in part similar to those which had rewarded Dr. Hall and in part different. In the angle between the stairs and the wall there lay two ten-foot columns of wood encrusted with mother-of-pearl, shale, and red stone, and other palm-log columns and beams overlaid with sheets of copper; piled in one heap there were four copper statues of bulls standing upright with their heads turned outwards over their shoulders; in a line along the wall were copper reliefs of reclining cattle, and mixed with these sections of mosaic friezes in which figures silhouetted in white limestone or in shell were set against a background of black shale and framed with strips of copper; and everywhere we found fragments or complete examples of the inlaid clay flowers with cone-like stems which had figured in the earlier excavations.

One day a workman unearthed before my eyes a small oblong tablet of white limestone bearing an inscription; I handed it to Mr. Gadd, who was standing beside me, and he read it out: 'A-anni-pad-da King of Ur, son of Mes-anni-pad-da King of Ur, has built this for his Lady Nin-kharsag.' It was the foundation-stone of the building, and the most important of all our discoveries.

At first reading it does not sound a very exciting thing, a list of rather unpronounceable names, but we were excited enough. The first name was unknown to us or anyone, but the second was familiar as that of the first king of the First Dynasty of Ur according to the Sumerian King-lists. I have, in the introduction to this book (p. 14) explained the extraordinary importance of the discovery of the tablet as establishing the historic character of a dynasty which had been regarded as mythical only, but because it belonged to the al 'Ubaid temple it did something more than prove the accuracy of the King-lists: it dated the building, so that the objects associated with it could be considered in their proper place in the development of Mesopotamian art, and that again meant that 'the First Dynasty of Ur' would not be merely an isolated fact but would have a content of its own; the phrase would denote a period in history whose character we could judge in the light of actual remains.

But the objects to which so much extra interest was lent by the finding of the foundation-tablet gave us a very anxious time; they lay so thickly in the ground that there might be half a dozen of them all exposed at one time and all calling for special care in their removal; and their condition was quite as bad as we had feared.

The uppermost of the four copper bulls was barely recognizable, only part of one leg and a mass of green powder betraying its existence. The second looked more promising, but the metal was broken into a thousand pieces and was so soft that it crumbled to dust at a touch (I spent three weeks preparing it and then when we lifted it the whole thing collapsed in atoms); with the next two we had better success and they are now in the British Museum and at Philadelphia, battered and distorted figures but still figures of bulls showing something of the fine quality of the originals and remarkable as being the oldest copper statues preserved to us. The copper reliefs were less difficult to manage and only one was rejected as too fragmentary for removal, and even then the head, cast in metal and more solid than the hammered sheets which formed the body, remained a first-class object.

The inlaid columns were crushed flat and the wood had perished, but most of the tesseræ were approximately in position, only those along the edges having been dislodged and scattered. They were removed in sections, sacking being waxed on to the tesseræ that lay face upwards and glued on to the backs of those which belonged to the lower face of the shafts: lifted thus in sheets, the decoration could be fixed on to a new core (it was found that circular petrol-drums were of exactly the right diameter, and these served our turn) without any disturbance of the individual bits of stone and mother-of-pearl, while other sheets and the loose tesserae collected from the earth were kept with a view to more drastic reconstruction.

The mosaic friezes were held together with wax and muslin for such treatment as the Museum authorities might choose to give them. The friezes were two in number. One was simple, a row of birds, probably doves, rather roughly cut in white limestone (which I think was originally painted in colour) against a black ground. The other was much more elaborate and showed much finer workmanship. It consisted for most of its length of a procession of cows carved in limestone, probably once painted, or in shell, which was probably left white, but in the centre there was a scene in which human figures are introduced; on one side of a reed-built byre, from the door of which two calves are seen issuing, men seated on low stools are milking cattle; the man sits under the cow's tail milking her from behind; the calves, duly muzzled, are roped to the cows' head-stalls so as to encourage them to give milk. On the other side of the byre two men, shaven and wearing the fleece petticoat which in later times seems to survive as the official dress of priests and priest-kings, are pouring milk through a strainer into a vessel set on the ground, while two others are collecting the strained liquid in great store-jars [*Plate* 14*a*].

It is a typical scene of pastoral life, but the costume of the actors makes it likely that it is something more than this. There were in later days at least sacred farms attached to the temples, and here we may have priests preparing the milk of the Mother-goddess Nin-kharsag which was the nourishment of kings. That the very domestic-looking picture of milking had a religious bearing is made more likely by the fact that in the same frieze there was introduced between the figures of walking cattle a small panel of a curiously incongruous character: it shows a bearded bull rampant in hilly country, on whose back is perched a lion-headed eagle apparently attacking him and tearing at his rump; this is certainly an illustration of some mythological legend and its presence here cannot but affect our view of the frieze as a whole.

It was obvious that all the objects found belonged to the temple, and it was equally obvious that the majority of them at least were of an architectural nature; taken by themselves they were of first-rate importance, but they would gain enormously in interest if they could be assigned to their proper places in the architectural scheme. At first sight this would seem to be a hopeless task, because of the building to which they belonged not a single brick was left in position, and of the platform on which the building stood the upper part had been destroyed so that not even the ground-plan was known. Luckily, however, the position in which each object lay was here more than usually informative. The temple had not been disintegrated by gradual decay but had been suddenly and violently overthrown; that was clear enough. The walls had been undermined and then pushed over from the inside, so that in front of the platform there lay, sloped downwards, great blocks of intact mud-brick walling to the lower face of which the fragments of the friezes were still attached—we had to cut away the brickwork to get at the back of the frieze. Where, as did happen, bits of two friezes occurred on the same masonry block, we were given the order and the exact distance between the two; the relative position of the row of copper heifers and the shell mosaic of cattle was thus fixed. Underneath the fallen wall-masses and lying for the most part at ground level came the other objects. Dr. Hall had found, on one side of the staircase, his great eagle relief, the copper foreparts of lions clearly belonging to a gateway, and fragments of mosaic columns; on the other side of the stairs we found two more mosaic columns and two sheathed in copper, all lying flat on the ground and more or less at right angles to the façade, and close by them the copper bull statues piled up in a heap. These were architectural features which if not exactly free could at least be easily detached; the enemy had wrenched off the lions, pulled down the columns (which brought the great relief with them) and had flung the lot down from the top of the platform; they had collected the bull statues into a heap, and then had undercut the walls and toppled them over. All that we had to do was to record the exact position of every object in relation to the wall and the exact angle at which it lay, and by calculating the slope of the debris against the wall face and the height of objects in it we could get a very fair idea of the place from which each had fallen. I think that the only real mistake made was about the terra-cotta flower rosettes which I pictured as standing free and upright, whereas they were quite certainly embedded in the brickwork with only the heads showing; all were found close to the platform wall and apparently loose, but this was because they had decorated the lower part of the temple wall which had been smashed to pieces when the upper part fell down. Of the interior of the building we can know nothing, but the restoration of the façade, at least, cannot be far wrong.

The temple proper occupied one corner of the platform and its main door stood at the top of the flight of stone steps

Plate 13

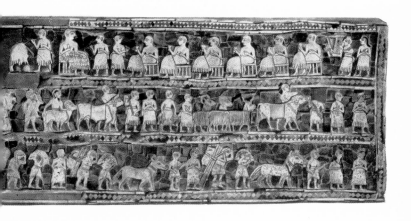

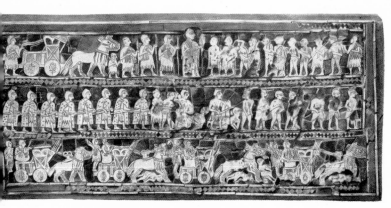

The 'Standard of Ur'

Plate 14

a. Mosaic frieze from the façade

b. The ruins of the temple platform

A-anni-pad-da's Temple of Nin-kharsag

it stood a little back from the platform's edge, and in front of its doors there was a porch with a pent-house roof whose beams and supporting columns were of wood overlaid with polished copper. Mosaic columns held up the lintel, and above this was set into the wall the copper relief of the eagle and two stags found by Dr. Hall, while the front parts of lions found by him had their place in re-entrant angles flanking the actual doorway, which they thus seemed to guard.

On the ledge along the top of the platform, against the background of the temple wall, stood the copper statues of bulls, and behind them, probably, the clay flowers were set in the wall-face so as to give the effect of animals in a flowery meadow. Higher up on the façade came the copper frieze of reclining cattle worked in relief; above these the mosaic frieze with the milking-scene; and higher up still the bird frieze with its bolder and more roughly-carved figures. The brick balustrades of the staircase were certainly panelled with wood, for we found along the foot of them the copper nails by which the wood was attached; the platform was of burnt brick below, and this may well have been left exposed; the upper part, of mud brick, was probably whitewashed, as was the mud-brick wall of the temple above.

We can picture the whole building as something very gay and fanciful, the gold and colour of its decoration vivid against the white walls, and we can admire the skill with which the elements of the decoration are graded according to their height from the ground—statues in the round below, then figures in relief, then flat figures seen as silhouettes against the black bands of the friezes—and the knowledge of perspective which prefers simpler and broader effects for the top row of all. At the time when we found it it was by far the oldest known building in Mesopotamia, the oldest in the world that we could re-create more or less as it really was. Since then, older buildings have come to light; but the al 'Ubaid temple remains unique as illustrating the archi- tecture and the art of the First Dynasty of Ur.

Al 'Ubaid gave us yet another discovery, not so sensational but none the less of great interest.

In a second and smaller mound which lay close to the

temple we found a number of graves. Compared with those of the early cemetery at Ur they were very poor, containing as they did few objects other than pottery, but they were, in spite of that, most important. It was natural to suppose that they should be contemporary with A-anni-pad-da's building, since the neighbourhood of a temple is holy ground and is therefore generally a favourite spot for burying the dead; but besides this, some of the clay vessels of very distinctive form found in the graves were actually represented in the milking-scene on the mosaic frieze; the graves could be confidently assigned to the First Dynasty of Ur, and, since they supplied us with a great variety of pottery types used in that period, we had an admirable starting-point for dating subsequent discoveries.

In all excavations, whether on building sites or in grave-yards, pottery forms the bulk of the objects found. In every country the forms of clay vessels in common use change from age to age as civilization advances or degenerates, new social conditions have to be met, new inventions are introduced or simply fashions alter: a few types may be fairly constant throughout a long period, but on the whole pots change with the times, and while the same is true of all other things, pots as being the most numerous and, since baked clay is for all its fragility virtually indestructible, the best preserved, are the most useful evidence for dating. In a country like Egypt, where the domestic pottery of every age has been carefully studied and recorded, it is possible to fix the age of a ruin merely by walking over the mounds and observing the sherds which strew the surface; in Mesopotamia in 1923 very little was known of the pottery of any period and that of the early times was absolutely unknown. To secure more than a hundred shapes of vases and to learn the kind of ware employed in making them, with the certainty that all belonged to a definite period in history, was most valuable, and when we came to excavate the rich tombs of Ur it was partly on the basis of the graves of al 'Ubaid that we were able to assign to them their true date.

At Ur, in the southern part of the Royal Cemetery area, there was spread over the tops of the grave-shafts a mass of

98

rubbish forming three fairly distinct strata, the middle one being of a dark colour, burnt brick earth and charcoal, the upper and lower strata of a light grey, lime rubble plentifully mixed with potsherds, seal impressions and tablets; the three together seem to represent temple store-rooms which had been burnt and razed to the ground. The buildings must have been later in date than the cemetery, since their ruins lay above the shafts, but they need not have been much later, for when they were destroyed the ground-surface from which the last graves had been dug was still exposed, not hidden by any such accumulation of rubbish as time would inevitably have produced. It is not impossible that they were chapels connected with the old royal graves, but of this no one can be certain; but in any case they must have been, or included, store-rooms in which were kept offerings made by kings, for the seal-impressions came for the most part from the stoppers of big jars and two of them bear the name of Mes-anni-pad-da, King of Ur and founder of the First Dynasty, while loose in the rubbish we found the actual seal, a lapis lazuli cylinder, of the wife of Mes-anni-pad-da and mother, as we may suppose, of the A-anni-pad-da who built the temple at al 'Ubaid. Here too then, in the capital of the State, the First Dynasty comes to life, but apart from the written record not very much of the period survives. We know that after the Jamdat Nasr period the Ziggurat and its surrounding religious structures were rebuilt, and of these we have recovered the ground-plans; in the case of a number of other temples there have been found remains of plano-convex brick construction proving that the foundation at least went back to Early Dynastic times, but we cannot connect any of them definitely with the First Dynasty. Although that dynasty is in the Sumerian King-lists put immediately after the First Dynasty of Erech and on that showing should introduce the Early Dynastic Period it is archæologically certain that it did in fact come relatively late in that period.[1] That is proved by evidence gathered

---

[1] Perhaps after the downfall of the Jamdat Nasr people (whom I would relate to the Erech Dynasty) there was an interregnum during which the several city states preserved their independence to the extent that no one of them, until the rise of Mes-anni-pad-da of Ur, could secure dominion over the

from many sites, but even at Ur we can see that the Royal
Cemetery, which is Early Dynastic, antedates the First
Dynasty—it may well be that the prosperous reigns of such
local kings as Mes-kalam-dug and A-kalam-dug enabled
Mes-anni-pad-da to establish his hegemony over the whole of
Sumer and so to figure in the King-lists. The buildings at Ur
therefore, which for the sake of convenience in reference we
have called 'First Dynasty', may be, and sometimes certainly
are, of earlier foundation though they may have been standing in the days of Mes-anni-pad-da and his son. But there is
one important exception.

The Early Dynastic Ziggurat is completely buried inside
that of Ur-Nammu, and we made no attempt to excavate it;
all that we can say is that it was a good deal smaller than the
Third Dynasty building which stands to-day, but was none
the less of imposing size, the main block, without the staircase, measuring about a hundred and fifty by a hundred
and twenty feet at ground level. It stood well back on a
raised terrace enclosed by a heavily-buttressed wall and
partly occupied by religious buildings; these we were able to
excavate and they told us a great deal. In the first place, we
had to deal not with one building but with two. I have
already described how the Ziggurat complex of the Jamdat
Nasr time had been deliberately destroyed and how the new
walls had been constructed with a certain admixture of flat
bricks below and with plano-convex bricks above ground
level. These walls necessarily belonged to the very beginning
of the Early Dynastic period, and they were sufficiently well
preserved for us to trace out the whole of their ground-plan.
But at a later time within the 'plano-convex brick period',
i.e., well within the Early Dynastic period (for the plano-
convex brick went out of fashion before the period ended)
the whole thing had been rebuilt on almost identical lines,
the new walls resting on the stumps of the old; there was here

whole country; on which theory the King-lists are literally correct. Or perhaps the order of the numerous early dynasties recorded in the King-lists has
got muddled: some of them must have overlapped or been strictly contemporary and the arrangement of them may be arbitrary; Ur may have been put
first because it achieved greater importance or because it was (as the lengths of
the reigns of its kings show) better documented.

no violent destruction by iconoclasts, no new religious departure requiring a different type of temple; it looked, quite simply, as if the original building had in the course of years fallen into disrepair and had to be rebuilt, but rebuilt with a pious conformity to tradition. We can have no certain assurance, but it is tempting and I think reasonable to assume that the costly work of reconstructing the central shrine of Ur was taken in hand by Mes-anni-pad-da when he ceased to be a vassal city-king and became the sovereign lord of Sumer. A Sumerian king was regarded as the regent of his capital's patron god (the god's 'tenant farmer' was the expression used) and his rise to power really meant that the city's god had become the chief of the pantheon of Sumerian gods; the new divine ruler would naturally require a house suited to his supreme dignity. For this reason I do not hesitate to call the buildings I am about to describe the Ziggurat buildings of the First Dynasty of Ur.

The wall surrounding the terrace was a colossal structure no less than thirty-six feet thick; its outer face was relieved by shallow buttresses and—an extraordinary feature in this stoneless land—the mud brickwork rested on a foundation of coursed limestone rubble masonry rising to a height of nearly four feet. The First Dynasty temple at al 'Ubaid has limestone foundations, but they are no more than a single course of stone laid at or below ground level, and we have found other examples of the same thing in Early Dynastic buildings at Ur, but there is nothing at all like this terrace wall with its six or seven courses of rough unshaped blocks. And the curious point about it was that it was a sham; the stonework did not go back into the wall but was a mere skin one stone thick. The wall had been built of mud bricks only —laid, in the initial stages, against the face of the First Early Dynastic wall, which was still standing to some height—and when they had got up to four feet the builders set the stones against the smooth mud brick face, levelled the top with mud mortar and then carried on with their brickwork, bringing it forward to line up flush with the stone; it was a rather naïve method of construction, but an easy one for workmen not accustomed to building in stone and obliged to make economical use of an expensive material. A stone facing of this sort, not bonded into the brickwork behind, gave no additional strength but on the contrary was a source of weakness, and since it was plastered with mud like the upper part of the wall it did not aim at spectacular effect; I can only suppose that it is a survival of a genuine constructional system (a temple of the Uruk period at Warka has real stone foundations) now reduced to a religious formula.

The entrance to the terrace had been in the middle of the north-east wall, immediately opposite the foot of the Ziggurat staircase; the gateway was a double one, for there was here an interior wall, so that the visitor passed through an entrance-lobby about twenty feet deep in the side walls of which were doors giving on to store- or service-chambers built against the inner face of the terrace wall. Once through the inner gate one had the Ziggurat directly in front and, on either side, temple buildings occupying the north and east corners of the terrace. The builders of the Third Dynasty Ziggurat, remodelling the terrace and raising its level, had had to destroy the old buildings, but the stumps of the walls remained underneath their higher pavement and we could recover at least the ground-plan of them. If one can judge by the analogy of later times the building in the north corner should, by its position, have been the special shrine of the Moon-god, Nannar, the patron deity of Ur to whom the Ziggurat of Ur was dedicated; so it may have been, but its arrangements do not correspond to those of a normal temple. Access was by a small and unpretentious door at the south-west end (see the plan, Fig. 5) and from it one went by a bitumen-covered 'causeway' across a lobby into what must have been an unroofed central court; this had a floor of clay only, and against its north-west wall there was a raised brick and bitumen tank with shallow runnels on either side which reminds one of a scullery sink and was probably used for the preparation of food or for the washing of utensils—we found in it half a dozen clay cups and a few small animal bones and fish scales. Two doorways in the north-east wall led to two small square chambers behind each of which was a very narrow passage-like room; each of the main chambers was

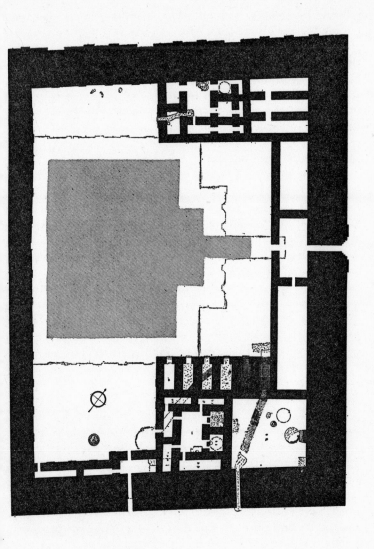

103

entirely taken up by a great fireplace, square in the one case, circular in the other; they were filled with ashes and cinders, the brickwork of the edging was reddened by heat, and that they were in constant use was shown by the fact that the floor of the square furnace had been relaid no less than twelve times. A door in the south-east side of the open court led into a series of narrow rooms, virtually a passage, which in turn may have led (of the end wall only the foundations remained, so that it was impossible to say whether there had been a doorway or not) to three large storerooms lying at the back of the building proper, in the north angle of the terrace wall.

There is nothing here that suggests a temple; the obvious term to apply to such a building is 'kitchen'. Now the sacrifices that men offered to the gods were in fact the food of the gods; the flesh of the votive animal had to be cooked, whether it was roast with fire or seethed in the pot, and the cakes and the show-bread had to be baked, so that a kitchen was an important part of a temple; we have an admirable illustration of this in the Larsa period, *v.* Plate 23*a*. In the present instance we have a kitchen and no temple. The explanation is, I think, that the temple, the real house of the god, was on the top of the Ziggurat; it was a small building, and the ground area was insufficient to supply space for the domestic offices, so—and it was far more convenient—the kitchen was put at the foot of the Ziggurat and only the prepared food would be carried up to be laid before the god.

The building in the east corner of the terrace was very similar in character. The main block here too was entered by a small door in the south-west end, and there was the lobby, the central court with side chambers and, facing the entrance, two rooms entirely taken up by big furnaces or fire-places, one square and one circular. Behind the building there was, instead of store-chambers, a large open court entered by a passage through the terrace wall from which a paved causeway led to the north-easternmost of a range of small cells built against the side of the main block, and through this one could pass on to the Ziggurat platform. In the open court there was a circular base of burnt bricks set in and overlaid with bitumen against which was a more or less rectangular brick platform, also remains of a second similar base, and, sunk in the floor, a circular basin of burnt bricks and bitumen. A third circular brick base lay in the open area south-west of the building, close to a row of service-chambers or store-rooms built against the inner face of the terrace wall, and here was a second narrow passage through the terrace wall itself, giving access from outside to the Ziggurat platform.

Here then we have a second 'kitchen', complicated by a range of small cells all opening on to the Ziggurat; and again later analogies can be invoked in explanation. In all later periods there stood on the south-west side of the Ziggurat terrace a temple dedicated to Nin-gal, the wife of the Moon-god, and for one such at least we have written evidence that the temple served also for those minor deities who formed as it were the court of the supreme god and his consort. The small cells (with the exception of the one that, having doors at both ends, was no more than a passage) were probably chapels containing the statues of those minor gods; Nin-gal herself may have had her shrine up on the Ziggurat. In the central court of the building we found a few fragments of just such inlay as was used for the mosaic frieze of the temple at al 'Ubaid and of wigs and beards carved in stone which came from composite statues, and of gold objects; other pieces of gold came from the central chapel; it was enough to show that some part at least of the building had been decorated in such fashion as beseems a temple. Where nothing more survives than a few tattered mud-brick foundations it is not easy to conjure up anything of splendour: but with the analogy of al 'Ubaid before us we may be sure that these few fragments do witness to a structure whose very richness would account for its utter destruction. Actually one discovery did hint at the wealth of its contents. In the middle of the big open court lying in front of the 'kitchen' there was a clay pot sunk below the pavement in which were quantities of beads, two miniature toilet-vases of white limestone, two seals of coloured alabaster in the form of lions' heads, and stone figures of a man, a squatting bull, a calf and a dog;

they must have been offerings dedicated by the faithful. A few other objects of First Dynasty date turned up elsewhere in the site; four of them deserve mention. Close to a brick pavement of the period, on the outskirts of the cemetery, there was found the lower half of a limestone slab on which is carved in relief a scene of the funeral procession of a king; the empty chariot, covered with a spotted leopard's skin, drawn by two beasts which look like lions but ought by analogy to be asses (their heads are broken away), is led along by attendants; there was another scene above which is lost.

Under the foundations of a house attached to one of the temples another discovery was made. The ground here had been terraced for the building, and tumbled together in the filling behind the terrace wall was a group of objects of First Dynasty date. Two of these were a pair, limestone figures of rams, only the heads and foreparts carved in the round, the rest left rough; they seem to be supports for a throne, probably the seat of some statue of a god whose sacred emblem was the ram. With them was a small relief in alabaster carved on both sides; it was badly weathered and only half of it was preserved, but it was curiously interesting. It represented a high-prowed boat made of reeds tied together and having an arched cabin or canopy amidships—a boat not unlike the silver model found in the tomb of the king A-bar-gi; on one side a man was shown standing in the stern and a sow in the cabin, on the other two fish took the place of the man and a goose that of the sow. Probably the little object was dedicated in a temple by one of the marsh folk and pictures the sort of life he led, for fish, wild geese, and wild boar are the staple products of the marsh-land; it was a strong temptation to call it a picture of Noah's Ark, but though that passed as a jest in camp, the other is the more likely explanation!

In spite of all the destruction that had been done by later builders working upon the same site our excavation of the Ziggurat terrace did yield more information than we might have expected regarding the layout of the Moon-god's shrine in the time of the First Dynasty; and it also threw an interesting light on what one might call political conditions. I have remarked above on the fantastic thickness of the wall enclosing the terrace, a thickness of thirty-six feet; it suggests a fortress rather than a temple. The south-east wall, between the eastern 'kitchen' building and the corner of the terrace, was double (as too was the north-east wall) where a gate passage led through from the city; the passage ended in a guardroom, and beyond this there were two narrow storechambers between the parallel walls; here there were found a number of jar-stoppers bearing seal-impressions, but also many sling-bolts of baked clay and clay balls, some of them quite large, missiles for use, perhaps, with some kind of catapult. The store-room had in fact served as an armoury.

The city was dominated by the temple of its patron god. But since the god was really the king it was quite natural that his temple should be the core of the city's defence as well as the centre of its worship. We can safely assume that the town was walled. Inside the town there was, then as later, the Temenos or Sacred Area which again was enclosed by walls: it was the second line of defence. Lastly, in a corner of the Temenos, rose the towering mass of the Ziggurat which, with its fortified terrace, corresponded to the keep of the mediaeval castle; here the fighting men of Ur would make their last stand against a victorious enemy. The city states of old Sumer were constantly at war with one another; the long succession of dynasties recorded in the King-lists reflects the instability of things as one vassal ruler after another rebelled against his overlord, overcame his neighbours and made his own city for a time the capital of the land, his own city god becoming by right of conquest the temporary head of the Sumerian pantheon.

Further light on the religious observances of the time was thrown by a discovery in another part of the field. On the line of the south-west wall of Nebuchadnezzar's Temenos there was a low mound in which years before Taylor had done some excavation, finding little, but making worse confounded one of the most confused sites I have ever dug. Under the Babylonian wall there was a tangle of broken and scanty remains of buildings of different dates amongst which we were able to identify a temple of the goddess Dim-tab-ba set up by Dungi, king of the Third Dynasty of Ur, of which however little was left. Later houses had complicated the site with their successive ruins, and house drains, driven down deeply into the soil, had made havoc of everything beneath. Consequently when we did come to the Early Dynastic levels we found walls and floors but all so fragmentary that no coherent plan of them could be drawn up. But in three cases we found underneath the foundations of these walls 'foundation-deposits' of a sort we had never encountered before. When the old builders had cut the trenches for the foundations of the proposed building—probably it was a temple, the prototype of Dungi's Dim-tab-ba shrine—but before they started to lay bricks, they would dig here and there on the wall line a square pit about three feet deep and on the bottom of it spread a mat, the 'table' of the desert banquet.[1] On this were put small clay vessels containing foodstuffs; an ox rib showed that these must have been the god's portion of the consecration sacrifice. Then over the spread table there was inverted a great bell-shaped heavily-ribbed bowl of clay and the pit was filled up with earth and the wall built across it. Under the floor of Dungi's temple we found terracotta cylinders containing animal bones which clearly echo this primitive rite of consecration.

The site, as I have said, was terribly cut up by the drains which had served the houses of Larsa and later dates, but as we dug deeper we found precisely similar drains connected with the Early Dynastic buildings. The nature of the drains is this. You begin by sinking a circular shaft about five feet in diameter to a depth of thirty or forty feet; then in it you pile one on another your drain-pipes, terra-cotta rings about three feet across with a heavy collar at one end (this to give a better balance) and small holes pierced through its sides, and as you put each in place you fill the space round it with broken potsherds, and so on up to floor level, when you cap it with a pierced lid or leave a hole in the tiled pavement for the intake. As the water poured down the drain runs out

[1] The Arabic word meaning 'table' is used by the tent-dweller for the table-cloth which he spreads upon the ground.

through the holes in the sides (kept clear by the potsherd packing) and so seeps away into the subsoil the drain will be effective for a very long time [*Plate* 21*b*].

We had not known that the system had been introduced so early, but what did surprise and puzzle us was the number of drains in a single prehistoric building; it seemed quite illogical that there should be two contemporary drains in a tiny chamber measuring only fifteen feet by three, and in the next room two more; neither a house nor a temple could require sanitation on that scale. Then as we dug deeper and came to the lowest rings of the drains (which of course we had had to destroy as we went down) we had another surprise. At the bottom of each there were quantities of small clay vessels of the two types which we knew to have been regularly used for religious offerings—for instance, on the 'tables of the gods' which I have just described—and terracotta model boats. They had been dropped down the drains, but not by accident, for in a single drain we might find as many as forty intact vases as well as fragments of as many more broken by the fall. I have occasionally found potsherds, and once a complete pot, in what were definitely domestic drains —accidents of course will happen; but this is something different. Now the Sumerian pantheon includes gods of the nether world, prominent among them Ea, Lord of the waters that are under the earth; in connection with him the ancient texts speak of the 'apsu', the dark and mysterious place that reaches down to the waters of the underworld. Now there is nothing strange in the idea of pouring libations to an earth god into a pit, a hole in the ground or a well—in this way your offering goes more directly to the god, and the practice is common to many peoples. I think that our 'drains' are a humble version of the 'apsu'. The use of a common drain for such a purpose may offend our modern susceptibilities, but the East is less squeamish about things of the sort and generally achieves its ends by the means most ready to hand, and a forty-foot pipe although it does not actually reach to the waters of the underworld does at least bring your offering appreciably nearer to god.

V

The Dark Ages

MASSIVE as were the walls of the Moon-god's citadel they could not assure any permanence of empire. If we can trust tradition, Mes-anni-pad-da's dynasty lasted for five generations in all, and then came the end. The King-lists which with our discoveries at al 'Ubaid had received the stamp of historical truth now break down again into a welter of dynasties concerning which we know nothing at all except that they are incredible; they speak of a Second Dynasty of Ur, but it is a mere name to which we cannot attach anything that we found on the site.

I must admit that some of my colleagues have called me seriously to account because in my official publication of the Royal Cemetery I classified one particular group of burials as 'Second Dynasty Graves'. I had however been careful to point out that I used the term merely as a matter of convenience—a rough-and-ready way of distinguishing graves which were intermediate between the First Dynasty of Ur and the Third, and was not at all insisting that they were necessarily connected with the unknown Second Dynasty, although such a connection was not impossible.

There were fifteen graves in the group, ten of them normal and distinguished only by their contents, which mark the transition between the Royal Cemetery and the Sargonid graves but come nearer to the latter, and five are shaft graves containing multiple burials which recall in their arrangement one or two of the royal tombs of the earlier period. None of the last can compare in wealth with the old royal tombs, but they are richer than any of the Sargonid graves. In the pottery, the metal vases and the tools and weapons alike

110

there are many types peculiar to this group; there are fairly numerous survivals from the earlier period but a greater number that are shared in common with the Sargonid; and the head-dresses of both men and women are all in the Sargonid fashion. The best of the single graves had a mud-brick-lined shaft in which was a gable-topped wooden coffin containing the body of a man. Outside the coffin were placed numerous clay pots, several of them red-painted and burnished, a large ribbed tray of copper on which rested copper bowls and vases, a knife and an arrow-head, and the complete bodies of two sheep; against the head of the coffin a row of spears had been planted upright, as they were in the grave of Mes-kalam-dug in the earlier cemetery. On the man's head there were six gold fillets arranged in tiers overlapping one another, a small gold ear-ring and a twisted gold ribbon originally wound round a lock of hair; four necklaces were round the neck, made of beads of various coloured stones, carnelian, agate, jasper, chalcedony, sard, and of gold, to one of which was attached an amulet in the form of a standing goat, a fine lively little figure solid-cast in gold. On the right shoulder was a silver toggle-pin that had fastened the cloak and on the arms were bracelets, a plain gold band on the right arm and on the left three of gold and two of silver, with which was a large lapis lazuli cylinder seal; by the waist was a gold-mounted copper dagger and a silver axe-head; other weapons of copper lay beside the body. Two gold ear-rings and a spirally-coiled gold hair-ring were put in front of the head (they were not worn) and various copper and clay vessels completed the furniture of the coffin.

The multiple graves might contain anything up to twenty bodies. The stratification showed that all these were of one period, had been buried at the same time; the principal bodies were in coffins, and their furniture was much the same as that described in the single grave above; the others were not all together in a 'death-pit', as in the old royal graves, but lay separate, generally wrapped in matting, not necessarily at the same level but at different stages in the filling-in of the tomb shaft; but although they thus obtained what seemed to be a more individual status yet for the most part the bodies, often richly decked with personal ornaments of gold and semi-precious stone, yet had none of the grave furniture considered essential for the dead—no such vessels for food and drink as the traveller to another world requires. All the offerings were with the principal burials. To this extent the graves of the group do seem to carry on, with certain modifications, the traditions of the royal tombs of the older cemetery and to link those up with the mausolea of the Third Dynasty which I shall describe later. It does look as if they were the tombs of rulers sufficiently important to be considered semi-divine and therefore to receive in death those honours which are appropriate to gods rather than to men; but that does not mean that they are the graves of the kings of the Second Dynasty of Ur. In date they seem to me to come very shortly before the time of Sargon of Akkad.[1]

One object of quite extraordinary interest was found in the upper filling of one of the multiple graves; here there had been some disturbance and it was difficult to be sure whether the object in question belonged to the grave or must be associated with the later rubbish introduced at the time of the disturbance, in which case it would be of Sargonid date. It was a steatite seal, circular, engraved with a figure of a humped bull done in the style of Mohenjo-daro and with an inscription in the characters of the Indus Valley. We had had evidence of contacts between Ur and India at an earlier date, for in the Royal Cemetery we had found beads of carnelian on which were geometrical patterns artificially bleached by a chemical process, exactly corresponding to examples from Mohenjo-daro, and it was inconceivable that the invention should have been made independently in the two countries at more or less the same time; at Ur we do not find such beads in any later setting, but in India the craft has been practised right down to the present day. Little things like beads can of course be carried far afield, passed from hand to hand, and their occurrence does not necessarily mean direct con-

---

[1] One authority would place them immediately after Sargon and before the Third Dynasty of Ur, on the strength of one of the cylinder seals which is very much in the Third Dynasty style; but against this I would set the evidence of the pottery, the metal weapons and vases and the stratification which seemed to me conclusive.

Plate 15

3

5

1. Shell cylinder seal from a soldier's grave, Royal
Cemetery period. 2. Sargonid green stone cylinder.
3. Stamp seal, Mohenjo-daro type. 4. Third Dynasty
seal. 5. Third Dynasty seal. 6. Seal of the Larsa period

Examples of Seals

Plate 16

The headless statue of Entemena, Governor of Lagash

tact between the two countries concerned. But it is different with a thing so strictly personal as a seal: and when we find, as we do, that from the Sargonid period on quite a number of them occur, sometimes real imports from India, sometimes imitation of Indian seals made by Sumerian craftsmen, then the conclusion is certain. By Sargon's time, if not before (as the seal from the tomb suggests) trade between Sumer and the Indus Valley had attained such proportions that Indian business firms at Mohenjo-daro or other towns there found it worth while to have their Indian agents in residence in the towns of the Euphrates Valley.

Until further evidence is forthcoming from some other site we must hold in suspension the question of the date of our 'Second Dynasty' graves and of the Indian contacts and must admit that, historically speaking, after the violent destruction of A-anni-pad-da's temple at al 'Ubaid there is a complete gap (the length of which is uncertain, depending as it does on a chronology regarding which differing views are held) up to the time when, about 2600 B.C., the city of Lagash becomes a leading power in the land. We found at Ur a small granite stela inscribed with the name of Ur-Nina, the founder of a long dynasty of Lagash rulers, and its presence here must mean that he ranked as the overlord of Ur. The carving on the stone is incredibly crude, and it seems tragic that Ur, which under the First Dynasty had produced such masterpieces of art, should now be subject to mere barbarians; perhaps the people did rebel, for Ur-Nina's grandson claims to have conquered Ur, but the attempt was not repeated and Lagash, although its dominion was so far limited that its governors do not figure in the King-lists, retained authority over Ur for several generations. In an outlying part of the site we found an inscribed clay cone—a sort of foundation-deposit—which recorded the building of a temple by Enan-natum I, the fourth in line from Ur-Nina, and it is significant that the temple was dedicated not to Nannar, Ur's patron deity, but to the god of Lagash. Enannatum was succeeded by Entemena, and to his dealings with Ur we have eloquent testimony. When we were clearing the area behind the Ziggurat, on the pavement of a gateway through the

encircling wall built by Nebuchadnezzar in the seventh
century B.C. we found a large diorite statue of a man wearing
the conventional Sumerian garment of sheepskin and bearing engraved on its back and shoulders a long inscription
describing the pious works of Entemena 'Governor of
Lagash, beloved of Nina, great governor of Ningirsu, son of
Enannatum governor of Lagash, eldest descendant of Ur-
Nina king of Lagash; at that time Entemena carved his
statue, "Entemena beloved of Enlil" he called its name'. The
text makes it clear that the statue was intended to be set up
in Lagash; either Entemena changed his mind and put it in
Ur or else it had been in Lagash and at some time or another
the people of Ur had sacked Lagash and carried off the king's
statue as a trophy; in any case it did come to Ur. It had been
a fine statue, well carved (Lagash had become civilized!)
but its head was missing, broken off in antiquity, and the
jagged stump of the neck was polished till it shone. One can
only suppose that when the yoke of Lagash was broken the
headless figure of the dethroned ruler was set up in the
passage way and every passer-by contemptuously stroked the
broken neck until the stone was as polished as the toe of
St. Peter's statue in Rome [*Plate* 16].

A rather different picture of the Lagash period is given by
a limestone relief found in the treasury of the temple of the
Moon-goddess. It is a plaque about ten inches square with a
hole in the centre for a peg, probably to fix it to the temple
wall. On it are two scenes carved in low relief; above, a male
figure, ritually naked, pours a libation before the seated
image of the god; he is followed by three smaller figures
wearing heavy cloaks; in the lower scene we have the same
figure pouring his libation, but instead of the god there is the
door of the shrine, and behind him come three figures of
which the leader, standing full face, is the High Priestess
wearing mitre and long cloak and the other two are servants
carrying a kid for the sacrifice and a chaplet [*Plate* 17*a*].
Later analogies make the meaning clear.[1] The man making
the sacrifice is probably the king himself, denoted as such by
his greater stature; the High Priestess is the king's daughter.

[1] See below, p. 115.

The position of High Priestess of the Moon-god at Ur was so important—and presumably so lucrative—that from very early days right down to the close of the city's history it was traditionally held by a member of the royal house, and if no daughter was available the king's son might be installed as High Priest. If the rulers of Lagash fell in with this tradition, as our plaque would show, for it is definitely in the Lagash style, it would seem that the overlords of Ur were at some pains to conciliate their subjects.

A roughly-cut inscription on fragments of a limestone vase apparently implies that after the fall of Lagash Ur passed under the control of Lugal-kisal-si, 'king of Erech and of Ur', but Erech enjoyed only a short-lived authority, for Sargon of Akkad defeated its forces, carried off its king and 'destroyed Ur'. Probably the 'destruction' meant little more than the dismantling of the fortifications, for a stone mace-head with an inscription of Sargon, once dedicated in the Moon-god's temple, is proof that he paid respect to the city's gods. More than this; in the Moon-goddess' temple we found a sadly-battered alabaster disc on one side of which was carved in relief just such a scene of worship by the High Priestess as was given on the Lagash plaque, but an inscription on the back tells us that the principal figure with her flounced dress and high conical hat is none other than En-he-du-an-na, daughter of King Sargon of Akkad. It was an astonishing piece of luck to get this personal evidence regarding Sargon, who was one of the outstanding characters of early Meso-potamian history, so famous that scholars had been apt to doubt whether he was more than the imaginary hero of old legend; now we have En-he-du-an-na, and she is a very real person; she lived at Ur and she had her court there, as be-seemed a princess. In the Sargonid cemetery we found two intact graves in which were cylinder seals and a third cylinder seal, from a plundered grave, loose in the soil; all the owners belonged to members of En-he-du-an-na's household, one being her steward, one her scribe and one her hair-dresser; the seals served the double purpose of confirming the presence at Ur of Sargon's daughter and of dating the cemetery with unexpected accuracy.

The Sargonid graves lay immediately above those of the Royal Cemetery but were quite distinct from them not only by stratification but also by the nature of their contents. The grave itself, and the ritual of burial, show no change; but the pottery is quite different; there is a whole new range of shapes (which implies a change in table manners!) and the vessels are much more carefully made and very often are rendered more attractive by being covered with a wash of red paint and then burnished brightly; it is perhaps a sign of diminished wealth, for it is when men cannot afford cups and dishes of stone or of metal that the humble art of the potter comes into its own. Certainly the graves are nothing like so rich as those of the Royal Cemetery; there are no vessels of gold or silver and even stone is rare; we still find beads of lapis lazuli and carnelian, and to those are added materials unknown or uncommon in the old days, hæmatite, agate and chalcedony, but when gold is used we generally find, instead of solid metal, the thinnest of gold foil plated over a copper core. The most surprising change is in the tools and weapons. In the Royal Cemetery these had been cast in bronze and the smiths had taken full advantage of the technique of casting to make the beautifully socketed axes and adzes which characterize the period: in the Sargonid graves only copper is used and the clumsily-fashioned blade is simply hammered round the end of the wooden handle and secured by a rivet or a tang is driven into the shaft; it is a sad decadence. The explanation seems to be this, that the Early Dynastic people imported the ore from the district of Oman on the Persian Gulf, and it was a natural alloy containing about five per cent nickel to ninety-five per cent copper. In the Sargonid period either the Oman ores had given out or the source of supply was cut off for some political reason (the Akkadian trade connections were naturally with the North) and copper ore was now imported from Asia Minor; but this was pure copper and therefore not amenable to casting, so that the smiths were obliged to use the hammering process to give shape and hardness to the inferior metal; it was a retrograde step in culture.

Since we cleared more than four hundred Sargonid graves

we were able to collect plenty of material for establishing the character of the period, and the most striking feature was the change in the fashion of head-dress. In the Royal Cemetery age men wore round their heads a ring of gold or silver chains and long 'bugle' beads of lapis lazuli or carnelian which, like the *agêhl* of the present-day Arab, kept the head-cloth in place, and the women, at least those connected with the court, had the elaborate garniture of broad gold or silver ribbon, wreaths of gold and stone beads with pendant leaves or rings of gold, hair-rings of coiled gold wire and enormous moon-shaped ear-rings of gold. The Sargonid men have nothing but a small oval frontlet of thin gold tied across the forehead, and the women have a similar frontlet (worn, as with the men, across the forehead, not in the hair), and ear-rings of gold, moon-shaped but very small, and a lock of hair starting from just above either ear was plaited and spirally bound with a very narrow gold ribbon and pinned in position above the forehead. Granted that these are relatively poor graves which could not be expected to rival the exuberant splendour of the Royal Cemetery, none the less so radical a change in fashion must reflect a change in social habits and in the general outlook on life.

And change is apparent in the cylinder seals also. As regards their subjects, the favourite motive of the older period, the ritual banquet with seated figures drinking through tubes, disappears altogether; we find not uncommonly the 'introduction' scene wherein the seal's owner is brought by his personal god into the presence of a major deity, a scene which is unknown in the Royal Cemetery time but is the most popular of all under the Third Dynasty; for the first time we get mythological scenes (borrowed perhaps from the mystery-plays performed in the temples)—the goddess Nidaba is seen seated on a corn-stack while divine attendant gods and her husband Ashnan come before her carrying ears of corn, or Shamash, the Sun, climbs the mountains, coming out from the doors of morning which his servant-gods open for his passage, or Shamash and Ishtar trample on a fallen enemy, or Zu, the robber, the bird-man god of storm and darkness, oppresses mankind who kneel to

him for mercy, whereon Shamash appears with wings of flame
and his servant-god is shown picking up the broken body of
the lord of storm. The old motive of Gilgamish and the lions
bringing down to earth the wild bull or the ibex persists into
the Sargonid period with undiminished popularity, but the
treatment of the motive is very different. In these, as indeed
in all the seals, the crowding together of the figures which in
the Early Dynastic seals makes the composition so intricate
and confused is abandoned, and instead the artist has learned
how to space out his design so that each figure, isolated
against a clear background, may gain in significance. This
use of space as an essential part of design is an innovation of
Sargonid art and its leading characteristic; we see it most
obviously in such a major work as the celebrated sculptured
stela of Naram-Sin, Sargon's grandson, but it pervades no
less effectively the tiny masterpieces of the gem-cutter
[*Plate* 15. 2].

During the reigns of Sargon's successors Ur continued to
enjoy the favour of her alien rulers, in spite of a rebellion
which broke out on Sargon's death, for not only was a princess of the royal house again installed as High Priestess of
Nannar at Ur, as we know from outside sources, but the
city's temples were regularly honoured. In the ruins of
E-nun-makh, the shrine of the Moon-god and his wife, we
found under a later pavement an enormous mass of fragments of stone vases which had been dedicated to the temple
and kept in its treasury; when the Third Dynasty of Ur
crashed and the Elamite forces broke into the city they
sacked the temples and wantonly destroyed the offerings of
ancient kings that were stored in them. The temples were
rebuilt, but with the broken stone *ex votos* nothing could be
done, so the fragments were collected and, because they were
holy and so could not be treated as mere rubbish, buried
under the new pavements of the shrines to which they had
belonged. There we found them. Stone mace-heads and
vases of steatite, limestone and alabaster, many of them bore
inscriptions recording the name of the donor; they were of
different dates, coming right down to the last days of the
Third Dynasty, but amongst them not a few belonged to the

dynasty of Sargon of Akkad. One mace-head was the gift of Sargon himself, many vases had been dedicated by Rimush, Sargon's son, treasure selected from the king's share of 'the booty of Elam' after 'the king of all had smitten Elam and Barakhsi'; one of them was a steatite bowl very curiously carved with demon and animal figures in the Elamite style, obviously brought back from the enemy country. Here then there was evidence enough of the pious regard paid to the temples of Ur by the Sargonid kings, but it is all the evidence that we found; nowhere was there any record of buildings erected by them. One cannot believe that in the course of the hundred and fifty years covered by the dynasty there was no building activity at all; the absence of any proof is probably due to the accidents of discovery. The custom of stamping the actual bricks did not come in very early, and there might well be no means of identifying a wall built to the orders of Rimush; clay foundation-cones duly inscribed would have been immured in the masonry, but the survival of any such to the present day, within the area of our excavations, is at best a matter of luck, and here luck was against us. Fortunately however this lack of evidence (which would have done no more than confirm what the vase-fragments told us) was atoned for by the discovery of building-inscriptions of Gudea.

The Sargonid dynasty was brought to an end by the invasion of the Guti, a savage hill tribe from the Elamite land, and with their victory the entire economy of Sumer was reduced to chaos. 'Who was king? who was not king?' plaintively writes the author of the King-lists. For a time there was, in fact, no general overlord; the old city states resumed their independence under local rulers who could claim no higher title than that of *patesi* or governor. Prominent amongst these city states was Lagash. Thanks to the French excavations at that site (now called Tello) we know the names of all the nine governors, members of one family, who in turn held office at Lagash; of one of them, Gudea, nearly a score of portrait statues have come to light, so that he is the figure most familiar to us in all the early history of Sumer. One might have supposed that here the 'accidents of discovery' had given to Gudea an importance in our eyes which his status as local governor would not warrant; but the evidence from Ur shows that the governors of Lagash, although they might in theory and profession be subject to the Guti, yet enjoyed a very real authority.

Amongst the fragments of votive stone vases found under the pavement of E-nun-makh no less than four bore inscriptions of 'En-anni-pad-da priest of Nannar, son of Ur-Bau governor of Lagash'. Ur-Bau was the founder of the line of Lagash governors, and it is clear that he controlled Ur also and, following the precedent already old, installed his son as High Priest of the Moon-god. Three inscriptions (found elsewhere on the site) gave us the name of Gudea. One of them was on a stone vase, an *ex voto* dedicated by some unknown follower 'for the life of Gudea governor of Lagash', which proves no more than that there were subjects of Lagash in Ur; but the other two are far more interesting, for both of them record the building by Gudea of temples at Ur, one being the foundation-cone of his shrine for Tammuz (Adonis), the other a stone tablet from the foundation-deposit of the temple of the god Nindar, son of the goddess Nin-kharsag who owned the temple at al 'Ubaid. The building was so important that one of the years of Gudea's reign was named 'the year in which he built the temple of Nindar', and we can conclude that his lordship over Ur ranked high in his claims to honour, and that it was substantiated by special favours accorded to the subject city.

The inept rule of the Guti lasted for about a hundred years and then, *c.* 2120 B.C., a single battle put an end to it and Utu-khegal of Erech set himself up as overlord of Sumer. Lagash had to submit—we hear no more of its independent governors—and that involved the submission of Ur likewise. A fragment of a diorite stela which we found not only proves this but gives us a dramatic insight into the history of the period.

'For Ningal the beloved wife of Sin, his Lady, for the life of Utu-khegal the mighty man, king of Erech, king of the Four Regions, Ur-Nammu, governor of Ur . . .' so the text runs, and it is virtually repeated on a fragment of a second stela

'For Nannar King of the Anunnaki, his King, for the life of Utu-khegal the mighty man, king of Erech, king of the Four Regions . . .' Ur-Nammu is governor of Ur as the vassal or servant of the king of Erech, and he is making offerings or building temples to secure the long life of his overlord. And then comes another inscription, this time on the stamped bricks specially made for the building of the great fortified enclosure of the Ziggurat—'For Nannar, most glorious son of Enlil, his King, has Ur-Nammu the mighty man, lord of Erech, king of Ur, king of Sumer and Akkad, built E-temen-ni-il his beloved temple'. Utu-khegal had reigned for seven years only; then the governor of Ur rebelled against his master and slew him and as king of the whole land founded the Third Dynasty of Ur. In the early days his pride in victory makes him claim the unusual title 'lord of Erech'— and it is noteworthy that his first act seems to have been to strengthen the defences of his capital city. Later that title is dropped, as the king's position became more assured, and 'the mighty man, king of Ur, king of Sumer and Akkad' is the invariable formula.

VI

The Third Dynasty of Ur

OR a hundred years, from 2112 to 2015 B.C., under the five kings of the Third Dynasty, Ur was the capital of a great empire and its rulers were at pains to make it a centre worthy of its political pre-eminence. We very seldom excavated the ruins of a temple without finding some record of that period; either it had originally been founded or it had been restored by some one king of the Third Dynasty. Ur-Nammu, the first of his line, was particularly active as a builder. 'For Nin-gal his Lady Ur-Nammu the mighty man, King of Ur, King of Sumer and Akkad, has built her splendid Gig-par', 'For Inanna the noble Lady . . . Ur-Nammu has built Esh-bur, her beloved temple', 'For Nannar the Lord of Heaven', 'For Anu King of the gods', 'For Nin-e-gal his Lady' and so on; it is a formidable list of works undertaken by the new ruler. His reign was not a long one, only eighteen years, and did not suffice for the programme on which he embarked; the Ziggurat itself and E-khursag the Palace were begun by him but finished by his son, and in some cases either haste or economy led him to construct in mud brick only and it was left to his successors to pull down the rather shoddy walls and rebuild in baked brick. Certainly by the time the Third Dynasty was drawing to its close the city of Ur was crowded with magnificent monuments testifying to the wealth and piety of its kings; it was but natural that when Ibi-Sin, the last of Ur-Nammu's line, was defeated by an alien enemy those monuments should be specially signalled out for destruction. With the exception of the Ziggurat there are very few Third Dynasty buildings of which the walls still stand up above ground level; when the time came to restore the ruined temples it was a case not of

patching but of pulling down all the old work and rebuilding; it is only in the foundations that we find the stamped
bricks bearing the names of the Third Dynasty founders.

The inscriptions tell us that Ur-Nammu built the walls of
Ur 'like a yellow mountain'. The walled city (Fig. 6) was in
shape an irregular oval, measuring about eleven hundred and
thirty yards in length by seven hundred and fifty yards in
width, and was surrounded by a wall and rampart. The
rampart was of mud brick built with a steeply-sloping outer
face; the lower part of it was in fact a revetment against the
side of the mound formed by the ruins of the older town,
but the upper part of it extended inland over the top of the
ruins to make a solid platform from twenty-five to thirty-
five yards wide rising twenty-six feet above the level of the
ground at the rampart's foot while its back stood only five
feet above the ground-level inside the city. Along the top of
this ran the wall proper, built of burnt bricks; where the
rampart was narrowest one had simply the wall with a berm
in front of it and behind it a passage for the manœuvring of
troops; where it broadened out it was because here there was
a temple or other public building standing on the rampart;
such might be incorporated in the system of defence, its
outer wall linking up with the city wall and its roof serving
as a tower. This massive fortification was further strengthened by the fact that the river Euphrates (as can be seen
from the sunken line of its old bed) washed the foot of the
western rampart while fifty yards from the foot of the
eastern rampart there had been dug a broad canal which left
the river immediately above the north end of the town, so
that on three sides Ur was ringed with a moat and only from
the south could be approached by dry land. It was a colossal
work and must have seemed to the builder impregnable, but
it was to fall in the end; the rampart, backed by a solid mass
of earth, could not be violently overthrown and although in
places wind and rain have weathered it almost all away yet
we seldom failed to find at least the lower part of its worn and
battered face; but of Ur-Nammu's wall not a trace remained.
We would come on examples of the very large bricks, specially moulded and inscribed with the king's name and titles,

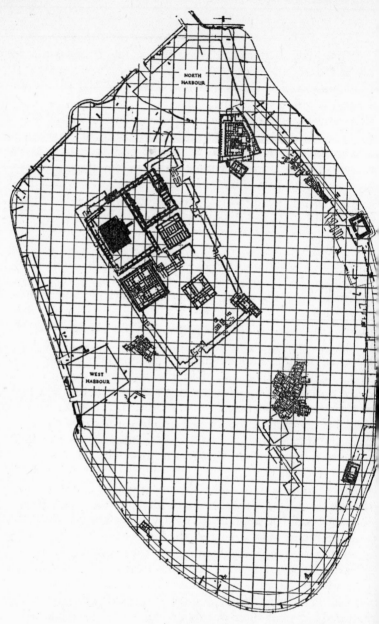

NORTH HARBOUR

WEST HARBOUR

Fig. 6. Plan of the City of Ur showing the principal
sites excavated

124

re-used in some later building, but none of them were
in situ; just because the defences of Ur had been so strong the
victorious enemy had dismantled them systematically, leaving not one brick upon another.

With the Ziggurat it was very different. Of all the great
staged towers which characterized the cities of Sumer that of
Ur is the best preserved, and it is for the most part the
original work of Ur-Nammu. Here a few words of explanation are called for. The Ziggurat is a peculiar feature of
Sumerian architecture which can now be traced back to the
earliest times, to the period of the chalcolithic al 'Ubaid
people. As we have seen, the al 'Ubaid people (whose skull
formation shows them to have resembled what is called
Caucasian man) had cultural affinities with Elam and therefore presumably came down into the Euphrates valley from
the east, came, that is, from a hilly country; like all people
who live in a mountainous land they would naturally
associate their religion with the land's outstanding features,
and as a matter of fact the Sumerian gods are often represented as standing upon mountains and would accordingly
be worshipped upon 'high places'. The immigrants to Lower
Mesopotamia found themselves in a vast level plain where
there was no hill on which god could be properly worshipped, and art therefore had to make good the deficiencies
of nature. Here even a private house, if it was to be safe-
guarded against the annual inundations, needed to be raised
on some sort of platform, and that being so the solution of the
religious difficulty was not far to seek—the platform merely
had to be made taller. In every town therefore which was
big enough to warrant the effort the inhabitants built a
'high place', a tower rising up in stages and crowned by the
town's principal shrine; they used 'bricks instead of stone and
slime (bitumen) had they for mortar', and to their work they
would give such a name as 'the Hill of Heaven' or 'the
Mountain of God'. This was the Ziggurat. Of them all, the
biggest and the most famous was, in course of time, the
Ziggurat of Babylon, which in Hebrew tradition became
known as the Tower of Babel; it was entirely destroyed by
Alexander the Great, but its groundplan survives and shows

that it was but a repetition on a slightly larger scale of the Ziggurat of Ur; and it too was built by Ur-Nammu.

The site of the Ziggurat of Ur was fixed by ancient tradition. I have spoken already of the ziggurats of the Jamdat Nasr and Early Dynastic periods; what Ur-Nammu did was to rebuild over these, probably incorporating their remains in the core of his new structure. The site was in the west corner of the Temenos called E-gish-shir-gal or Sacred Area of the city; the king rebuilt the enclosing wall of the Temenos (which formed the second line of the defences of Ur) and although very little of that wall survives we found traces of it sufficient to give us its outline and the proof that it was indeed the work of Ur-Nammu. The Sacred Area as a whole was dedicated to the Moon-god Nannar and his wife Nin-gal —at least, this seems to be the case, for Ur-Nammu expressly states on his brick-stamps that he built it for Nin-gal, while other inscriptions of the Third Dynasty speak of it as belonging to Nannar; presumably the two deities shared it in common. But the north-east end, called E-temen-ni-il, was the peculiar property of the Moon-god; here, in the west corner, rose the terrace on which the Ziggurat stood, and in front of the terrace, to the north-east, occupying about two-thirds of the terrace length and extending to the far wall of the Sacred Area, was the Great Court of Nannar; the great court was low-lying, actually sunk somewhat below the general level of the Temenos, and there must have been a flight of steps in the monumental gateway that gave access from it to the terrace, for the latter was raised three feet above Temenos level. The terrace was surrounded by a massive double wall of mud brick with intramural chambers; much of it had gone, but on the north-west side it was well preserved, standing still to a height of five and a half feet. It was of mud brick, built against the core of the old First Dynasty terrace wall; the front sloped steeply back (the angle was 35 in 100) and was relieved by shallow buttresses sixteen feet wide and little more than a foot deep which must be considered decorative rather than constructional, since they can have added nothing to the building's strength [*Plate* 17*b*]. The face of the wall was smoothly rendered with mud plaster ;

126

much of this had fallen away and we very soon cleared off the rest, for beneath the plaster there was a dramatic discovery to be made. At regular intervals of two feet there appeared the small rounded heads of clay 'nails' driven into the mud mortar between the brick courses; these were 'foundation-cones' and on the 'nail's' stem was the inscription 'For Nannar the strong bull of Heaven, most glorious son of Enlil, his King, has Ur-Nammu the mighty man, King of Ur, built his temple, E-temen-ni-il'. Such cones were familiar enough as objects on museum shelves, but now for the first time we saw them in position just as the builders had set them four thousand years before. That they should be found *in situ* is of course most important scientifically, for we not only learn that a particular king built a particular temple, but they positively identify a building which we have excavated and they give it a positive date; but at the same time one felt a quite unscientific thrill at seeing those ordered rows of cream-coloured knobs which even the people of Ur had not seen when once the terrace wall was finished and plastered.

The excavation of the Ziggurat itself was a formidable task. In the middle of last century Mr. J. E. Taylor, then British Consul at Basra, was engaged by the British Museum to investigate some of the ancient sites of southern Mesopotamia, and amongst others he visited Ur, in those days a place difficult and dangerous of access. Struck by the obvious importance of one mound, which from its height, overshadowing all the other ruins, he rightly judged to be the Ziggurat, he attacked it from above, cutting down into the brickwork of the four corners. The science of field archæology had not then been devised and the excavator's object was to find things that might enrich the cases of a museum, while the preservation of buildings on the spot was little considered. To the greatest monument of Ur Taylor did damage which we cannot but deplore to-day, but he succeeded in his purpose and at least made clear the importance of the site whose later excavation has so well repaid us. Hidden in the brickwork of the top stage of the tower he found, at each angle of it, cylinders of baked clay on which were long inscriptions giving the history of the building. The texts date from about 550 B.C., from the time of Nabonidus, the last of the kings of Babylon, and state that the tower, founded by Ur-Nammu and his son Dungi, but left unfinished by them and not completed by any later king, he had restored and finished. These inscriptions not only gave us the first information obtained about the Ziggurat itself, but identified the site, called by the Arabs al Mughair, the Mound of Pitch, as Ur 'of the Chaldees', the biblical home of Abraham.

Taylor's excavations did not go very far. Those were the days when in the north of Mesopotamia Rawlinson was unearthing the colossal human-headed bulls and pictured wall-slabs which now enrich the British Museum, and, dazzled by such discoveries, people could not realize the value of the odds and ends which alone rewarded the explorer in the south, and the work at Ur was therefore abandoned. Towards the close of the century an American expedition again attacked the top of the mound and exposed some of the brickwork, but apart from that apparently fruitless attempt at excavation the site was deserted and what showed of the upper stages of the Ziggurat was left to the mercies of the weather and of Arab builders in search of cheap ready-made bricks; when British troops advanced to Mughair in 1915 only a few ragged bricks could be seen protruding from the top of a huge mound of undisturbed sand and rubble up whose gently sloping sides a man could ride on horseback. In 1919 Dr. H. R. Hall initiated the real excavation of the monument and cleared part of the south-east end down to the level of the terrace floor and discovered that the lower part of the brick casing, protected by the rubbish heaped against it, was wonderfully well preserved. It was manifest that the work begun by Hall must be continued by the Joint Expedition, and we started on it almost at once, but it was a task that could not be completed in a hurry.

The amount of rubbish which had to be removed was very great, running into thousands of tons, all of which had to be lifted in small baskets and then carried by our light railway to a safe distance where it would not hamper later operations. In this mass of fallen brick and wind-blown sand there were

Plate 17

a. Limestone relief of sacrifice, Lagash period

b. Ur-Nammu's wall supporting the Ziggurat Terrace

Plate 18

The Ziggurat of Ur-Nammu;
back and front views

no objects of any sort to be found, so that, until we were down to floor level, the job was mere navvy work unimpeded by any considerations of archæological method, and actually the end of our 1923–4 season saw the great building standing free of the rubbish which had shrouded it for so many centuries. Of course a vast amount remained to be done on the surrounding buildings, but I fondly imagined that our work on the tower itself was finished, and taking advantage of the assistance of Mr. F. G. Newton, the most experienced of archæological architects, ventured to reconstruct on paper the Ziggurat as it had originally been.

The reconstruction was wrong. Because of all the ziggurats in Iraq that of Ur seemed to be the best preserved the Government had very properly seen to its protection and we had been instructed that on no account were we to move any of the brickwork remaining *in situ*. The cylinders found by Taylor told us that Ur-Nammu and his son Dungi had between them built the staged tower and that Nabonidus had restored and finished it, but they did not say that other kings too had worked upon it. A fair proportion of the burnt bricks of Ur-Nammu bore his stamp, and so did some of Nabonidus' bricks, but the vast majority of the bricks bore no name. We were in our early days at Ur and had still everything to learn; for us a plain brick was just a brick, and we had not got the experience to decide by its measurements and proportions to which period of history it ought to be assigned. Consequently when, high up on the Ziggurat, we brushed the surface of the bricks which we might not move (and the stamps were most often on the under side!) we assumed, or I assumed, that what did not belong to Nabonidus necessarily belonged to the Third Dynasty, and when it came to working out the reconstruction of the Third Dynasty building some of the evidence on which I relied was brickwork of an entirely different period. Later on, of course, I recognized that this first attempt was premature and we returned to the study of the Ziggurat fortified by all that we had learned in the meantime about Sumerian and Babylonian brickwork and able to eliminate all that was not of Ur-Nammu's date, and in 1933 could put forward a new

version of the Ziggurat reconstruction which in all essentials
is demonstrably correct.

In form the Ziggurat is a stepped pyramid having three
stages. The whole thing is solid. The core is of mud brick
(probably laid round and over the remains of the First
Dynasty Ziggurat) and the face is a skin of burnt bricks set in

Fig. 7. Reconstruction of the Ziggurat of Ur-Nammu

bitumen mortar, about eight feet thick. The lowest stage,
which alone is well preserved, measures at ground level a
little more than 200 feet in length by 150 feet in width and is
about fifty feet high; from this rose the upper stages, each
smaller than the one below, leaving broad passages along the
main sides and wider terraces at either end; on the topmost
stage stood the little one-roomed shrine of the Moon-god, the
most sacred building in Ur, for whose setting the whole of
this vast substructure had been planned.

On three sides the walls rose sheer to the level of the first
terrace [*Plate* 18*a*], but on the north-east face fronting the
Nannar temple was the approach to the shrine. Three brick
stairways, each of a hundred steps, led upwards, one projecting out at right angles from the building, two leaning

against its wall, and all converging in a great gateway between the first and the second terrace; from this gate flights of stairs ran straight up to the second terrace and to the door of the shrine, while lateral passages with descending flights of stairs gave access to the lower terraces at either end of the tower; the angles formed by the three main stairways were filled in with solid flat-topped buttress-towers [*Plate* 18*b*].

When first we started the work of drawing out the plan and elevations of the Ziggurat we were puzzled to find that the different measurements never seemed to agree; then it was discovered that in the whole building there is not a single straight line, and that what we had assumed to be such were in fact carefully calculated curves. The walls not only slope inwards, but the line from top to bottom is slightly convex; on the ground plan the wall line from corner to corner of the building has a distinct outward bend, so that sighting along it one can see only as far as the centre; the architect has aimed at an optical illusion which the Greek builders of the Parthenon at Athens were to achieve many centuries afterwards, the curves being so slight as not to be apparent, yet enough to give to the eye an appearance of strength where a straight line might by contrast with the mass behind it have seemed incurved and weak. The employment of such a device does great credit to the builders of the twenty-second century before Christ.

Indeed, the whole design of the building is a masterpiece. It would have been so easy to pile rectangle of brickwork above rectangle, and the effect would have been soulless and ugly; as it is, the heights of the different stages are skilfully calculated, the slope of the walls leads the eye upwards and inwards to the centre, the sharper slope of the triple staircase accentuates that of the walls and fixes the attention on the shrine above, which was the religious focus of the whole structure, while across these converging lines cut the horizontal planes of the terraces.

No one looking at the Ziggurat can fail to notice the tall and narrow slits which at regular intervals and in rows one above another pierce the brickwork of the walls; they run clean through the burnt-brick casing and deep into the mud brick of the core, where they are loosely filled with broken pottery. These are 'weeper-holes' intended to drain the interior, a necessary precaution, for with damp the mud brick would swell and make the outer walls bulge if it did not burst them altogether.

This is the obvious and correct explanation and for a long time it satisfied us; but then the difficulty arose, how was the damp likely to get into the core? There was no real danger at the time of construction, for though there would then be plenty of water in the mud mortar used for the crude bricks, this would dry—indeed, with so vast an area to build over, one course would be virtually dry before the next was laid above it—and the tendency of the core would be to shrink rather than to expand. It is true that torrential rains fall in Mesopotamia, but in the days of the Third Dynasty it was usual to lay pavements of burnt brick two, three, or even five courses thick set in bitumen mortar, and no surface water could penetrate this and do harm below. If there had been such a pavement, the precaution was needless; and if there was not such, why not? And further, at each end of the tower there is in one of the buttresses a deep recess in the brickwork running from the edge of the first terrace to the ground, and at the bottom of this there is what engineers call an 'apron', a mass of brick waterproofed with bitumen and built with its top at a slant calculated to carry off smoothly and without splash water falling from above: evidently there was water on the terrace.

In the doorway of a room of late date lying against the back wall of the tower we found a great diorite hinge-stone bearing an inscription of Nabonidus in which he refers to his repairs of the building and states that he cleared the 'Gig-par-ku' of fallen branches. As the excavations progressed we were able to establish that the Gig-par-ku was a part of the temple complex dedicated to the Moon-goddess, and that it lay close under the south-east end of the Ziggurat; somehow the site of this building had become encumbered with branches of trees. There may have been trees in the Gig-par-ku itself, but as most of it was roofed in, this is not very likely; and the only other place from which the branches could have fallen into it was the Ziggurat itself.

This explains the weeper-holes. The terraces of Ur-Nammu's staged tower were not paved with brick but were covered with soil, and in this trees were planted; the long recesses in the buttresses may have carried off the waters of a violent storm, but they may equally have served as water-hoists for the irrigation of the terrace; and what made possible the swelling of the core of the tower and therefore necessitated the weeper-holes in its facing was just this irrigation—the water poured at the roots of the trees would percolate through the top soil into the crude brick, and if it had no outlet would really endanger the building.

Thus we have to imagine trees clothing every terrace with greenery, hanging gardens which brought more vividly to mind the original conception of the Ziggurat as the Mountain of God, and we shall recognize how much better the sloping outer walls harmonize with this conception, rising as they do like the abrupt bare sides of some pine-topped crag, than if they had been uncompromisingly vertical, the walls of a house of man's building.

The lowest stage stands to-day to its original height, the tops of its walls indeed being weathered away but fragments of paving against the foot of the second stage sufficing to give its true level. Of the second stage just enough remains to give its outline, and of the third stage the lower part of the mud-brick core, bereft of its facing, gave both the measurements of this stage and the approximate level of the second-stage floor. Of the three flights of stairs the two built against the sides of the Ziggurat still had much of their burnt-brick treads, though these were not original but restored by Nabonidus in the sixth century B.C.; the central stairs had suffered more severely but the solid staircase survived although its upper surface had perished. The gate tower under which the three flights converge is frankly a restoration; it had been ruined away almost to its foundations, but those massive piers remained; the four doorways (of which the jambs could be distinguished) were of course essential to the plan and while a pointed corbelled arch is likely enough we do possess evidence that the round (true) arch was used under the Third Dynasty and a little roofed cistern of Ur-Nammu's date on the Ziggurat terrace gives us a contemporary analogy for the suggested dome. We found the start of the stair-flight going up to the second stage, and part of the stairs going down to the main floor of the first stage; the topmost stair-flight and the actual shrine to which it led are frankly restorations (Fig. 7).

The building is absolutely symmetrical except for one thing. At its south-east end, on the lowest platform, there was a small building leant up against the wall of the second stage which had no counterpart at the north-west end. Only enough of this remained for us to say that it did exist and had had its entrance at the south-west end; there was nothing found in its ruins to explain its use. It seems to me possible that it was the shrine of Nin-gal. Nannar had his house on the summit of the Ziggurat which was dedicated to him; it is possible that his wife, who at Ur was held in very great honour, had her place on the same 'Mountain of God' but at a lower level.

The recovery of the form of the Ziggurat was one of the most gratifying results of our work at Ur, for besides giving us a clear picture of the city's most important monument it helps to solve problems on other sites where similar buildings once stood. Thus of the Ziggurat of Babylon only the ground-plan survives, but it is identical with that of Ur (though somewhat larger) and as it too was built by Ur-Nammu we can safely conclude that its elevation also was the same, so that looking at the Ziggurat of Ur we can visualize the Tower of Babel. And just as the Tower of Babel was remembered in Hebrew legend as a work so colossal as to seem to challenge Heaven itself, so the Ziggurat of Ur, dominating the city as it did, must have impressed itself on the imagination and the memory of all who dwelt there. When Jacob at Bethel dreamed of ladders (or staircases, the word is the same) set up to Heaven with angels going up and down, surely he subconsciously recalled what his grandfather had told of the great building at Ur whose stairs went up to Heaven—such was indeed the name of Nannar's shrine—and how on feast-days the priests carrying the god's statue went up and down those stairs in a rite meant to assure a bounteous harvest and the increase of cattle and of human kind.

On the north-west side of the Ziggurat, between it and the terrace wall, there was a building, many times repaired by later rulers, of which the foundation went back to Ur-Nammu; scanty as the remains of the original were they can be restored in the light of the later reconstructions and bear a striking resemblance to the First Dynasty building on the same site. Undoubtedly the character of the building is the same and we have here the 'kitchen' in which the food of the god was prepared. Next to it, in the thickness of the chambered wall of the terrace, there is a small room whose unusually solid walls suggest that it was a building of considerable height and a niche in one wall seems to mark it out as a shrine; we called it 'the shrine of Nannar' and it may well be such; associated with the 'kitchen' it may have been the shrine in which were offered the prepared foods that were in due course to be allotted to Nannar's priests. We had arrived at this conclusion when a further discovery confirmed it in a very gratifying manner. In the back wall of the 'kitchen' block and again in the angle wall of one of its rooms we found brick boxes containing big inscribed copper cylinders; three of them bore the name of Nur-Adad king of Larsa (c. 1750 B.C.) and one that of Marduk-nadin-akhe of Babylon (c. 1100 B.C.); apart from the difference of names the texts were practically duplicates, and they speak of the 'great cooking-pot' and of the preparation of 'the evening and the morning meals' of the god. Evidently Nur-Adad had repaired Ur-Nammu's building and duly recorded the fact; centuries afterwards the Babylonian king carrying out similar repairs had discovered Nur-Adad's four cylinders and had piously replaced three of them but for the fourth substituted a copy bearing his own name.

Whether or not there was a second kitchen building to the south-east of the Ziggurat in the Third Dynasty time as there had been in the time of the First Dynasty it is impossible to say, for only a single meaningless fragment of Ur-Nammu walling was left, and in later times this area was occupied not by a kitchen but by a regular temple of Nin-gal the Moon-goddess. That something stood here in the days of Ur-Nammu seems to be certain, for the angle taken by the Ziggurat drain was apparently dictated by the presence of some building, and we did find here a well originally made by Ur-Nammu (it had been restored by a whole succession of later rulers) and a four-compartment cistern of burnt brick and bitumen also of his work.

It is probable also that there were buildings in front of the Ziggurat, though again nothing really survives, and although Ur-Nammu's Ziggurat at Erech has a pair of temples flanking the central staircase and at Ur such temples do occur in Late Babylonian times we should not be justified in attempting any reconstruction. Instead, our problems are complicated by the presence here of a most peculiar feature. In the floor of the terrace there had been very neatly made a rectangular hollow measuring about fifteen feet by eleven and three feet deep. In this were laid three courses of large untrimmed limestone blocks above which, filling the pit, was very clean reddish burnt earth. There was nothing underneath to explain this, so that the reason for it must have been something above, presumably rectangular in shape and (in view of the loose burnt earth) not very heavy; the size suggests an altar and the pit comes precisely below the site of the altar of the Late Babylonian shrine. Sumerian texts insist on the ritual importance of burnt earth for the foundations of a religious structure; Hebrew ritual supplies parallels for the use of unworked stone for altars, and there were Habiru in Sumer in the time of Ur-Nammu. It is possible, though by no means proved, that we have here an altar-foundation prepared in accordance with ideas held by Sumerians and by Hebrews.

E-temen-ni-gur, the Ziggurat terrace, was entered from the Sacred Area by a single gateway in its east corner where there was a solidly-built gate tower in which a flight of steps led up from the lower level outside; as built by Ur-Nammu it was merely an entrance, but under later rulers 'the Great Gate' was, as we shall see, destined to assume an importance of a different sort. The other entrance to the terrace was in its north-east wall where, again with a double flight of steps under a massive tower, one passed into the Great Court of Nannar occupying the rest of the north-west end of the Sacred Area. This was a very large open court, brick-paved, with chambers all round it and a monumental doorway facing the terrace doorway which gave on the outer town; its only internal feature of interest was a brick altar-like structure set immediately in front of the door leading to the upper terrace, this being a reconstruction of a similar but smaller 'altar' dating back to before the Third Dynasty Period. Inscriptions on clay tablets found here made clear the purpose of the building; it was a store-house into which were brought the offerings made to Nannar and the dues paid to him. The tenant farmers who tilled the temple lands would bring their rent in kind, cattle and sheep, grain and cheese; the merchants would bring the tithes of their stock-in-trade, the pious would bring their free-will offerings; all would be duly recorded by the priests in charge who would weigh the goods and issue receipts in the form of clay tablets the duplicates of which were filed in the temple archive; the great court with its score of magazines can have been none too large for all the business to be conducted there. The 'receipt of customs' was not the least important part of Nannar's establishment.

Actually of the 'Great Storehouse' built by Ur-Nammu very little survived, and it would have been impossible to understand the tattered remnants of his walls but for the fact that after its destruction by the Elamite invaders later kings had rebuilt on a somewhat larger scale but on almost identical lines. Ur-Nammu himself had not, apparently, lived long enough to finish the building which, like several other of his works, was completed by his son Dungi. His grandson Bur-Sin found the main structure complete and in good condition and so did no more than add a second 'altar'; and then the whole thing was razed to the ground by the Elamites. The thoroughness of their destruction is intelligible enough if one glances at the plan (Fig. 8) with its huge walls, the flat roofs of the intramural chambers giving plenty of room for the manœuvres of defending troops; for a victorious enemy to dismantle such fortifications was an obvious precaution.

When the Elamite rulers of Isin and Larsa felt that their position was secure they could afford to rebuild at Ur even these semi-military works; the Great Court was not only reconstructed but it was actually enlarged at the expense of the Ziggurat terrace, the front of which was cut back some twenty-four feet, and its north-east wall was thickened and the gate-tower apparently heightened. Further, the inner face of the south-west wall through which ran the passage leading to the Ziggurat terrace and the outer faces of the other three walls were all decorated with an elaborate system of attached half-columns divided down the middle by double T-shaped niches; carried out in brick this is an extremely effective form of ornament, relying as it does not on applied colour but on the varying depth of shadow cast by the sun; it set the pattern for temple builders for many centuries to come.

The first record that we found of these repairs dated to about sixty years after the fall of Ur, when Ishme-dagan was king of Isin. Reverting to old tradition he had made his daughter Enannatum High Priestess of Nannar at Ur,[1] and naturally the High Priestess was active in rebuilding her temples; we find her name on bricks in the Great Court, but it may well be that essential repairs had been done by other Isin authorities before her. Of the Larsa kings several have left their mark—and their names—on the Great Court. One of them, Sin-idinnam, also worked on the north-west retaining-wall of the Ziggurat terrace. There Ur-Nammu's buttresses wall had been of mud brick, and with time it had suffered severely; Sin-idinnam added to it a revetment of burnt brick, following exactly the pattern of the old work. Centuries later a Kassite king, Kuri-galzu, added another skin of burnt brick, again on the same lines though with a less pronounced slope; when

---

[1] Enannatum seems to have been of the type of the famous Vicar of Bray. She always calls herself, with pride, 'the child of Ishme-dagan King of Sumer and Akkad', but when her brother Libit-Ishtar, who succeeded Ishme-dagan on the throne, was defeated and deposed and Gungunum of Larsa seized the overlordship Enannatum still retains her office and now makes her offerings 'for the life of Gungunum, the mighty man, King of Ur'.

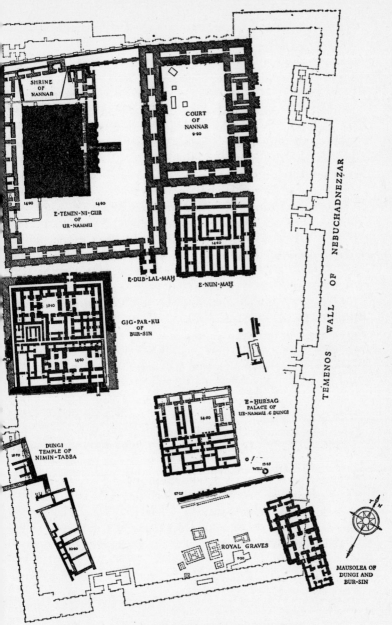

Fig. 8. Plan of the Third Dynasty Temenos

139

we excavated the site we found the three constructions of such different dates one behind the other, archæological strata arranged vertically instead of horizontally.

But the most striking work in this area was done by Warad-Sin, last king but one of the Larsa Dynasty. He probably found but little to do in the Great Court itself (though we did find there broken foundation-cones both of him and of his father Kudur-Mabug) but he made great changes in the terrace adjoining it. On the north-west side of that terrace he threw out a brick bastion corresponding in width to the interval between the wall of the Great Court and the front line of the Ziggurat; it was a huge gate-tower giving a new access to the Ziggurat terrace. The whole of the lower part of the tower was solid brickwork except for the gate-passage running through the middle of it and a staircase leading up to the guard-chamber over the gate;[1] in the heart of the brickwork, carefully arranged in lines parallel with the frontage, we found *in situ* numbers of clay foundation-cones inscribed with the dedication of the building. 'For Nannar the princely sun who shines in a clear sky, who listens to prayers and supplication . . . I, Warad-Sin the reverent prince . . . when the god of the new moon had revealed to me his favourable omen, had directed on me his look of life, had commanded me to build his temple, to restore its place, then for my own life and the life of Kudur-Mabug, the father who begat me, his house, joy of the heart, E-temen-ni-gur, I built for him. As the ornament and wonder of the land it stands for ever . . .'

It certainly was a splendid building. The entire façade (Fig. 9) was decorated with half-columns divided down the middle by double T-shaped grooves.[2] In the re-entrant angles of the porch, flanking the lower of two flights of stept that led up to the terrace, there were slender free-standing

---

[1] There was only *one* staircase to serve the two halves of the tower, between which there could be no communication below the roof of the passage dividing them; the first room therefore must have been above the passage, the towers being solid up to that level.

[2] The style was identical with that of the Larsa walls of the Great Court already described, but it does not necessarily follow that both buildings are the work of the same man.

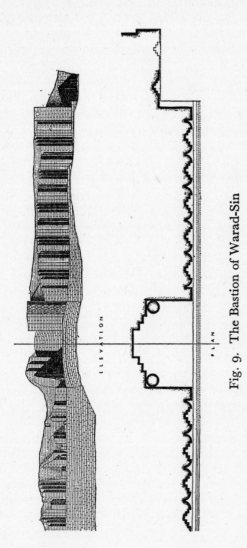

ELEVATION

PLAN

Fig. 9. The Bastion of Warad-Sin

141

columns built of mud bricks specially moulded and producing on the surface a pattern of triangles in shallow relief to imitate the effect of palm-tree trunks. For us this was an astonishing discovery. Until recently all authorities were agreed that the column was an architectural feature unknown in Mesopotamia until the sixth century B.C. at least. Then we found columns in the First Dynasty temple at al 'Ubaid and the German excavators at Warka found the huge mud-brick columns of the Jamdat Nasr age; but it could still be maintained that after the First Dynasty the column fell out of use and in the classical age of Sumer and Babylon was unknown. The discovery of Warad-Sin's free columns in his gate-tower was therefore all-important for the history of architecture, and its imitation of a palm trunk was really a rebuke to scholars, for in a country where the palm is indigenous the invention of the column for building purposes needs no great feat of imagination or research—Nature supplies the column ready-made. Some years later we found another column built of mud bricks specially moulded, this time in the ruins of a temple of the Third Dynasty [*Plate* 22*b*]; Warad-Sin therefore was no innovator, the use of the column was continuous, and the credit of the Sumerian as an all-round architect is well established.

The other building operation in which Kudur-Mabug and his son Warad-Sin were associated was the terrace entrance in the east corner, known as Dublal-makh, the House of Tablets. Ur-Nammu had built it simply as the gateway leading to the terrace of the Ziggurat and his building was of mud brick, except for the floors which were of burnt bricks set in bitumen; he named it Ka-gal-makh, 'The Great Gate'. The first change was made by Bur-Sin, Ur-Nammu's grandson, and was not inconsistent with the original purpose of the structure. The Great Gate led into the area peculiarly sacred to Nannar; as one mounted the steps one was passing on to holy ground, and it would seem natural enough that there should be there a statue of the god to which one could pay reverence before entering his domain. Again, it is the immemorial custom of the East that 'the judge sat in the gate to give judgement'; it might be the gate of the city, but the gate of the Holy Place would confer a special sanction on the judgements pronounced there, and so it came about that the Great Gate served also as a court of law. An inscribed door-socket stone told us just how these ideas took shape in the course of time. 'To Nannar his beloved King; Dublal-makh, from of old an enclosure where daily offerings were laid before his heavenly emblem, this house had not been built. Bur-Sin . . . the king of Ur, the king of the four quarters of the world, Dublal-makh, the House, the wonder of the land, the place of his judgements, his net from which the enemy of Bur-Sin does not escape, this house he built for him, he completed, he adorned with gold and silver and lapis lazuli . . .' Bur-Sin had in fact pulled down his grandfather's mud-brick gatehouse and rebuilt it in good burnt brick, and he added a fore-chamber where perhaps there had been the unroofed enclosure to which his inscription refers; he made it a real shrine and a law-court. The Elamites, when they sacked Ur, destroyed Dublal-makh and carried off the statue of Nannar to Anshan, their own city, but as soon as the dynasty of Isin was established its kings took the work of repair in hand. We found two door-sockets of Gimil-ilishu, the second king of the dynasty, the inscriptions on which state that 'Gimil-ilishu the mighty hero, king of Ur, when he had brought Nannar from Anshan to Ur built for him Dublal-makh, his place of judgement', and the name of his successor, Ishme-dagan, appears on some of the bricks in the walls. Then, according to the brick-stamps, Sin-idinnam of Larsa did a certain amount of rebuilding, and finally (of the Larsa kings) Kudur-Mabug. Of these, Ishme-dagan made a radical change which his successors followed; he walled up the doorway at the back of the gate tower so that the building could serve as a gate no longer but became simply a shrine, and a new entrance to the Ziggurat platform was made by cutting a doorway through the enclosing wall against the south-east side of the Great Court. Such was the building which Kudur-Mabug in his turn restored, the city's law-court and the 'House of Tablets'.

Under the pavement of a Larsa annexe to Dublal-makh we found a mass of clay tablets which had belonged to the business archives of Nannar's temple. They were of unbaked clay and were in very bad condition, reduced by infiltered moisture to the consistency of mud and impregnated with salts, and many had been broken or chipped when they fell from the shelves on which they had been stored; we had to lift them with the earth still about them and bake them in an extemporized furnace before any cleaning could be attempted,[1] but in this way we did salve several hundreds of interesting documents of the Third Dynasty.

It was no polite fiction that made Nannar the King of Ur. He controlled its destinies more effectually than did his mortal representative and he must therefore have his ministers and his court; he was a great landowner and therefore needed stewards to manage his estates; apart from the High Priest and his clerical associates we read of the Sacristan and the Choirmaster, the Treasurer, the Ministers of War and of Justice, of Agriculture and of Housing, a Controller of the Household, a Master of the Harem, and Directors of Livestock, Dairy Work, Fishing and Donkey Transport. All these carried on their duties in the temple precincts, and so the temple is not a single building like the self-contained temples of Greece and Rome, but a huge complex which is at once temple and palace, government offices and stores and factories. Something of this sort has already been assumed in our descriptions of the ruins and is proved by the plans here published; fortunately just as our plans grow more complete and more complicated, the tablets turn up to throw light upon the use of those many courts and chambers.

As landowner the god received as well as tithes either rent or a part share in the produce of the soil, and since money was unknown these were all paid in kind; and since the temple was also a fortress, enormous quantities of food-stuffs were stored within it, ready to meet the normal requirements of the temple staff but also to act as a reserve in case of war. For everything that was brought in a receipt was given, a

---

[1] This is now a recognized process but in 1924, when this discovery was made it was a novel experiment only justified by the desperate condition of the tablets, and, incidentally, by its success.

Plate 19

Dungi's Mausoleum; the stairs seen from the
tomb chamber below room 5

Plate 20

Bur-Sin's Mausoleum; the stairways leading
to the tomb chambers

small tablet carefully dated recording that so-and-so has
paid in six pounds of the best butter, so much oil, sheep,
cattle or what not; and every month a full balance-sheet of
all returns was drawn up in parallel columns showing each
farmer's contribution under separate headings. While
farmers and cowmen paid in country produce, the townsfolk
used another currency; there are receipts for all sorts of hides,
for gold and silver from the jewellers, for copper from the
smiths; in one room we found a smelting-furnace, and in
other rooms big jars full of scrap copper and ingots of the
metal presumably of some standard weight: evidence that
this quarter of the building served a special department of
the temple affairs.

But if the revenues are scrupulously recorded the outgoings
are not less carefully checked, and these are just as illuminating for the life of the time. Naturally the temple officials
drew their rations from the stores, and the issue vouchers
were all preserved in the registry; every man had his regular
allowance of foodstuffs, flour and oil, etc., for which he or his
servants had to sign, and special issues were authorized in
cases of sickness—thus a man may draw an extra quarter-
pint of best oil as liniment for his headache. But the most
interesting records deal with the industrial side of the establishment. Numbers of women devotees were attached to the
temple, and these were employed in regular factories inside
the precincts; there were slaves similarly employed, and
piece-work was given out to private contractors who had
smaller factories outside the temple area: all these had to be
supplied with the raw materials which had been brought in as
tithe, and with the food which was their wage. The main
industry illustrated by the tablets found this season was
weaving. In the building E-karzida alone 165 women and
girls were kept at work, and we have the accounts made out
for the month, quarter, and year of the quantity of woollen
thread supplied to each and of the amount of cloth produced, each sort distinguished by quality and weight, with
due allowance for the wastage of thread in weaving. The
rations are in proportion to the output, the older women
receiving less than the young ones (who would have larger

appetites but did more work)—no more in fact than did the youngest children; thus if four pints of oil a day was the standard allowance for adults, children of different ages got two pints, one and a half, or one, and the really old woman one also. For the sick there were special rates: if any one died, her name was kept on the books until the end of the financial year, but the date of her death was recorded and an entry made against the name to the effect that henceforth no rations were drawn, or were drawn only for an accredited substitute. The whole system was coldbloodedly business-like, but the records of it are not without their dramatic side and go far to re-create the life which was lived within the temple walls.

Some seventy years after Kudur-Mabug's death the House of Tablets was again destroyed, and again after that was rebuilt in a somewhat altered form. Those later vicissitudes do not concern us here and will be described in their proper place, but it is worth while noting that even in the fourteenth century B.C. Kuri-galzu calls it Dublal-makh, but also Ka-gal-makh, the Great Gate, the Ancient One. Just as the names of the gates of London have long outlived their reality so Ur-Nammu's gateway preserved its identity through the ages.

All the rulers of the Third Dynasty of Ur were active builders and we found few temples which did not owe their foundation to one or other of them. But in most cases the remains were scanty. To restore a temple was a work of piety which ensured the favour of the gods, and the temples therefore were constantly and thoroughly repaired by later kings who often pulled down in order to rebuild; the city was sacked and its monuments destroyed first by the Elam-ites, at the close of the Third Dynasty, then by Hammurabi of Babylon, and again by his son Samsu-iluna as a result of the city's revolt against the Babylonian yoke; it is not sur-prising that little of the Third Dynasty work was left, and such traces as survived were intelligible only because the later builders piously reproduced the original plan, even using the footings of the old walls as a foundation for their own. Most of these buildings therefore such as E-nun-makh and the E-gig-par-ku will be described hereafter under the heading of the period to which the best-preserved of their ruins belong; but there are two exceptions, two Third Dynasty structures which were never touched in after generations and so should be described here.

The first of these is E-khur-sag. It was a large square building distinguished from all the others in the Sacred Area in that it occupied a salient projecting from the south-east side of the Temenos proper. Possibly it existed, or at least had been planned, before the Temenos Wall of Ur-Nammu was built, and that wall had been specially deflected in order to enclose it; otherwise (and judging from the ground-plan this is more likely) the Temenos Wall originally ran straight on and the salient was an addition built up against it with a view to the erection of E-khur-sag as something not strictly a part of the Temenos but very closely connected with it. The building, which measures a hundred and ninety feet square, was orientated, as usual, with its angles to the four points of the compass; the whole of the north corner, comprising about a third of the ground plan, is completely destroyed, but can be fairly confidently restored.

The ground plan (see Fig. 8) shows a building divided into three distinct sections. To the north-west, occupying nearly two-thirds of the area, is what looks rather like a temple with outer and inner court and, behind double walls enclosing small lobbies, a room corresponding to a sanctuary; along the two sides of this are the magazines normal in temple construction. In two of the south-eastern 'magazines' there are doorways leading to two similar but not quite identical complexes which are divided by a wall and have no direct communication with each other; each consists of a large room which must have been an open court or light-well and seven or (in the larger complex) nine other chambers.

The building was of one story only. It was very well built, all its walls of burnt brick,[1] the outer face of the external walls is decorated with shallow buttresses resembling those

---

[1] So far as they are preserved; it is possible that the upper parts of the walls were of mud brick, as in the case of private houses.

of the Ziggurat, its corners are rounded; all the rooms were paved with burnt bricks set in bitumen and two rooms against the south-east wall have immensely solid floors raising them above the general level and approached by steps in the doorways. Judging by the ground plan alone one would say that we have here a temple with, attached to it, residential quarters for two priestly families; but there are strong arguments against that conclusion.

Ur-Nammu founded the building and the bricks of the walls bear his stamp, but apparently he died before it was finished, for the pavement bricks bear the stamp of his son Dungi. Ur-Nammu's inscription is the stock one mentioning the building of the temple of Nannar and the city wall; those bricks could have been used for any construction in the Temenos or even outside it, since the text implies only that the work done is in the service of the god. On the other hand Dungi's pavement bricks bore the inscription 'Dungi, the mighty man, King of Ur, King of Sumer and Akkad, has built E-khursag, his beloved house'; no god's name is mentioned and one is led to suppose that E-khursag, 'the House of the Mountain', was really the royal palace.

Now there are generally three ways in which the authorship and character of a Sumerian temple can be identified— by the brick-stamps, by the door-sockets and by the foundation-deposits. The Sumerian door consisted of a wooden leaf fixed to a pole rather higher than itself; the projecting top end was held by and revolved in a metal ring attached to the lintel, the lower end was shod with metal and went down through a hole in the pavement to rest and turn on the hinge-stone. This was a boulder of (imported) hard stone, limestone or diorite, in which a cup-shaped hollow had been cut to take the pole-shoe, and generally one part of it had been smoothed and inscribed with the name of the king who dedicated the building and of the god in whose honour he built it. Door-sockets then can give us all the information we require; but they have to be used with caution because imported stones were valuable and an old stone would often be taken away and re-used for some building other than that for which it had first been intended, so that the old inscription no longer applies. In the case of E-khursag all the hinge-stones were in position, but they bore no inscription at all.

Foundation-deposits are found in the corners of buildings. Built into the wall-foundations there is a small box of burnt bricks, lined with matting and waterproofed with bitumen; in it is set a copper figure of the king modestly represented as a labourer carrying on his head a basket of mortar; at his feet is a stone tablet in the form of a plano-convex brick; on the brick and on the king's skirt is an inscription recording his name and that of the temple. In the two surviving angles of E-khursag the boxes duly came to light, but figures and tablets alike were plain and uninscribed.

Hinge-stones for doors were of course in general use, but only in the case of a consecrated building would they bear the dedication-text, so that uninscribed door-stones are common enough. On the other hand we have never, except at E-khursag, found the deposit of figure and tablet in any building other than a temple, but with this one exception they have invariably borne the name of the royal builder and of the god to whom the temple was dedicated; here Ur-Nammu has broken the rule, and he must have had a reason for doing so. If we remember that the king was nothing more than the vice-regent of the god who was the city's real lord we shall, I think, understand this building. Ur-Nammu planned a palace for himself, but because he represented Nannar the inscription on his bricks was not inapposite; for the same reason a foundation deposit was appropriate, but because it was to be a house for a man a dedication would have been out of place; so he compromised with blank figures. Dungi had no qualms and said plainly what he was about. Because he represented the god the king's Hall of Audience and the god's temple should be on the same lines; for the same reason his palace ought to be attached to the Temenos; but, because he was also a mortal it could not be actually on the holy ground inside the Temenos proper. I would therefore identify E-khursag as the palace of the Third Dynasty kings, the north-west part of it being the official Hall of Audience, the two residential blocks the living-quarters of the king and of his harem respectively.

This would explain the subsequent desertion of the site. Had it been a temple it would almost inevitably have been restored at a later date. If it was the royal palace it would have been most thoroughly destroyed by the Elamites and there would have been no reason for its reconstruction, firstly because it had no religious tradition behind it and secondly because after the Elamite invasion there was no king at Ur and so no royal palace was wanted.

The other undisturbed Third Dynasty building was the royal mausoleum. Just outside the Temenos, to the south-east, close to the great wall holding up the terrace on which the palace stood, we found the burial-place of the kings. This was the site of the old Royal Cemetery and probably the tradition of those ancient days still held good; the small group of graves which I labelled 'Second Dynasty' (see above, p. 110) together with the graves of Sargon's time help to bridge the gap between Queen Shub-ad and Ur-Nammu; at any rate this was the spot chosen for the huge tombs of the Third Dynasty kings.

As is shown by the ground plan (Fig. 10) there were three distinct buildings forming a single block. The largest one, in the centre, is built with bricks bearing the stamp of Dungi; at the north-east end of this, and communicating with it by a single doorway, there is a smaller building almost identical in plan, and at the south-west end there is the third building, awkwardly tacked on to the west corner of the first (with which it has no communication) and less symmetrically arranged; both the last two buildings are constructed with bricks bearing the name of Bur-Sin, Dungi's son. It seems likely, though it cannot be proved, that the central building is the tomb of Ur-Nammu, built by his son, that on the north-east is Dungi's tomb built by Bur-Sin, and that on the south-west is Bur-Sin's tomb built by his son Gimil-Sin with bricks set aside by Bur-Sin for the purpose. The order in time of the three parts is quite clear—the Dungi building is the earliest, as is shown by the others being built up against it, and it is obvious that the builder of the north-east tomb had the choice of sites and took the better, while the builder of the south-west tomb had to make shift with the only site

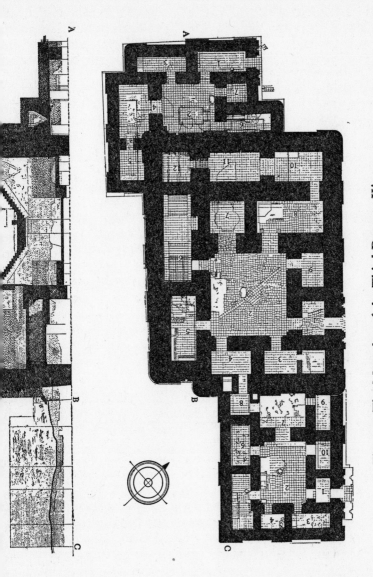

Fig. 10. The Mausolea of the Third Dynasty Kings

left to him. That Dungi was not building for himself is proved by the fact that the underground tomb had to be occupied and filled in before the building proper could be erected; the same is true of the others, and we should therefore have expected to find a third name on the bricks of the south-west mausoleum, but since here Bur-Sin's name again appears and the building could not have been constructed in his lifetime if it was indeed his tomb, that he had made the bricks ready for it seems the only possible explanation.

As nothing like these tombs has yet been found elsewhere in Mesopotamia I shall describe them at length; an account of the Dungi building will go far to explain the others.

The building consists of two parts, the underground tomb-chambers which were constructed first, and the super-structure which only took its final form after the tomb-chambers had been filled in. The latter is a building measuring a hundred and twenty-five feet by eighty-five; its walls, of burnt brick set in bitumen mortar, are no less than eight feet thick so that the structure, though only one story high, must have been very lofty; the walls, relieved by shallow buttresses, are battered, having a pronounced inward slope, like the walls of the Ziggurat, and further resemble the Ziggurat walls in not being straight but having a slight entasis or outward curve; the corners are not square but rounded, and where on the south-east side there is a salient that too is rounded—the effect is almost Romanesque!

On the north-east side is the entrance, its buttress jambs decorated with T-shaped grooves; through an entrance lobby in which was a drain one passed into a paved central courtyard open to the sky. The pavement sloped down to the centre, as did tiled surface drains meant to carry rain-water from the roof, to a sump-pit lined with terra-cotta rings; by this was a terra-cotta bitumen-lined bath for ablutions. In every wall were doorways leading to the rooms which surrounded the court, on three sides a single range but a double range on the north-west; in the doorways we would find, amongst the ashes of the woodwork, fragments of gold foil showing that the doors had been overlaid with gold. Between the doors in the south-west wall were the remains of a brick altar with bitumen runnels in front of it exactly like the altar in room 5, and in the angle of the door-jamb a brick pillar such as we find in the chapels of private houses in the Larsa Period.

Most of the rooms do not call for detailed description, but in room 3, in the ashes covering the floor, there were stone hammers on whose striking surface could be seen traces of gold; clearly they had been used by the despoilers of the building for breaking up the precious metal for loot. In rooms 5 and 8 were fragments of wall decoration, fairly thick sheet gold cut into open-work patterns with shield-shaped holes into which were set inlays of agate or lapis lazuli; in room 9 tiny stars and sun's rays in gold and lapis lazuli may have come from the ceiling; in any case there had been here a wealth of ornament which amply rewarded the plunderers, and the few traces of it that remain suffice to give us a very different idea of the appearance of the building from that which we get by looking at the stripped walls of bare brick.

Room 4. In the doorway were found fragments of an inscribed alabaster vase of Dungi. In the south-east wall was a doorway leading out of the building into that of Bur-Sin; it was peculiar in having no reveals and might be thought therefore not to have been part of the original plan, but there was no visible sign of alteration, and if indeed the door had been cut through the wall the jambs had been re-faced with a very clever imitation of the old brickwork. Close to the door there was in the thickness of the wall a low corbel-vaulted chamber which certainly was original. On the outside it was closed by a mere skin of brick which had been damaged when the wall of Bur-Sin's annexe was built up against it; on the inside it had been closed by a similar skin only one brick thick, and to mask this every alternate brick in the corners of the jambs had been chipped back so that the new brickwork might show no break of bond, a trick employed several times in the Dungi Building. Possibly the chamber had been intended for a foundation-deposit; in any case it had been broken open and looted by the Elamites. When we found it, the entrance had been very roughly blocked up again with mixed bricks projecting beyond the wall face, and inside were two bodies and a number of clay pots of the Larsa period. Some Larsa householder digging into the ruins below his foundations must have found the little chamber and re-used it as a burial vault.

Room 5 was the most interesting in the building. The whole of the north-west end was occupied by a raised brick base divided into three parts, a lower ledge along the front, a low platform along the north-east wall, and a higher platform in the west corner; the back was destroyed by plunderers who had dug through it into the tomb below, but the front was almost intact. The brickwork was overlaid with bitumen, and sticking to this were found fragments of gold leaf, so that the whole must have been gilded. In the top of the front ledge were six channels running parallel with the front and arranged two deep. Starting as shallow depressions they deepened as they ran and then, turning outwards at right angles, came to the edge and were continued as grooves down the front of the platform, emptying into six small brick compartments which formed a row on the floor in front of the platform; in these compartments we found wood ashes. On the top of the lower platform in the north corner there were the remains of one and apparently of two similar channels running down into brick compartments. Along the south-east half of the south-west wall and along the south-east wall was a low bench of brick covered with bitumen in which again there were long channels starting in front of a raised base which faced the door of the room, but these ended not in brick compartments but in cup-like hollows in the top of the bench [*Plate* 21*a*].

The explanation which suggested itself for the channels, etc., in the west corner was that over each runnel there would be set a porous (or pierced) vase containing scented oil which, escaping from the vase, would run along the channel and trickle down into a fire made in the brick compartment below, and so would go up as incense before a statue placed on the high base behind. This theory is amply supported by a text published by Professor Langdon,[1] in

---

[1] *Babylonian Penitential Psalms*, Oxford Edition of Cuneiform Texts, Vol. VI, p. 51, l. 15–p. 56, l. 19.

which a worshipper describing a sacrifice he has offered says 'seven kinds of sweet oil . . . have I burnt upon seven fires'. Remains of similar altars were found in room 8 and, as I have said, in the central court, and there were others in the Bur-Sin buildings; in every case they had been dug through to floor level. Evidently some votive object of intrinsic value was embedded in the brickwork and the Elamites, well informed as to where treasure might be found, overlooked nothing.

The long runnels in the wall benches must have been for liquid offerings and the raised pedestal for solid foods. The was clearly the dining-room of the dead king, and while the smoke of the incense rose into his nostrils his more material needs were satisfied with food and drink passing ceaselessly before him; very properly, the dining-room was directly above the tomb in which the king lay.

There was a flight of steps in the doorway of room 6 and the floor of the room was about six feet higher than that of the central court; below this high pavement lay the approach to the tomb. The pavement had been pulled up and plunderers had dug down for a little way below it, but stopped, seeing that their fellows had found a quicker way of getting at the spoil; we soon came on clean and undisturbed earth filling. The massive brick walls went steadily down. Between rooms 6 and 7 there was a doorway which had been bricked up and carefully camouflaged; below floor level the blocking was undisguised and at length we found the foot of a flight of steps in the door passage and, in front of it, a landing from which stairs ran down to left and right into the earth; now the pit which we were digging had walls on either side, to north-east and south-west, but at either end there was a high corbelled vault built of bricks and bitumen, and it was into the earth filling those vaults that the stairs descended. The vaults had been built over a timber centring which had of course decayed away and we could not by any means be sure that they would not collapse when once the earth filling had been removed; so work had to be interrupted until we had shored up the brickwork—which we did on the same lines, using the old joist-holes for the brackets that supported the sloping roof-beams. Clearing a little at a time and adding fresh centring as the work went forward (it was a ticklish job, for the bitumen mortar had dried and lost all its cohesive qualities so that the bricks were virtually loose) we were at last able to empty out all the filling and expose the bricked-up doors of the tomb chambers. There were two of these. The north-west stairs ended in a landing with a doorway on the right; under the blocking-wall more steps went down into a corbel-vaulted chamber thirty-four feet long running under rooms 11 and 10 of the superstructure; the south-east stairs ran up against a block-wall directly facing one and, continuing through the doorway passage, ended in a thirty-foot chamber similarly corbelled, lying under room 5 [*Plate* 19]. Both chambers had been broken into from above, through the floors of the superstructure, and their roofs were in a dangerous condition, so that more reinforcement work was needed before any clearing could be done; when it was done we discovered, as indeed we had expected, that our robber predecessors had done their job most thoroughly and, apart from human bones and fragments of clay pots, there was nothing left for us to glean.

One curious and almost comic point about the tomb-chambers was this—when we entered them for the first time we were frankly disappointed by their mean proportions; the bones and pot-fragments lay on a floor of mud brick which was about on the level of the springers of the arches—the chamber was long indeed but so low that only in the middle could one stand upright. Then we noticed that the stairs in the doorway ran down below the floor; we made a hole in the floor, which was many courses thick, and then came on burnt bricks set on edge with open spaces between them; there were two courses of these, and then the real pavement of the chamber, five courses of burnt brick set in bitumen and bonded in to the side walls. The explanation was that Dungi's architect had been too ambitious and had put his tomb chambers too deep down—nearly thirty feet below ground level, and that when the river Euphrates washed the city walls—with the result that when the chambers were to be used they were awash with infiltered water and the only thing that could be done at short notice was to raise the floors by five or six feet at the sacrifice of the proportions of the building.

In Dungi's building, as in each of the buildings of Bur-Sin, there were two tomb-chambers one of which was certainly destined for the king, the other contained a number of bodies; both chambers were closed at the same time and neither of them could afterwards be re-opened; the burials in both were part of the same rite. It seems clear that, in spite of the silence of the cuneiform texts, the 'death-pits' of the old Royal Cemetery had their counterpart in later times and that even the kings of the Third Dynasty of Ur went to their graves accompanied by a royal retinue. Moreover here, as in the case of the old royal tombs, there was a complicated ritual something of which can be deduced from the character of the building. The tombs, though designed as part of a plan which was to be completed later, were the *raison d'être* of the building and were constructed first, together with a superstructure, some of which was purely temporary, but some was to be incorporated in the later building. To judge by existing remains, the temporary superstructure may have been confined to the area overlying the tombs proper; slight changes of line in the brickwork of the pit walls may indicate that even the temporary building was not strictly contemporary with the tomb construction but was added, perhaps after the funeral. In any case the presence of the building suggests that the funerary rites which it served lasted for a considerable time after the actual burial. The two vaults were occupied at the same moment and their doors were walled up, but the staircase to the doors remained open and the presence of the door in the superstructure wall implies that people came down the upper flight of steps to perform ceremonies in front of the doors or on the central platform and on wooden galleries which prolonged it above the tomb entrance—evidence for such galleries was given by the holes in the side masonry which took the supporting beams.

Then the superstructure as we have it was built, and when it was virtually complete, with its floors at a higher level than those of the temporary building, the doors of the latter were bricked up, the galleries in the stair-pit dismantled and the pit itself filled in and paved over. At this moment a dramatic incident occurred. When we dug away the filling we found that in the upper part of the blocking of the door of each of the tomb chambers there had been made a small breach just large enough for a man to get through; the dislodged bricks were lying in front of the door covered by the clean earth imported for the filling. The tombs had been robbed and, obviously, robbed just as the earth was about to be put in; nobody would have dared to rob them when the pit was still in use, nor, if such sacrilege had been done, would the bricks have been left scattered on the floor and the breach unfilled; the robbers must have chosen their moment when the inviolable earth would at once hide all traces of their crime and they could afford to be careless.

The rulers of the Third Dynasty were deified in their life-time and worshipped as gods after their death. The tomb then was intended to receive the king's mortal body; the temporary structure was for the ceremonies of his burial, the permanent building was for the perpetuation of his cult. In this regard the form of it demands notice. It is built not on the lines of a temple (and the temples of the Third Dynasty are known to us by several examples) but on those of a private house; it surely must have been conceived of as the residence of a deity whose human origin could not be for-gotten, any more than when he was alive on earth his divine character could be overlooked. Death here meant no change of attributes, only a recasting of their relative values; and although the form of service would necessarily be modified, the 'temple' was in all essentials the palace of the god-king.

The south-east Bur-Sin building is, though on a smaller scale, so nearly a replica of that of Dungi that no description of it is required. The entrance to the two chambers was under the pavement of room 5 [*Plate* 20] and the chambers themselves underlay rooms 6 and 4 respectively. The north-west building was less regular in that it had no rooms opening off the south-east side of the central court where it was built up against the external wall of Dungi's building; also it con-

tained three tomb-chambers instead of two; one underlay
room 5, its approach being under room 4, one was below
room 6 and one in the middle of the courtyard; but all alike
had been made, and occupied, before the superstructure was
erected. In this last building, as also in Dungi's, we found
inscribed tablets bearing dates which took us up to the last
year of the reign of Ibi-Sin the last king of Ur-Nammu's
dynasty, who was defeated and carried off prisoner by the
Elamites; they prove clearly enough to whom the destruction
of the tombs was due. After the destruction the site was
deserted for a century or more, and when at length it was
re-occupied it was by private houses of the Larsa period.
The cult of the Third Dynasty kings was honoured no longer.

When we were clearing the ruins lying under the shadow
of the Ziggurat on its north-west side we found, re-used as
hinge-sockets in a late doorway, two fragments of limestone
carved in relief. A hundred and fifty yards away, in the
courtyard in front of Dublal-makh, many more carved fragments appeared which actually fitted on to the first two, and
another fragment apparently belonging to the same monument turned up in the ruins of E-nun-makh. These widely-
scattered bits made up a considerable part of a round-
topped stela almost five feet across and ten feet high, sculptured on both sides, which in pictorial and written form
commemorated the achievements of Ur-Nammu. Sadly
incomplete as it is, it is none the less the most important
piece of sculpture found by us at Ur; it has been restored, so
far as possible, in the University Museum in Philadelphia.

On either side plain raised bands divide the slab into five
registers in which different activities of the king are represented. On both sides, however, the topmost register is the
same. Under the crescent of the Moon-god Ur-Nammu
makes his prayer to Nannar on one hand and to Nin-gal on
the other; of the deities only the lower part of Nin-gal's
seated figure is preserved, nursing a child who may be
Dungi, the king's son; above the duplicated figures of Ur-
Nammu are angels flying down and pouring on to the ground
water from vases which they hold in their hands. On a broad
band between the registers there is an inscription giving a list

of the canals in the neighbourhood of Ur built by the king's orders, and this text explains the scene—Ur-Nammu has been responsible for the actual work of digging the canals, but it is the gods who grant the blessed gift of water and bring fertility to the land.

The second scene on the front of the stela is the best preserved. At the two ends of the register are the figures of Nin-gal and Nannar [*Plate* 22a] and Ur-Nammu, introduced by his personal patron goddess, makes his libation to each, pouring water into a vase in which are the fruits of the earth. But Nannar in answer holds out to the king the measuring-rod and curled line of the architect; he bids him build him an house. And in the next register the king carries out the god's order. In the corner that remains intact we see him behind the (seated) figure of Nannar (distinguished by his horned head-dress of divinity) bearing on his shoulder the tools of the builder, pick and compasses and mortar-basket, while a clean-shaven priest helps him with the load; of the rest of the scene only scattered fragments survive, but they show against a background of brickwork men climbing ladders and carrying baskets of mortar; it is the scene of the building of the Ziggurat, and we have here a contemporary picture of the founding of the finest monument whose actual remains we unearthed at Ur. The connection between the king's libation and the god's order is emphasized by an inscription on a clay foundation-stone which we found; it reads 'For Nannar his king, Ur-Nammu the mighty man, King of Ur, King of Sumer and Akkad, who built the temple of Nannar . . . he saved the vegetables in the garden plot . . .'; once lodged as a god should be, Nannar will guarantee the earth's increase.

In the fragmentary registers on the reverse of the stone we have a scene of sacrifice in which a priest cuts open the prostrate body of the bull so as to read the omens on its liver; a scene in which prisoners with their arms tied behind them are brought before the seated god, evidently the record of success in war; one in which drummers beat on an enormous drum, perhaps victory again, and finally a scene of sacrifice in which it is possible that the king himself is figured as a

Plate 21

a. Dungi's Mausoleum; the offering-tables in
room 5

b. A typical drain of terra-cotta rings

Plate 22

a. Scene from the Stela of Ur-Nammu

b. A mud-brick column of the Third Dynasty

god—and we know that Ur-Nammu was deified after his death if not in his lifetime.

The regular boast of a Sumerian ruler was that 'he had honoured the gods, he had defeated his enemies, he had done justice to his people and he had dug canals'; three of these meritorious acts are celebrated on the stela, but what about the fourth?

When Nannar holds out the rod and line he is certainly giving orders for the building of his temple, these being the proper tools of the architect. But when Hammurabi of Babylon had his great code of law inscribed on stone the text is headed by just the group which we have here, the king, and the god holding rod and line, and in that case there is no question of temple-building. The point is that these things can be taken both literally and symbolically. As symbols, the rod stands for straight dealing, the measuring-line for fair measure; such is to be the spirit of Hammurabi's Code, and such too is the conduct enjoined on Ur-Nammu which presumably he observed no less exactly than he did the explicit command to build. The stela is meant to sum up the whole duty of kingship.

As I have said, the stela is the most important piece of sculpture found by us at Ur and its historic interest is the greater because we have very few monuments of the Third Dynasty. But artistically it cannot rank as high as I was inclined to put it in the first excitement of discovery; its technique is excellent but it is wholly uninspired. A generation or two earlier Gudea, the governor of Lagash, had made for himself a stela which like this one recorded the achievements and virtues of the ruler, and the formula used was identical; the scenes and the treatment of them are the same. Ur-Nammu's sculptor was a skilful worker in stone, but he worked in a stereotyped tradition and could make no original contribution to art. Ur as the capital of the empire could command the best, and we may well imagine that no former age in Sumer had produced buildings so vast, combining such solid strength with an architectural *finesse* unequalled until the Greek period and, probably, with a wealth of ornament that no previous Sumerian ruler could have afforded;

but if we compare Ur-Nammu's stela, correct and conventional, with the fresh invention of the shell plaques from the Royal Cemetery [*Plate* 11], just as if we set the finely cut but dull cylinder seals of Ur-Nammu's time [e.g. *Plate* 15. 4] against the Sargonid seals with their vivid and dramatic pictures, we shall realize that under the Third Dynasty Sumerian art was in its decadence.

VII

The Isin and Larsa Periods

'When they (the Elamites) overthrew, when order they
  destroyed,
Then like a deluge they consumed all things together.
Whereunto, Oh Sumer, did they change thee?
The sacred dynasty from the temple they exiled,
They demolished the city, they demolished the temple,
They seized the rulership of the land.
By the command of Enlil order was destroyed,
By the storm-spirit of Anu hastening over the land it
  was snatched away;
Enlil turned his eyes towards a strange land,
The divine Ibi-Sin was carried to Elam.'

SO DID A contemporary poet give voice to the bitterness
of his spirit and there was no poetic exaggeration in his
lament; there is not a single building of the Third
Dynasty but bears the marks of violent overthrow. Ur
must have been pretty thoroughly destroyed, but such was its
importance that when the city of Isin took over the kingship
of Sumer and Akkad and when later the city of Larsa wrested
the hegemony from Isin, practically every ruler of either line
was at pains to restore one or another of Ur's ruined monuments; and when the native dynasty of Larsa was ousted in
its turn and an Elamite, Kudur-Mabug, installed his son
Warad-Sin as king, the foreigner proved himself the most
active of them all in the piety with which he rebuilt and
enlarged the temples of the ancient capital.

Royal inscriptions on bricks, clay cones and hinge-stones
from temple doors found by us amply proved the zeal of successive kings. Gimil-Ilishu boasts that he brought back from

Anshan the statues of Nannar, carried off by the Elamites, and that he rebuilt Dublal-makh and set up its doors. Idin-dagan makes a dedication to Nannar. Ishme-dagan speaks of himself as 'he who exalts the head of Ur' and we have an alabaster vase given to Nannar by him. His daughter, Enan-natum, was, as we have seen, High Priestess of the Moon-god at Ur, and the Gig-par-ku, the great temple of Nannar which she built, will be described later. Libit-Ishtar 'renewed the place of Ur' (this may refer to the rebuilding of the city wall) and calls himself 'the just irrigator of Ur'. Sumu-ilu built a store-house and a temple, Nur-Adad restored the temple of E-nun and built another for Nin-gal. Sin-idinnam was particularly active both in the restoration of existing shrines and the building of new ones; seven buildings are recorded as having been the objects of his care and the wide dispersal of bricks stamped with his name implies an even ampler programme. Warad-Sin was the most energetic of the kings; his great gate-tower for the Ziggurat terrace has been described above, and a dozen other works by him are known; Rim-Sin's inscriptions claim nine temples to his credit. Clearly, during the two centuries or so of the Isin-Larsa Period Ur more than recovered from the disaster that ended the Third Dynasty. It may well be that the temples of that time, when Ur was the capital city and its kings en-riched by successful war, were more splendid than those put up by alien rulers, but two centuries of comparative peace enabled the townspeople to attain by trade and manu-facture a prosperity less sensational perhaps but scarcely less real.

Our excavations produced no material evidence for such a city wall as some of the inscriptions seem to imply. Ur-Nammu's great wall had been carefully destroyed, not a brick remaining in place, but his rampart, being really the revetted slope of the town mound, was indestructible. The easiest and most economical form of defence was what the people of Ur actually put into effect; along the top of the rampart they built their houses in a more or less unbroken line, and the outer walls, blank at least to the level of the second floor, made a satisfactory substitute for a purely military fortification. Such was indeed a normal thing in the Near East; we may call to mind Jericho, where the house of Rahab the harlot was 'on the wall' and had a window of the upper story looking out over the country.

On the north-east side of the city we dug houses which gave us a continuous wall line for the space of nearly two hundred yards; then there was a salient made by a later (Kassite) fortress, but behind it the house walls ran on and were followed by us for another two hundred yards, beyond which we only tapped it at intervals, but with the same result. Sometimes, where the rampart broadened, it might be surmounted by a public building, but even so that would be incorporated in the system of defence. Thus towards the south limits of the town there stood on the wall line a temple dedicated to En-ki, the Water-god of Eridu—Eridu, by tradition the oldest of Sumerian cities, lies twelve miles away to the south, its ruins visible from the mounds of Ur, so that the site of the temple seems to have been chosen as one from which En-ki could see his own Ziggurat rising in the distance. This was a Third Dynasty foundation restored in the Larsa period; fallen against the wall we found clay foundation-cones which presumably had been embedded in the brickwork higher up, and in one corner of the building an intact box of burnt bricks set in the mud brickwork of the wall's core in which was the copper figure and inscribed stone tablet of Rim-Sin king of Larsa. At the very south end of the town there was another temple, also originally of Third Dynasty date and restored in Larsa times (it was again restored in the Kassite period and finally rebuilt by Nebuchadnezzar) unfortunately not identified by any inscriptions, which too stood on the rampart and was incorporated in the wall.

I think that when we started work at Ur we assumed that all the temples would be found inside the Temenos or Sacred Area. The Isin-Larsa building inscriptions were enough to show the error of such an assumption because that Area was not large enough to contain so many temples. And now the discovery of temples on the city wall made the truth evident. The Temenos was the peculiar precinct of Nannar and his

wife Nin-gal; the minor gods of their court might be honoured in chapels attached to the shrines of the great deities,
but they were inside the Temenos only because they were in
the Moon-god's service. Other gods of course were worshipped at Ur and had their temples there, but those temples
might be anywhere in the town. And they were not necessarily inside the old city walls. Since very nearly all our work
was done inside the walls we had small opportunity to find
them, but the one bit of serious excavation outside proved
the point. A small trial dig just a mile away from the
Temenos, to the north-east, hit on the scanty remains of a
very large and important building with elaborately-but-
tressed walls of burnt brick; the stamps on the pavement tiles
state that it is the Nig-ga-ra-kam 'the great and noble abode
of treasure', built by Sin-idinnam of Larsa, 'for the life of my
father and for my life'; it was a religious building of some
sort, and it lies far outside the city proper. It must be
remembered that al 'Ubaid itself, four miles away, was really
but a suburb of Ur; we may safely imagine that throughout
the whole of the sprawling town there were scattered temples
dedicated to one or another of the innumerable gods. None
the less, the first efforts of the Isin kings were directed to the
repair of the major shrines lying inside the Temenos, and of
those the temple of Nin-gal the Moon-goddess was second in
importance only to that of Nannar himself; it happens that
the ruins of the Isin version of the building are so complete
that we get from them a more detailed picture of a Sumerian
temple than is afforded by any other of so early a date.

The temple was originally built in its present form by
Bur-Sin, Ur-Nammu's grandson, in mud brick; now Ishme-
dagan's daughter Enannatum, High Priestess of Nannar,
determined to rebuild it on the old lines but in better
material, using burnt brick throughout. Excavating the site,
we found her building standing on the stumps of the older
walls which had been used by the new bricklayers as a
foundation, and so recovered at one time the ground-plan of
both temples.

The building was a rectangle measuring 240 feet either
way, and was surrounded by an enormously heavy wall

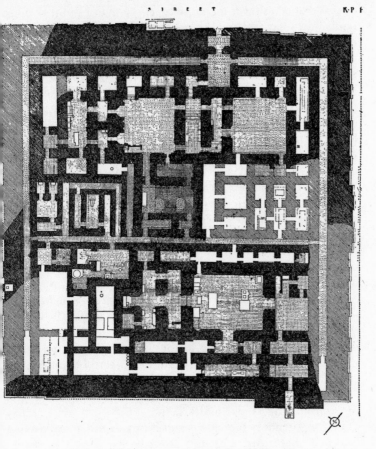

Fig. 11. Enannatum's Temple of Nin-gal

through the heart of which a narrow paved corridor ran round three sides of it, leading from a gate-tower over the main entrance to two fortified towers at the far corners; a similar corridor cut straight across the building, dividing it into two unequal parts and affording quick access from one tower to the other. From the outside at least the temple must have looked more like a military than a religious structure. Inside, however, its purpose was unmistakable. The larger section was again subdivided by a cross-wall, on

167

one side of which was a complete temple lying just inside the main entrance and on the other minor shrines and living-quarters for the priests.

The temple, with its outer and inner court, its two little antechambers and its long shallow sanctuary, was identical in its arrangement with the audience-hall of Ur-Nammu's palace. At the same time it presented certain curious features. Between the outer and the inner court were two long chambers, of which the first had a wide doorway opening on to the outer court, and against the back wall, facing the door, a brick base for a statue; it looked as if this was a 'Court of the Gentiles' to which the general public would be admitted to pay their devotions before the statue in the half-way shrine, while the inner court was reserved for the priests. To reach this one passed through the second narrow chamber, round which ran a raised brick bench water-proofed with bitumen and having along its edge a runnel for water; the floor also was covered with bitumen and sloped gently to the door leading to a tiny room in the centre of which was a terra-cotta drain going deep down into the earth. Obviously this was a lustral chamber, and here the worshipper would purify himself before going farther on to holy ground. The inner court and the sanctuary had been terribly ruined, but enough remained of them to show the place of the great altar of sacrifice in the court and inside the sanctuary the bases of the statues, the stepped altar, and the 'vestry' or treasury adjoining, while behind the sanctuary was the long passage-like chamber from which it is supposed that the priests worked the oracle.

In all this part, and in the next section of the building, excavation was made difficult by the presence of later walls whose foundations went down nearly as deep as the old work, while in some places the old floor-level had actually been re-used and the new walls simply set on the existing brick pavement. It was no easy matter to unravel the tangle of ruinous brickwork and to assign each fragment to its proper period, but when this was done the early plan was found to be remarkably regular and what had seemed mere confusion took on a very definite character.

The residential quarters of the priests were the most ruined of all, for there had been here a motive for more thorough-going destruction. In accordance with the fashion of the times the priests had been buried beneath the floors of their houses, and the brick vaults must have contained riches which tempted the avarice of the enemy who plundered the temple. In every case the pavements had been dug up and the tombs broken into and rifled so completely that there was scarcely anything overlooked—indeed, the only object worth mentioning which we found was a human face in glazed frit. Interesting in itself as being one of the earliest examples of polychrome glaze discovered in Mesopotamia, it was a tantalizing sample of what the graves must once have contained, for the little statue from which it had been broken off was probably a rich and elaborate work of art.

Next to the living-quarters we found, very much better preserved, a building of a quite novel sort. From the corridor which ran through the temple precincts there opened off a narrow passage between blank walls with a door at the farther end; going through the door, one found oneself in a similar and parallel passage leading in the opposite direction, again with one door at the far end of the side wall; this took one across a narrow room and down two more passages back into the corridor: it was a regular little maze of which the long central room contained the secret. Standing between its two doors, one looked down the length of a chamber, now of course roofless and with undecorated brick walls standing only some 5 feet high. The pavement was of brick, but the farther half of it was covered with bitumen on whose surface could be distinguished the impress of the reed mats which had once been spread there. Standing upright above the pavement, in which it was firmly bedded, was a large slab of white limestone, once round-topped, and side by side at its foot there lay fixed into the bitumen of the floor two other round-topped slabs of grey marble, and on each of the three stones, in characters intentionally defaced but still legible, there was an inscription which read 'Bur-Sin King of Ur, King of Sumer and Akkad, King of the Four Quarters of the Earth, has built this to his lady Nin-gal.'

Against a side wall there was a low bench or table of bricks, and that was all.

What it meant was beyond doubt. The temple of the lady Enannatum reproduced exactly the older temple founded by Bur-Sin (*see* Fig. 8) ; in that there had been a little sanctuary set aside for the worship of the royal founder, who was also a god. When the Third Dynasty came to an end and the Elamites sacked Ur, they broke up the sanctuary and tried to erase the name of the king, but Enannatum, repairing the building, repaired the shrine also and set up once more the dishonoured stones. Probably a statue of the king was enthroned against the upright stone, and on either side of it would be set poles capped with the symbols of power, mace-heads and the heads of beasts; offerings would have their place on the brick table, and walls and floor would be gay with hangings and rugs; the pious would come down the winding passages and, pausing at the far end of the shrine, would pay their homage to the memory of the deified ruler.

The rest of the great four-square building beyond the cross corridor consisted of a second temple of a different pattern. From the main court three arched doorways led to the sanctuary, where the statue of the goddess set on a high brick base looked out to the court. All round and behind the sanctuary were service chambers and magazines devoted to various uses. In one a queerly-shaped pit sunk in the pavement puzzled us until modern analogy proved that it was a weaver's pit, wherein the weaver sits with his legs below floor-level while he works at his low loom. Another set of rooms formed the kitchen [*Plate* 23*a*] : in an open court there was a well, and by it a bitumen-proofed tank for water, and a big copper ring let into the pavement may have been for the rope, so that the bucket might not be lost down the well, but, perhaps more probably, was for the rope fastened round the neck of the bullock intended for sacrifice, so that the beast might be thrown down and held fast for its throat to be cut; this was the Jewish custom, and is likely to have been that of the Sumerian priests. Against one wall were two fireplaces for boiling water, and against another the brick 'cutting-up table', the criss-cross marks of the butcher's knife clearly visible on its top; in a side-room was the beehive-shaped oven for baking bread, and in another room the cooking-range with two furnaces and circular flues, and in the flat top of it rings of small holes where the cauldrons were to be set; after thirty-eight centuries one could yet light the fires and recon-struct with all its activities the temple kitchen of the seven-teenth century before Christ, just such a kitchen as there was at Shiloh when the Ark of the Covenant was there and the sons of Eli quarrelled with the Israelites over their share of the sacrificial meat.

But it was the sanctuary and the courtyard that gave us the best results. We had been a long time getting down to them, for close under the surface there were remains of the late Babylonian period which had to be planned and noted before they could be removed, and they were so fragmentary that we were hard put to it to make sense of them.

Below this more shoddy buildings had to be removed, and then we came on a series of fairly massive mud-brick walls which proved to be those of a great house built probably for the temple priests in about 1400 B.C., with separate dwellings all giving on a central court. We were still high up in the mound, some six feet or more above the level of the pavements of Enannatum's temple, and this was a good sign. In this part of the building the walls, except for the open space of the courtyard, were close together, enclosing small chambers, and the walls were very thick; consequently when the upper parts of them were overthrown the debris filled the rooms to a considerable height and the builders of the succeeding age could not be bothered to remove it; it was simpler to build on the top of the mounds and where the old court left a low-lying hollow to put in a flight of brick steps down to it. Thus we found the walls of the chambers round the sanctuary standing six feet high and the fallen rubble between them undisturbed, and as we went down through this we were delighted to come across a layer of ashes and burnt wood spread over the entire area.

Nothing helps an excavator like violent destruction. If a building has fallen slowly into decay, one can be sure that the impoverished inhabitants have removed everything of value. The best thing that can happen is a volcanic eruption which buries a place so deeply that nobody goes back to salve his belongings; but the ideal conditions of a Pompeii are seldom met with, and one must be thankful for smaller mercies. If an enemy sacks a temple or a town, he is sure to overlook some objects at least which were of small intrinsic value for him, but may be very precious for the archæologist; and if he was so considerate as to set fire to the place and overthrow its walls, there is the further probability that his search was hurried and that no one else troubled to look for what he left behind.

So it was here. The ashes represented the ceilings and the panelling of the walls, and below them, lying on the brick pavement, there were hundreds of fragments of alabaster and soapstone vases and splinters of broken statues. One small statue we found entire, a heavy and clumsy figure carved in black stone representing the goddess Bau seated on a throne supported by geese; only her nose (which was made separately) was missing, and round the head were the small drilled holes to secure the gold crown which the robbers had torn off before discarding the statue. Bau was the patroness of the poultry farm, and this figure of her in its flounced and pleated dress reaching to the ankles, squat and thick-set, has an appropriately domestic look; it is far from being a first-class work of art, but as it is one of the very few Sumerian female statues in the round which time has preserved to us, it must rank high amongst our discoveries.

More fragmentary, for most of the head had vanished, but of far finer work, was a little seated figure of Nin-gal herself, which bore a long inscription stating that it had been dedicated by no less a person than the lady Enannatum, the second founder of the temple. This was pieced together from many fragments widely scattered. As the splinters of stone were collected and cleaned there began a regular jigsaw game, and it was most exciting to watch them gradually growing up into complete vessels, sometimes inscribed with the names of ancient kings. A Sumerian temple, like a modern cathedral, was a veritable museum of antiquities;

for centuries pious kings and others had been offering their treasures for the service of the god, and the temple strong-rooms would contain objects of all ages. It was here that we found the alabaster lunar disc of Sargon's daughter, and here too the limestone relief showing sacrifice being done by a princess of much older date—the latter was nearly seven hundred years old and the former five hundred when the robbers broke into the treasury where both were preserved.

One object was of peculiar interest. We found part of a stone cup inscribed with a dedication by the daughter of King Dungi, herself a high priestess of the Moon-god; another cup fragment bore the name of Sargon of Akkad, the great king who reigned 200 years before Dungi; and then it was found that the two fragments joined together and that both inscriptions belonged to one and the same cup. How it came about that the princess owned what had been so long before the property of King Sargon we cannot tell, but that she did so is another proof of the way in which in the ancient as in the modern world objects might long survive their generation: we shall see later how another royal priestess of Ur indulged in a passion for 'antiques'.

The stone fragments lay thickest in the neighbourhood of the sanctuary, but in the courtyard also they were fairly abundant: at one end of this we found bits, unfortunately not very numerous, of a large alabaster slab inscribed with a list of the royal benefactions which had enriched the temple, and in the middle of the court scanty remains of a much more interesting document. There stood here a big base of solid brick, and on it and round it we picked up pieces of fine-grained black stone covered with inscription; clearly the stone had originally been erected on the base, and enough re-mained of the text to show that it enumerated the conquests of the famous king and law-giver, Hammurabi of Babylon, perhaps the same as that Amraphel who is mentioned in the fourteenth chapter of Genesis as a contemporary of Abra-ham: Hammurabi reduced Ur to subjection, and this was his war memorial set up in one of the chief temples of the city [*Plate* 23*b*].

Scattered at random in the chambers of the temple we

found a number of inscribed clay tablets, part of the ordinary business records of the building. Such tablets are very often dated by the years of the reigning king, and on these we had represented most of the kings of Larsa, several years of Hammurabi, and the reign of his son almost continuously down to the eleventh year, and that was the last of the series. Now, the eleventh year was marked by a rebellion of the southern cities against Babylon, and the twelfth year was named 'that in which the king destroyed the walls of Ur'; here, then, we had a fixed date and a touch of drama. Ur had rebelled, and the destruction of Hammurabi's war memorial must have been an act of defiance on the part of the citizens; within twelve months, in the year 1737 B.C., so nearly as we can reckon it, the Babylonian troops burst into the city, looted Nin-gal's temple, flinging away what it was not worth their while to carry off, and set it on fire; the challenge and its punishment were clearly written in the ruins.

Indeed, when Samsu-iluna boasts that he 'destroyed the walls of Ur' he is understating the truth. In the houses of the Larsa period we found quantities of tablets, and the dates on these take us down regularly to the reign of Samsu-iluna and sometimes to his eleventh year; but not one later than that is found in any of them. Many, though not all, of the houses show evidence of destruction by fire; either therefore they were burnt, or they were deserted; Ur must have been left an empty ruin. For the modern archæologist this is a most fortunate thing, for it gives him an exact date for all those objects of every-day life which normally he can arrange in a typological series but cannot assign to a definite point in time; the private houses of the Isin-Larsa Period were not all built at the same moment, but all were in use together and all were abandoned simultaneously in the twelfth year of Samsu-iluna so that everything in the possession of their last occupants dates to the year 1737 B.C.

It is thanks to the city's violent destruction that our excavation of the private houses proved so illuminating. We can picture the life of the ordinary citizen of Ur in the eighteenth century B.C. with an accuracy and a vividness such as is surpassed only by Pompeii or Herculaneum; even the well-preserved houses of Tell al Amarna in Egypt tell us less, because they do not yield the tablets which at Ur give the personal touch that really brings the past to life.

In the season 1926–7 we dug a group of houses that lay just outside the Temenos, against its south-west wall, occupying most (probably all) of the relatively narrow space between the Temenos and the West Harbour. The houses were in all respects normal, and there was nothing in the lay-out that would suggest an official quarter, but the position, on the outskirts of the Sacred Area, might justify one in supposing that there was here something in the nature of a cathedral close. Certainly the inhabitants seem to have belonged to the priesthood and may have been those most closely concerned with the temples inside the Temenos; several of them possessed small libraries of ecclesiastical literature and from them we recovered a whole series of hymns in honour of different gods such as were used in temple services.

In the season 1930–1 we excavated an area about halfway between the south-east end of the Temenos and the city wall; the space cleared measured something like ten thousand square yards and gave us a very fair idea of the character of the residential part of the city (Fig. 12).

Anyone looking at the plans can see at once that there was no such thing as town planning at Ur. There may have been, there probably was, a Processional way leading to the Temenos, but the town in general preserved the form, or lack of form, of the primitive village, and there are no straight streets or broad thoroughfares, only winding lanes whose course has been dictated by the accidents of land-ownership. Sometimes the building-blocks which they enclose are so large that there had to be blind alleys giving access to houses in the middle of the block. The streets were unpaved, with surfaces of trodden mud which in wet weather would make deep slush, and they were so narrow that no wheeled traffic along them was possible [*Plate* 25a]. Wheeled vehicles had of course long been familiar (incidentally, a model chariot was found in the quarter) but it must have been debarred from the city, where everything must have been carried by human

Fig. 12. Town plan of the Larsa Period

Plate 23

a. The kitchen, showing the cistern and well, the cutting-up
table, the cooking-range, quern and grindstone

b. The inner court, looking towards the sanctuary;
the brick base is that of Hammurabi's war memorial

Enannatum's Temple of Nin-gal

Plate 24

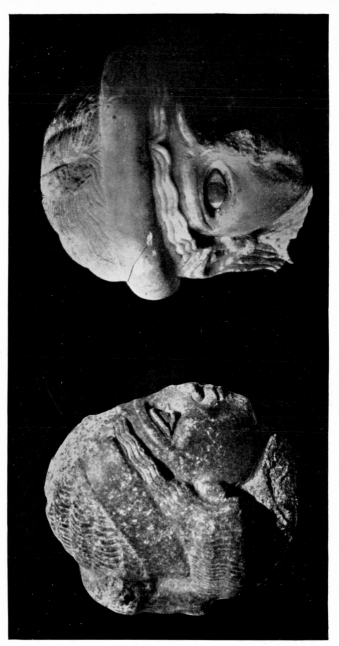

Sculptured heads in diorite and marble, Third
D̲y̲n̲a̲s̲t̲y̲ o̲r̲ L̲a̲t̲e̲r̲, a̲ m̲i̲d̲

porterage or on donkey-back, for which reason the masonry at street corners is nearly always carefully rounded so that passers-by should not graze themselves on sharp brickwork; for those who did not care to go on foot the 'white asses' of the prophet took the place of carriages, and accordingly we find against a house wall a low flight of brick steps which is clearly a mounting-block for the convenience of riders. Ur was, in fact, a typical Middle East town; its narrow winding lanes are the prototypes of those of modern Baghdad, and in Aleppo no more than seventy-five years ago the sight of a wheeled cart or carriage in the streets was so rare as to draw a crowd. One difference was that there were no domestic drains emptying into the roadway and there running down an open channel, as in so many oriental towns to-day, but then as now the sweepings of the house floors and the contents of the rubbish-bins were simply flung into the streets and, since there was no system of municipal scavenging, remained there to be trodden under foot. The result was the gradual raising of the street level, a phenomenon common to all old towns, London being no exception, but at Ur the process was more than usually rapid. A new house wuold naturally be built rather above the level of the street, but the rise of the latter meant that in wet weather a stream of filth would invade the house, so that the only thing to do was to raise the threshold by adding a fresh course of bricks. This worked for the moment, but in time another course was needed, and then another; there was indeed no end to it. During the time that the houses fronting on Paternoster Row were inhabited the street level rose more than four feet, and the threshold of No. 15, for example, had been gradually raised to match, so that entry was effected by a flight of six steps leading down to the original house floor [*Plate* 25*b*]. We found that the relation between house-floor and street was a most useful factor for dating the building. It also explained the rebuilding of houses. The time came when with the raising of the threshold and the lintel remaining as it originally was there was not enough headroom to allow of entry at all; reconstruction became imperative. The method employed was to pull down the old walls to the level of the ceilings of the ground-floor rooms and rebuild on them, laying the new ceiling-beams at the proper height above a new floor made flush with or above the existing street; constantly we found that if we pulled up the brick pavements of a house the walls were seen to go down with no apparent change to a buried pavement three feet below, and perhaps to a third pavement lower still.

For the building of the houses both burnt brick and crude mud brick was used. The front, facing on the street, was of burnt brick throughout—at any rate, to the height to which the walls were preserved, which is virtually that of the first-floor rooms; it may have been of mud brick above that level. The interior walls were of burnt brick below and mud brick above; the former might be no more than a damp-course three bricks high, or it might go up for four or five feet, this apparently depending on the wealth of the owner more than on any structural consideration; the mud brick at any rate, and perhaps the entire wall, would be plastered and whitewashed. No house windows opened on the street, at least on the ground floor; if there were any upper windows (but the walls do not stand high enough to give evidence on this point) they would have been blocked with shutters of reed-work set in a wooden frame (we found such in a Kassite window) corresponding to the wooden lattices of the modern Arab house. Consequently the streets were uninteresting, shut in by continuous walls blank except for the doorways of the houses; occasionally there might be an open-fronted shop, but most shops were in the regular bazaars where narrow passages, probably sheltered by awnings, were bordered by little lock-up booths, the whole being provided with doors that were closed at night; the only example that we found is Bazaar Alley, between Paternoster Row and Baker's Square, but this must have been typical.

We were greatly struck by the discovery that all the houses at Ur of the Isin-Larsa Period are built on the same lines. No two are exactly alike; the architect had to accommodate his groundplan to building-plots of very different sizes and often of irregular shape, but he always kept before him an ideal type approved by experience and suited to local con-

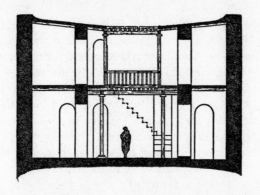

CROSS SECTION.

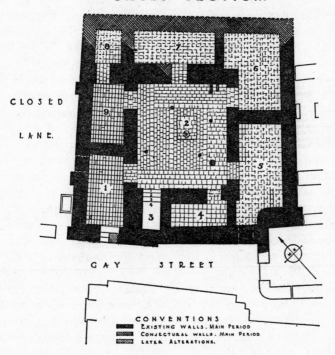

CLOSED

LANE.

GAY STREET

CONVENTIONS
EXISTING WALLS. MAIN PERIOD
CONJECTURAL WALLS. MAIN PERIOD
LATER ALTERATIONS.

Fig. 13. Plan of a private house

ditions and approximated to it as closely as he could. The type (Fig. 13) is that of a house built round a central court-yard on to which all the rooms open. Three conditions seem to have dictated this form, namely the climate of southern Mesopotamia, the desire for domestic privacy which has always characterized the Middle East, and the custom of domestic slavery; we shall easily see to what extent these factors influenced the building.

A characteristic house of medium size such as No. 3 Gay Street [*Plate* 26*b*] will serve to illustrate them all so far as its arrangements go, though for detail I shall draw freely upon other houses; and in my description I shall quote from the 'House Omen Texts' which under the guise of superstitious aphorisms embody some of the principles which the Sumerian architect had to observe.

The front door was small and unpretentious ('if the door of a house be very large, that house will be destroyed') and opened inwards ('if the door of a house opens outwards the woman of that house will be a torment to her husband') and you passed into a little brick-paved lobby having in one corner a drain over which would be set a jar of water so that you might wash your feet before going farther; the second door, leading to the house proper, was in a side wall so that there might be no clear view in from the street; either you or the porter on duty would give warning so that the womenfolk might decently retire. Against the jambs of the second door there would be hung terra-cotta masks of the god Puzuzu, a charm against the south-west wind which brings fever, and there was a step down in the doorway ('if the threshold of the court be higher than that of the house the mistress shall be above her lord') taking you into the central court. This was brick-paved, the pavement sloping slightly to the middle where was the intake of a drain that carried water away into the subsoil ('if the courtyard lets the water collect in the middle of the court, that man will have great good fortune') and all round it were the doors of the ground-floor rooms. The uses of all these rooms can be determined.

On the side of the court facing towards the front of the house a single doorway, wider than the rest, is that of the

Plate 25

a. A street scene in the Larsa town

b. Steps down from the street into
No. 15 Paternoster Row

Plate 26

a. Clay 'teraphim' of the Larsa period

b. View of No. 3 Gay Street, from the guest-chamber

reception-room to which visitors were admitted. It is always a wide and shallow room with the door in one of the long sides, precisely like the modern Arab *liwan* or guest-room; in the daytime a 'runner' rug would be laid against the back wall for guests to sit on, and its width is such that at night mattresses could be laid across it for the guests to sleep in a row. In some of the richer houses such as No. 3 Straight Street there is at one end of the guest-room a door into a brick-paved closet provided with a drain, the visitors' lavatory and wash-house, and at the other end a recess probably for the storage of bedding. Facing the guest-room there are two doors in the courtyard wall, one that of the household lavatory, a narrow chamber with a paved floor in which is just such a latrine opening as can be seen in any modern Arab house. The second door is that of the staircase. The stairs run over the lavatory; they start in the doorway, brick-built, and, because in order to secure head-room for the lavatory it was essential to have the maximum possible rise before the turn of the stairs, the bottom step is made too high to be practical and a moveable wooden step had to be placed in front of it—which again is precisely what one sees in the modern house, where the same arrangement holds good.

Of the remaining ground-floor rooms one (marked 5 in No. 3 Gay Street) was the kitchen, identified as such by its two fireplaces and by the querns found on its mud floor. One, having low brick benches for beds against the wall, was the slaves' sleeping-quarters; another was a general working-room in which might be found querns and store-jars.

It is clear that the ground floor of the house was given over to the domestic staff and to visitors; the family proper lived upstairs.

This is an unexpected conclusion. Later Babylonian houses were of one story only, so far as we know; the same is true of houses of the Sargonid age excavated at Tal Asmar by the Oriental Institute of Chicago; it might therefore seem rash to assert that at Ur in the Larsa Period the majority of the houses were on two floors. The existence of a staircase is not in itself a conclusive argument, for it might have led to a flat roof which could be used in fine weather for sitting-out and for sleeping; the Neo-Babylonian roofs were flat and doubtless were so used. But they had no staircases, and access to the roof must have been by wooden ladders (as is often the case to-day). At Ur there is a solidly-built flight of stairs and it takes up the space of a room which could ill be spared when the ground-floor accommodation was so limited; the only justification for such a staircase is that it led to a part of the building not less important than the rooms on the ground floor. The thickness of the walls is amply sufficient for them to rise to second-story height, but as the ceilings were hardly calculated to support the weight of walls the plan of an upper story must have reproduced that of the ground floor. There was no space for an internal passage and although all the rooms could be communicating that is inconvenient, and the Omen Texts expressly state 'if the door of a room opens on the court, that house will be enlarged; if the door of a room opens into another room that house will be broken away'; but somehow one must be able to get at the rooms.

The analogy between the ancient houses of Ur and the houses of the modern town Arabs has hitherto proved so close that one can fairly apply it further. In the modern house the stairs lead up to a wooden balcony that runs all round the court, and the doors of the upper rooms open on to that; we asked ourselves whether this could be true of the Larsa house. In No. 3 Gay Street we found, toward the south corner of the courtyard, a single brick bedded to the pavement with stiff clay, and round it were fragments of charred wood; in all likelihood the brick had served to jack up a post which had been cut too short for its purpose. Restoring posts in corresponding positions in the other corners we found that they were so arranged as not to obstruct any of the ground-floor doorways and would support a gallery three feet wide, which is just the width one would expect; incidentally, for the short post jacked up on a brick modern analogies would be innumerable.

I have perhaps gone into overmuch detail on one point to show on what sort of arguments we had to base our reconstruction; actually every point had to be argued out in the

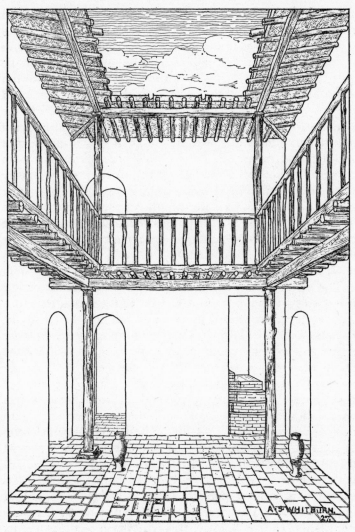

Fig. 14. Reconstruction of a private house.
(No. 3 Gay Street)

183

same way. In the end we could practically prove that the roof was not flat but sloped gently inwards, projecting beyond the walls so as to shelter the balcony, and having along its inner edge a raised coping through which at intervals gutters projected which would direct the rainwater into the drain in the middle of the courtyard; the central opening in the roof, not unduly large, provided all the light and air required. One fortunate discovery was that of a burnt-brick arch fallen almost complete in a doorway, proving a fresh architectural point. A rough brick compartment in one corner of the courtyard, a feature common to many houses, puzzled us until in one we found the fragments of huge clay pots; clearly, the day's water-supply brought from the public wells was stored here in the porous vessels that would keep it cool; and a very modern touch was given by the presence in one courtyard of flower-pots bedded with clay to the pavement round the central drain (Fig. 14).

The picture that we have of a private house of the period is indeed remarkably complete so far as the actual structure goes; of furniture we naturally found nothing, but it would have been for the most part of a very simple nature. Folding chairs and tables are represented on seals and we know of chests of wood or wickerwork for storing clothes; many-coloured rugs would be laid on the floors and plenty of cushions; for light at night there were oil lamps, little saucers with a wick floating on the oil. Granted that the streets were narrow and dirty and that the house-fronts presented little of interest, yet when once one had crossed the threshold things were very different. Such a house as I have described, with its paved court and neatly-whitewashed walls ('If the plaster of a house is painted white, it brings luck,' but 'If in the interior of a house the walls show the plaster falling off, destruction of that house'), its own system of drainage, its ample accommodation of a dozen rooms or more, implies a standard of life of a really high order. And these are the houses not of particularly wealthy people but, as the tablets found in them prove, of the middle class, shop-keepers, petty merchants, scribes and so on whose fortunes and idiosyncrasies we can sometimes trace quite vividly.

No. 1 Broad Street was a house, larger than most, belonging to a certain Igmil-Sin, a scribe or priest. We were puzzled at first by various alterations that had been made in the building; the doorways of the ground-floor rooms opening on the court had been bricked up, thus isolating from the main living-quarters the court itself, the lavatory and the guest-room, which was now entered by a door in its south end, the only means of communication between the two parts of the house; and in the north wall of the court a new doorway had been made giving directly on the street. The explanation was given by the tablets found in the building, nearly two thousand in all. Igmil-Sin was headmaster of a boys' school and had adapted his house accordingly; classes were held in the courtyard and guest-room while the remaining quarters were reserved for domestic use. Some hundreds of the tablets were of the regular 'school exercise' type, the flat sun-shaped tablets used for fair copies, etc.; there were very many religious texts probably used for dictation or for learning by heart, some historical texts, mathematical tablets, multiplication tables, all these belonging to the school, while a number of business tablets apparently referring to temple affairs showed the schoolmaster's standing.

In No. 1 Old Street structural alterations were due to quite another cause. This house, approached by a long narrow passage from Old Street proper, was an old building (its foundations went down very deep) originally of considerable size; but towards the end of the Larsa Period the doorways on the south-east side of the central court were bricked up and the rooms there were incorporated in the next-door house, No. 7 Church Lane. Here again the tablets came to our help. In the reign of Rim-Sin of Larsa the house belonged to one Ea-nasir who was a merchant primarily engaged in the copper trade, for which he had agents in various towns; but his private papers show all sorts of side activities; he speculated in house property and garden land, lent money on usury and once at least conducted a deal in second-hand clothing, this apparently at the expense of his main business, for one letter from an agent abroad complains that he has written three times on the subject and has had no reply. It is not surprising that Ea-nasir had to cut down his premises and sell part of his house to a neighbour.

Such changes were not uncommon and naturally resulted in structural alterations which upset the original plan of the building. Thus No. 7 Church Lane was twice enlarged at the expense of neighbours and became very irregular in consequence. No. 1 Bakers' Square, which had been a good house, was entirely remodelled as a factory; most of the rooms were given over to furnaces, and judging by the miniature models of tools found in the owner's grave the business was that of a smithy. No. 14 Paternoster Row was cut down in size, the rooms on the south-east side of its courtyard being incorporated in the Bazaar Chapel, and afterwards it was turned into a restaurant; for this, a wide window was opened on to the street with a brick counter immediately inside it for the display of cooked dishes; room 4 became the kitchen, most of its area taken up by a solid brick range in the top of which were the troughs for the little charcoal braziers on which the cooking was done, and alongside this the circular bread-oven; it was exactly like the cookshops of a modern bazaar. No. 3 Store Street, the house of a grain-merchant, had big brick bins below the floors of most of its rooms—we were puzzled to find the plastered walls going down six feet underground, until we saw the actual grain sticking to the plaster.

In a few cases the houses did not conform to the usual pattern. No. 11 Paternoster Row should perhaps not rank as an exception because it may well have been not a private house but an inn or *khan*; some of the ground-floor rooms were apparently stables, and while part of it was probably the living-quarters of the innkeeper the rest seemed more suited to public use. The walls of this building were exceptionally thick and suggested that it rose to the height of a third story. On the other hand No. 15 Church Lane was never more than one story high, for there was no staircase; the owner, Ibku-Adad, seems to have had business dealings with Warad-Sin son of Lamatumza, who lived at No. 3 Niche Lane, and also with one Atta who was perhaps the father of Nuratum, owner of the large and prosperous house No. 1 Store Street. It is significant that another small and possibly one-story house, No. 1 Niche Lane, the meanest and shoddiest building in the area, was the home of a professional money-lender. Certainly while digging the site we got the impression that in Rim-Sin's time this quarter of Ur was socially on the down-grade, with the result that what had been the best houses tended to be divided or to be turned to non-residential uses. We do not know how far a like tendency could be observed in other parts of the city, but it is likely enough that the fast-growing power of Babylon under Hammurabi's rule was curtailing the trade and undermining the prosperity of Ur; the increasing pressure from the north may be illustrated by the fact that Gimil-nin-gish-zida, the smith of No. 1 Bakers' Square, had a Sumerian-Semitic grammar, presumably because some of his business was conducted in the Semitic language. A commercial slump resulting from the supremacy of Babylon might account for the part played by Ur in the revolt against Hammurabi's son; apparently the city headed the movement in revenge for which all these Larsa houses were utterly destroyed.

Thus far I have described the domestic part of the Larsa house, but there is another part of it which is even more interesting.

In early days, and right down to Sargonid times, the custom of the Sumerians was, as we have seen, to bury their dead in regular cemeteries. In the Larsa Period the dead are buried inside the houses. The practice seems to have been started under the Third Dynasty of Ur, if we may judge by the great mausolea of the kings of that dynasty, which take the form of private houses built above the tomb vaults; by the time of the Larsa kings it had become the invariable rule. The proper place for burial was a long and narrow paved yard lying at the back of the house, generally behind the guest-room;[1] two-thirds of this were open to the sky, one end, however, was covered with a pent-house roof, and here the

[1] In the case of No. 3 Gay Street, the plan of which is given in Fig. 13, p. 179, the back wall of the guest-room and the burial-yard behind it had been completely destroyed.

pavement was raised up a few inches to distinguish it from the open part. The open part was the burial-ground, the roofed part was the domestic chapel. If at the end farthest from the chapel you pull up the floor-bricks and dig down you find yourself in front of the door of a brick-built vaulted tomb the roof of which is only two feet or so below the pavement [*Plate* 27*a*]. The door is blocked with rough brickwork and against it are two or three clay pots for food and drink; inside there may be as many as ten or a dozen bodies. It is a family vault, brought into use whenever an adult of the household dies; then the tomb was re-opened, the bones of the last occupant somewhat unceremoniously shoved into a corner and the newcomer laid in seemly fashion in the middle, only to be put aside in his turn when next a burial took place. Very often against the side of the vaulted chamber there are one or more clay coffins containing single bodies; this, I imagine, was because two deaths had occurred in a short space of time and the opening of the chamber seemed inadvisable; for small children (and the rate of infant mortality was very high) the chamber was never opened but the body was put into a clay pot and buried below the floor, often just in front of or actually inside the chapel. The fittings of the chapel were in all cases the same [*Plate* 27*b*]. Against the back wall there was a low bench of brickwork on which we sometimes found the cups and little plates for offerings still *in situ*; immediately above this there was in the back wall a square recess like a fireplace from which an open channel ran up the wall but ended before it reached the roof; it was a fireplace for the burning of incense, and the channel would serve to create sufficient draught while at the same time it would let the smoke escape into the upper part of the 'room'. In one corner was an altar built of brick (usually mud brick) and mud-plastered, the plaster elaborately moulded so as to give the effect of panelling; in one instance we found fixed to the pavement bitumen holed sockets for fixing horizontal rods just above the floor, and the only possible explanation of them was that the rods were for the lower ends of curtains which would be drawn across and hide the altar when it was

Plate 27

a. The family burial-vault beneath the floor

b. The altar, offering-table and incense-hearth
The Family Chapels of the Larsa period

Plate 28

a. The statue of Pa-sag

b. The Pa-sag chapel seen from the street

not in use. Sometimes there was in the other corner a door
leading to a tiny closet which might have been a vestry but,
as we often found there quantities of tablets, was more
probably the family archive. In the houses and in the chapels
small terra-cotta figures and reliefs of deities or of votaries
were common; in one house (No. 3 Paternoster Row) there
was one of unusually large size, the upper part of a figure of
a bearded god still retaining a good deal of the original
painted surface; some at least of them must be connected
with the chapel services, i.e., must represent the family or
personal gods of the householder, the *teraphim* of the tale of
Jacob and Rachel when she stole the household gods of
Laban her father [*Plate 26a*].

The discovery of these domestic chapels, about which
literature had told us nothing, threw an entirely new light
on the more personal religion of the Sumerians. Obviously
there is here an emphatic insistence on the unity and the per-
petuity of the family. The head of the house, when he dies,
is not carried off to some outlying cemetery where he might
soon be forgotten and in any case would be cut off from his
descendants; instead, he continues to be a member of the
family, remaining in the house and sharing in that family
ritual of which he once was High Priest and now his son is
High Priest after him. When first we started digging Larsa
graves we were disappointed by their poverty; apart from
one or two clay pots and those purely personal things such
as seals, ear-rings or finger-rings which could not decently
be taken off the corpse the most elaborately-built vault underlying a large and wealthy house would yield us nothing at
all; the best of them could not compare with the poorest
grave in our old Royal Cemetery. The explanation is simple
enough. The dead man of the Larsa age needed no tomb
furniture because everything in the house was still at his dis-
posal. The food and drink at the tomb door were required
so that the spirit if it came forth might refresh itself and be
satisfied (the Omen Texts assure us that it was no uncommon
thing to meet the ghost of a dead forebear in the house) and
so mix with the family in kindly mood; but back in the house
it shared everything with them. To some extent the services

at the family altar may even have been addressed to the dead below the floor—the eldest son had the title 'the pourer of oil to his Father'; but primarily they were directed to that personal god who was the embodiment of the Family and its patron. On the cylinder seals of this period, as of the Third Dynasty, the most common subject is that of the seal's owner being introduced into the presence of Nannar or Nin-gal by the nameless personal god who acts as mediator and inter-cessor: those great gods were too great and too remote to be approached by ordinary men, and a divine intercessor was called for; but the intercessor, as family god, was one to whom the members of the family had direct access and it was he who, in the chapel of the house, received the prayers and offerings of all generations alike—he was the god 'of Abra-ham, of Isaac and of Jacob'.

Another discovery important for our understanding of the religion of the Sumerians—and again one for which there had been no evidence in the literary texts—was that of the popular wayside shrines. Every now and then there would be opening off the street a doorway distinguished (sometimes, if not always) by large terra-cotta reliefs attached to the door-jambs, replacing the modest Puzuzu heads found in private houses. A few brick steps in the doorway led up into an open paved court which might be a court and nothing more, as in the cases of the Bazaar Chapel at the corner of Paternoster Row and the Carfax Chapel, or might be a more elaborate affair with a walled-off sanctuary and subsidiary chambers as in the Pa-sag Chapel and the Ram Chapel in Church Lane. A description of the Pa-sag chapel will serve for all [*Plate* 28*b*].

Like the other chapels it was of a date late in the Larsa Period. One came into the court not directly but through an entrance lobby; in the corner to the left what had been a mere recess had been turned into a closed cupboard in which we found numerous votive objects, a clay model of a chariot, model beds, a clay rattle, whetstones and rubbing-stones and more than thirty stone mace-heads, one of them inscribed with a dedication to Pa-sag. Facing you as you came in was the sanctuary, its doorway, distinguished by jambs having bold reveals, flanked by two brick pedestals two-and-a-half feet high, one flat-topped, the other having in its top a rectangular bitumen-lined hollow, clearly meant for liquid offerings. Immediately in front of the sanctuary was a brick altar, its top covered with bitumen; by it was a clay cup, and other clay cups and the skull of a water-buffalo lay close by. Near the sanctuary door lay a rectangular lime-stone shaft two-and-a-half feet high having a cup-like hollow in its top and on each side crudely-carved reliefs of birds and human figures—it is a libation-altar such as is shown in one of the scenes on the great stela of Ur-Nammu. Towards the east corner lay a (very ugly) limestone figure of a goddess which had stood on a hollow wooden plinth; inside the plinth was a small statuette of a goddess made of copper, but the arms, which must have been in some other material, were missing. A few more clay pots, some large querns or mill-stones of black lava and some stone pounders were found also in the court. The sanctuary had been closed by a door consisting of a wooden frame set with panels of reed-work. In the back wall, facing the door, was a niche of which the lower part was filled by a base of bricks, mud-plastered and whitewashed; on this stood the limestone figure of the goddess Pa-sag. It was a small figure, not very well carved, and it had been broken in half in antiquity and roughly mended with bitumen; its feet were missing also, and it had therefore been embedded in the mud base so as to keep it upright in position [*Plate* 28a]; a poor thing artistically and never of much intrinsic value it had nevertheless been respec-ted, and its humble worshippers had done their best to make good the damage it had undergone. On the floor were found numerous small beads (the necklace of the goddess), various clay pots, including an incense-burner, and 64 inscribed tablets dealing with the affairs of the little shrine.

Pa-sag's chapel, like the others, was founded by some pious citizen, who might sacrifice for the purpose part of his own domestic premises, and it was maintained by voluntary sub-scriptions. It was served by a visiting priest, for whose use probably the two back rooms with a separate entrance on Straight Street were provided, his salary being paid out of the gifts made by visitors or from the modest endowments which the founder of the shrine or other benefactors had furnished.

We have long been familiar with the character of the great temples of Sumerian and Babylonian cities. They were dedicated to the major gods, they were built by kings and they were immensely wealthy, the city god himself being the chief landowner of the State. At the other end of the scale we now have the household chapel for the worship of the personal god who had no name other than that of the family he represented. The wayside shrine is different from either of those. It starts from private initiative but serves a public end; it is dedicated not to any of the great gods nor to the patron god of any family but to one of those minor deities whom the Sumerian could count by the thousand. Pa-sag for instance had as her function the protection of travellers in the desert; only if one were proposing such a venture would one have any need to invoke her aid, but in that particular juncture she would of course be invaluable and a prayer put up and an offering made in her shrine would be but a prudent measure of insurance. These minor gods were departmentalized Powers the need for whom was casual but real enough when it did arise; because they were minor they could be approached by the private suppliant but they held no position such that the State was obliged to make provision for them; that their temples were founded and maintained by the piety of individual laymen is proof of their importance in popular religious belief. There was nothing in life that did not come within the special province of one god or another—that is why there are so many gods—and the wise man would invoke the appropriate god for help in whatever he proposed to do.

Our excavations in the residential quarters have given us a very detailed picture of the conditions of life at Ur in the Larsa period but the excavated area was comparatively small and to get an idea of the town as a whole we must call for other evidence.

The ruin-mounds of Ur are very extensive, but even they do not represent the entire town, for quarters which were inhabited for a relatively short period did not form mounds at all, or mounds so low that they have been obliterated by the general rise in the level of the plain. Thus, we dug in the flat ground half a mile south-west of the Ziggurat and found Larsa houses there. A mile away to the north-east of the Temenos we found the 'Treasure-house' of Sin-idinnam of Larsa, and to the east of this again there was a wide extent of low-lying land in which the houses of the same period are as densely built as those in the Paternoster Row area. The walled city of Ur—the 'Old Town'—formed not more than one-sixth of 'Greater Ur' as the latter is defined by our trial digs; but beyond the closely built-up area stretched more open suburbs—thus, we could distinguish traces of more or less scattered buildings right up as far as the temple of al 'Ubaid, which is four miles away, and there were small satellite towns within five or six miles of Ur (we tested several of these) which themselves can have been little more than suburbs of the capital city. If we assume that our excavated area is fairly representative of the 'Old Town' as a whole so far as the density of population is concerned then the 'Old Town', excluding the Temenos, would easily have contained four thousand two hundred and fifty houses; allowing eight persons to a house, which is a moderate figure for a country where large families were held desirable, concubinage was freely practised and slavery was the rule, we arrive at a total for the walled city of 34,000 souls. At that rate the population of Ur must have exceeded a quarter of a million and may have been twice that; it was indeed a great city.

It is obvious that all those people could not have made a living by agriculture. Ur was a trading and manufacturing centre and its business extended far afield, as is shown by the tablets found in the houses of its merchants. Raw materials were imported, sometimes from oversea, to be worked up in the Ur factories; the bill of lading of a merchant ship which came up the canal from the Persian Gulf to discharge its cargo on the wharves of Ur details gold, copper ore, hard woods, ivory, pearls and precious stones. It is true that the sceptre had passed away from Ur, but neither Isin nor Larsa could be commercial rivals for this city with its old traditions of trade and its key position with navigable waterways keeping it in touch with the sea; the Ur of Rim-Sin's time was actually larger and probably more prosperous than it had been in the days of Ur-Nammu.

VIII

The Kassite and Assyrian Periods

THE twelfth year of the reign of Samsi-iluna of Babylon, son of the great Hammurabi, the year 1737 B.C. according to our reckoning,[1] was officially named 'that in which he destroyed the walls of Ur'. The ruins bear eloquent testimony to the thoroughness of that destruction. The fortifications were dismantled—this indeed one might expect; every temple that we found had been plundered, cast down and burned; every house had been consumed with fire; the whole of the great city ceased to exist. In the houses it often happened that where walls were not left standing very high we could note lying over the tops of them horizontal strata of dust and sand and ashes, sure proof that for some length of time the ruins had been undisturbed, long enough for the gradual processes of wind and rain to fill in the hollows and thereafter start the ordered burial of the dead town. Of course people did come back to what had been their home, but they had neither the morale nor the means to rebuild it. Where the house walls were still standing fairly high they would squat in the ruins, patching the broken walls with old bricks, stamping a new mud floor over the wreckage that filled the old rooms, but would content themselves with the one story which meant less work and less material; we never find in Kassite houses those staircases which had characterized the houses of the Larsa age. Even the later Kassite houses which were not mere adaptations of old ruins but independent foundations set up when Ur was comparatively prosperous were on one floor only; the ground-plan might be traditional, with the central court and rooms opening off it, but so far as we could tell (admit-

[1] On Sidney Smith's system of chronology; v. pp. 16 and 251.

tedly, the number of such houses dug by us was limited, and to generalize from them is perhaps dangerous) the two-story building had passed out of fashion.

Of course too there had to be temples; whatever happened, the gods must have somewhere to live. One might have supposed that the problem would be solved easily enough, for the land at least was still there and the gods were the great land-owners, so that in the hardest times there ought to be revenues sufficient for a good building programme. But this seems not to have been the case at all. Whether or not it was that Babylon laid hands on all incomings, Marduk as conqueror appropriating the wealth of Nannar, at any rate Nannar's priests could not meet the charge. The Gig-par-ku, the temple of Nin-gal, was the only one that gave us concrete evidence of attempts to make good the damage done by the Babylonian troops, and there it is only too clear that the means of the restorers were straitened to the last degree; their building is the poorest patchwork, there are no dedication-stamps on the bricks and old material is freely employed. In other temples we found no traces of such work, Kuri-galzu's brickwork being laid directly on that of Larsa; where the old ground-plan was so faithfully followed one imagines that there must have been a building standing above-ground to serve as a guide, something more than mere tradition as to the temple's form: I think that there was something, but something of such poor quality that when proper reconstruction was in view the first step was to sweep away the shoddy walls which had been all that impoverished piety had been able to set up.

Samsu-iluna utterly laid waste the city of Ur, but the effects of his victory went far beyond this. I have constantly, and especially in the last chapter, had to refer to the tablets found by us in the course of the excavations; there were thousands and thousands of them.[1] Down to the time of Samsu-iluna these documents, letters, contracts, accounts

---

[1] A volume published by Dr. Legrain deals with 1,800 tablets but those are exclusively business texts of the Third Dynasty of Ur, and even so are but a selection. Those of the Isin-Larsa Period are far more numerous; about 880 of them have been published by Dr. Figulla, who has also published 200 business documents of the Late Babylonian Period.

and what-not are written in the Sumerian language, the language of the people of Ur. After that date the tablets are in the Babylonian language. Even under the kings of Larsa the old native speech, it is clear, was being hard pressed by that of the Semitic North and the business man of Ur might profit by being bilingual; but after the downfall of Ur the supremacy of the North was complete. The Sumerian language was still preserved for religious purposes, exactly as Latin has been preserved for the services of the Roman Catholic Church, but it was a dead language. Outside the temples nobody used it at all, and even the priests had to learn what had been the natural tongue of their kinsmen a few generations before, and they did not learn it very well; even when they were copying an old text they might be guilty of the veriest schoolboy 'howlers'. The old expression for universal dominion, 'King of Sumer and Akkad' was now an anachronism, for Sumer had ceased to exist. We cannot be surprised that the stragglers who returned to the ruins of Ur and even the later generations who built themselves houses more or less on the old model on the mounds that hid the forgotten tombs of the Third Dynasty kings had not the heart, even if they had the means, to repair its ancient monuments. Certainly the gods had to be housed—mere prudence insisted on that insurance policy; but there could be no idea of reviving the glories of a past with which every link had been broken.

The First Dynasty of Babylon petered out ingloriously. Samsu-iluna himself had been hard put to it to keep out an invading people called the Kassites; his successors found their dominions filched from them, 'by the Kings of the Sea-lands' on the one side, by the Kassites on the other, but in time the latter established themselves as sole rulers and heirs of the Babylonian empire. Good fighting men they must have been, to achieve their position, but they seem not to have known how to use it. The early Kassite period is a blank page in the history of Mesopotamia; politically the kings were insignificant, the arts stagnated, no great buildings gave lustre to the names of the rulers and no records were kept of their uneventful rule. Thus it is that at Ur for the space of nearly two hundred and fifty years the rather squalid houses of its private citizens are the only evidence that excavation could produce to show that the city was in existence at all.

And then, about 1400 B.C., we have a complete change. There arose a Kassite king, Kuri-galzu II, who was an impassioned builder. Ur is full of his monuments, and he was no less active in the other southern cities which had so long been neglected by the central government. It is always interesting to speculate why a ruler should suddenly strike out a new line for himself, and Kuri-galzu must have had his reasons. Perhaps it was that Assyria, a vassal state of Babylon, was beginning to show signs of independence, that to the north-west the Mitanni had grown to be a formidable power and that, in the heart of Asia Minor, the Hittites had built up a state which had already interfered in Syria and was evidently prepared to back its political intrigues by physical force without regard to distance. With storm-clouds gathering in the west and north the Kassite king may have felt that to consolidate the south in his interest was the course of wisdom; the easiest and the traditional method of ingratiating himself with the subject cities was to espouse the cause of their gods, and the rebuilding of temples would appeal both to the people and to the gods themselves. I imagine that Kuri-galzu's motive was more political than strictly religious, but in any case he did embark on a very ambitious building programme. In its execution quality had to be sacrificed to quantity. It is true that Kuri-galzu worked for the most part in burnt brick, which is more than his successors did, for mud brick is the standard material of the Late Babylonian builders; but he could very seldom afford bitumen mortar, plain mud taking its place; and whereas in the Third Dynasty temples the brick courses are carefully laid right through the wall's thickness, the Kassite walls, which have so solid a look, generally consist of two skins of properly laid bricks enclosing a core of brick rubble and mud; the broken bricks for the filling are taken from the old buildings which were being repaired, and any unbroken old bricks were used in the face of the wall, so that one can see there bricks of different ages and different sizes indiscriminately mixed. In spite of this, however, much of Kuri-galzu's work survives in better condition than that of any former age.

Naturally the king's first care must have been the restoration of the central shrine of the Moon-god. Of the Ziggurat itself we can say no more than that, for the re-modelling of the building in the Late Babylonian time involved the sweeping away of everything subsequent to Ur-Nammu and his son Dungi; but in the surrounding buildings the hand of Kuri-galzu is much in evidence.

The revetment which the Larsa kings had added to Ur-Nammu's buttressed wall upholding the Ziggurat terrace had fallen away in ruins; this was now refaced with specially-moulded bricks reproducing the half-columns and niches of Warad-Sin's gateway tower. When we excavated the terrace edge we found Kuri-galzu's wall and at first supposed that our job was done; then in places where the wall-face had fallen away exposing the packing of brick rubble behind it, we found that the latter hid an older but similar burnt-brick wall which was of Larsa date; and finally, where this too had perished, we could see behind it Ur-Nammu's mud-brick terrace wall studded with his clay cones of dedication; it was a curious case of vertical stratification.

Not only the retaining-wall of the terrace but the whole circuit of the chambered wall above was rebuilt, and so too was the whole of the great courtyard of Nannar lying below the terrace, with its surrounding magazines and its monumental gateway; this was done following the old lines but no attempt was made to reproduce on the external walls the elaborate decoration of attached half-columns which had distinguished the Larsa work. None the less, the solid double buttresses which relieved the plain stretch of the walls must have been quite as imposing as the rather fussy effect of the columns; certainly this was the impression we got when, clearing the façade of the great court, we found Kuri-galzu's square-buttresses wall actually resting on the older columned wall which served it as a foundation; the contrast was all in favour of the later work.

Kuri-galzu was primarily a restorer, as he is always at

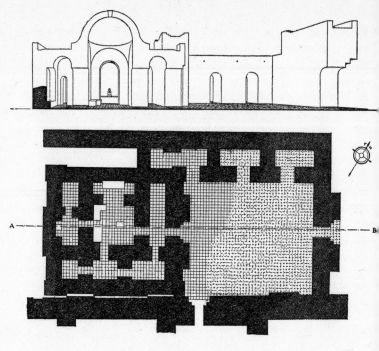

Fig. 15. Plan and restored section of Kuri-galzu's
Temple of Nin-gal

pains to state, and his brick-inscriptions record that 'he has
renewed for Nannar E-gish-shir-gal, his beloved house'
(which is the whole Ziggurat enclosure) or, as a gate-socket
says more explicitly 'E-gish-shir-gal, the temple that from
days of old had been in ruin he built and restored to its
place', but the reconstruction was on such a scale that he
could fairly claim—as he does on another door-socket which
we found here—that he 'had built E-gish-shir-gal'. One
building in it seems to have been an innovation on his part,
for no earlier remains were found underlying it; this was a
temple to Nin-gal occupying the free space to the south-east
of the Ziggurat. Except for one wall of the outer court we
recovered the whole plan of the temple, a small and compact
building unlike any other at Ur (Fig. 15); judging by the

Fig. 16. Reconstruction of main court of the Nin-gal Temple

thickness of its walls and the arrangement of its rooms it
had a central dome surrounded by barrel vaults, an architectural design curiously like what we find in early Arab
times; the suggested reconstruction on Fig. 16 is not at all
what we should have expected to find in Mesopotamia of the
fourteenth century B.C. The axis of the shrine was at right
angles to that of the building as a whole, the sanctuary being
on the north-west side of the central chamber; in a niche in
the back wall was a brick altar or statue-base embedded
between the bricks of which we found fragments of gold
foil, a little silver vase, vases of glazed frit and of variegated
glass, objects put here according to some ritual of dedication.
For the service of the Nin-gal temple a new gateway was
made through the double enclosing wall of E-gish-shir-gal,
an imposing entrance surmounted by a gate-tower; a smaller
and simpler gate, approached by a flight of steps, about
forty yards away to the east, led straight on to the open

terrace, taking the place of that which once had passed through Dublal-makh, 'the Great Gate'.

Kuri-galzu's reconstruction of Dublal-makh 'the great main gate, the ancient one, which from of old had been in ruin' was most striking.

When we first came to Ur one of the most prominent features of the site was a little mound not far from the east corner of the Ziggurat which we could identify as one which had been excavated by Taylor, the British consul at Basra, when he dug here for the British Museum seventy years before. He reported having found in it a small two-roomed building of burnt brick with arched doorways, which he had taken to be a house of late date; the walls stood so high that his workmen had roofed the place with mats and used it as a shelter. We cleared away the drift sand which had filled the two rooms and then proceeded to lay bare the outer face. Of the brick arches over the two side doors noted by Taylor one had since fallen, but the other was intact, and the bricks of the door-jambs and of the walls, good burnt bricks set (exceptionally) in bitumen mortar had stamped on them the dedication-inscription of Kuri-galzu, which Taylor of course could not read; it was not a late building but one of the fourteenth century before Christ. For us at the time the outstanding feature was the arch, by nearly a thousand years the oldest arch standing complete above-ground; since then we have found, in the Royal Cemetery, other arches two thousand years and more older than this, but in the winter of 1924 we could hail our discovery as one which revolutionized the history of architecture.

The little building, whose walls were relieved by the T-shaped vertical grooving which in time we learnt to recognize as the peculiarity of a temple, was surrounded by a brick pavement. Following this outwards we came to its edge, formed by a fresh wall, also having the T-shaped grooves, which went down for some five feet and ended at another brick pavement; it was the containing-wall of a platform or pedestal which jutted out from the high level of the Ziggurat terrace and it was on this platform that Kuri-galzu's building stood, high above what proved to be a great paved court in front of it [*Plate* 29*a*]. As the floor of one of the two rooms had been destroyed by Taylor's workmen we dug down through it and immediately below what had been floor level found that the character of the wall-bricks changed and they bore the stamps not of the Kassite king but of the Larsa king Ishme-dagan; deeper down still were one or two courses of bricks stamped with the name of Bur-Sin, of whom we found also one of the inscribed door-sockets. What had happened is accurately described by Kuri-galzu on his bricks: 'E-dublal-makh, the ancient house which from days of old had been decayed, I built on the four sides, I restored to its place, I made good its foundation.' The old temple was in such parlous state that even the lower courses of its walls would not have stood up to the weight of a new building erected on them—but, piety demanded that the new building should be founded on the old. Kuri-galzu therefore built a new wall round the temple and filled the space between them with solid mud and rubble packing, laying over this a pavement flush with the floor of the Ziggurat terrace; he filled up the inside of the temple likewise, to the same level, and trimmed down the old walls to a course or two below the pavement; thus solidly encased they would serve perfectly well as foundation for his new work, and since the 'Great Gate' had long ceased to be a gateway at all the fact that it was now raised up on a pedestal did not matter; in fact, it was an improvement, for seeing that Dublal-makh was the Court of Law and the sentences of the Court were proclaimed from its gate, the extra height would only add to the dignity of the announcement.

Scattered about in the rubbish at the foot of Dublal-makh we found a number of Kassite bricks with patterns moulded in relief; most of them had parallel zig-zag lines, others high embossed motives of which we could not make any sense at all. The explanation came from another site. At Warka, the ancient Erech, the German excavators found a Kassite building the façade of which was decorated with life-size figures of deities, standing out in high relief from the wall face, built of specially moulded bricks; they stood in a row, holding vases from which came streams of water repre-

sented by just such zig-zag bands as we found at Ur. We
unearthed only a few fragments whereas the Erech reliefs
could be rebuilt in their entirety, but the identity of the two
discoveries could not be questioned; somewhere in the immediate neighbourhood of Dublal-makh Kuri-galzu set up a
building adorned in this striking and apparently original

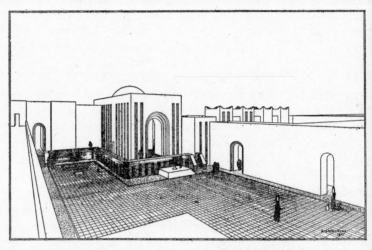

Fig. 17. Reconstruction of the Dublal-makh Court

manner. The moulded bricks did not belong to Dublal-makh
itself; of this we could be sure, for Kuri-galzu's walls were
still standing eight feet high and showed no signs of orna-
mental reliefs; possibly they came from the façade of a small
temple adjoining it on the east which was a new foundation
dating from the Kassite time and so badly ruined that nothing could be said about its appearance—at least, there was
nothing to disprove any theory regarding its decoration that
one might care to put forward. What had happened was
this. Up to the end of the Larsa period there had been an
open space between the ancient temple E-nun-makh and the
wall of the Ziggurat terrace; Kuri-galzu repaired E-nun-
makh and for the most part followed faithfully the original
plan, but he pulled down the south-west wall and extended
the building right up to the terrace wall, the new wing

forming an attached but separate shrine which he called
E-mu-ria-nabag. As we know from an inscribed door-socket
of Gimil-Sin there had long been at Ur a shrine of that
name, but it must have been completely destroyed and
perhaps even its site had been forgotten, so Kuri-galzu had a
free hand and thought fit to tack on this shrine of Nannar to
the joint temple which Nannar shared with his wife. The
addition did alter the look of the façade, which now continued beyond the old south corner so as to include the gateway of the new shrine and, beyond that, to abut on the side
wall of Dublal-makh; along that façade ran a broad road—a
'Sacred Way'—spanned by two double gateways, which led
through a third gateway into the great courtyard in front of
Dublal-makh. The greater part of the lay-out had been
decided by the Larsa kings and was followed by Kuri-
galzu, but whereas the Larsa work had been systematically
destroyed the Kassite remained in fairly good condition; it
was possible to recover not only the groundplan but, to a
considerable extent, the elevation of the buildings in this
area, as shown in Fig. 17. The brick-paved courtyard, with
magazines round three of its sides and in its south corner
what may have been an office building, was not merely a
temple court but served as a continuation of the Sacred Way
that ran past E-nun-makh. In its west corner a gateway
through the Ziggurat terrace wall gave access by means of a
flight of brick steps [*Plate* 29*b*] to E-temen-ni-gur, the terrace
itself, and a second gateway in the south-west wall gave on a
broad passage running right through to the wall of the Temenos; on either side of the passage were gate-towers, that on
the right leading into Kuri-galzu's temple of Nin-gal on
the Ziggurat terrace, that on the left to his version of the Gig-
par-ku of Nin-gal. The Gig-par-ku built by the Larsa
priestess Enannatum had been so ruthlessly laid waste by the
Babylonians that its repair was out of the question; tradition
preserved the memory of what had stood there, but the
shapeless heap of ruins must have daunted even so con-
scientious a restorer as Kuri-galzu, and the building which
he erected on the site had very little in common with the old.
Even the outlines were not the same; the Kassite building is

rather longer and much narrower than that of Larsa; it has none of the massive fortress-like appearance that Enannatum gave it, and it contains one temple only instead of two. The whole of the south-east end of the block is given over to somewhat flimsy buildings in mud brick which perhaps served as living-quarters for the priests; there had been such in the Larsa temple, as we know from the tombs beneath the pavements of the living-rooms, but now they cover a much larger area and are quite differently planned. It was perhaps because he suppressed the second shrine in the Gig-par-ku that Kuri-galzu built on the Ziggurat terrace the temple of Nin-gal which I have described above (p. 200); the fact that the doorways of the two buildings face each other across the Sacred Way would seem to associate the two shrines almost as closely as when they were under the same roof.

Indefatigable builder as Kuri-galzu was—and there are few monuments at Ur that do not show signs of his handi-work—either he cared little for the arts other than archi-tecture or else there were no other arts for him to patronize. Judging by what remains, the Kassite period was one in which artistic production had sunk to the lowest level and nothing that we have found gives evidence of any imagina-tion or originality. The one example of stone carving is a 'boundary stone', typical of Kassite times, an oval-topped stela bearing a long inscription which is really the title-deed of a landed estate giving the owner's name, the defini-tion of the boundaries and the stereotyped curses on whoso-ever should remove his neighbour's land-mark; at the top are carved in relief the symbols of those gods who in the text are called upon to protect the land-owner's rights. As a work of art such a thing is of little or no value, but it seems to have been all that the Kassites could produce. We excavated many Kassite tombs, built like those of the Larsa age underneath the houses wherein the family lived, but not one of them yielded any object of note; undecorated clay pots, generally of coarse and clumsy make, and the few purely personal things that decency would leave upon the body—a string of beads, a copper finger-ring or a pin fastening the shroud, these and nothing else constituted the grave furniture. So far as the evidence goes it was not the wealth of the people of Ur that was responsible for the rebuilding of the old temples; on the contrary, the rebuilding seems to have been the only thing that averted the complete decay of the city. Whether or not it fulfilled the king's political purpose it did enable the chief monuments of Ur to survive yet another long period of neglect.

The Kassite rulers who succeeded Kuri-galzu were not interested in the buildings of what must now have counted as a second-rate provincial city, and there is a gap of two hundred years in our records. It is true that Nabonidus states that in the course of his work on Dublal-makh he discovered the foundation-inscriptions of Nebuchadnezzar I, 1146–1123 B.C., and presumably the statement is correct, but our excavations produced nothing to corroborate it. Marduk-nadin-ahhi, 1116—1101 B.C., certainly did repair E-nun-mah, for we found his inscribed door-sockets in position in the ruins. A copper cylinder discovered by us, also *in situ*, in the foundations of Nannar's temple kitchen on the N.W. side of the Ziggurat terrace gives us the name of Adad-aplu-idinnam, 1083–1062 B.C.; he calls himself 'the Nourisher of Ur' and claims to have 'renewed E-gish-shir-gal', but a patch of brick pavement against the north-east face of the Ziggurat and a second patch in the great courtyard below are all that to-day bear witness to the truth of his boast. There was then in the twelfth and eleventh centuries B.C. a certain revival of royal interest in the well-being of Ur, although so far as material remains go the part played by the late Kassite rulers was not a very important one. In any case they were the last of their stock to be in a position to show favour to the south country; the dominion passed from their hands to those of the kings of Assyria, and none of those undertook any public works at Ur until the time of Ashur-bani-pal in the middle of the seventh century before Christ.

In the seventh century the governorship of Ur seems to have been a hereditary post; it had been held by one Ningal-dinnam, and his son Sin-balatsu-iqbi succeeded him in office in the reign of Ashur-bani-pal, king of Assyria. Sin-balatsu-

iqbi evidently found the monuments of his city in a parlous
state and, being an unusually active person, he embarked on
a comprehensive scheme of restoration. It is interesting to
note that of the many foundation-inscriptions of his that we
found only two say that the work was done 'for the breath of
life of Ashur-bani-pal, King of kings, his King'; in all other
cases the governor gives his own name and title and the name
of his father, implying that the building was carried out by
him on his own initiative and, presumably, at his own expense without the aid of any subvention from the central
government; he seems to have enjoyed a large measure of
independence. And how necessary the work was is clear
enough. 'The great walls of E-temen-ni-gur (the Ziggurat
terrace) and its platform were in ruin since long ago, its
foundation was buried. I sought for the place of its destroyed
gates, I built the retaining wall of its platform, I raised its
superstructure. A door of boxwood, best wood from distant
mountains, which was planted on a bronze shoe—its battens
were strong, its prop was of gold, its bolt of clear silver—
I set with silver, that the gate of the oracle chamber built in
the house of divination might stand for ever.' So he boasts
in the inscription of a door-socket which we found in
position in Dublal-makh, the actual socket that had served
his door of boxwood and precious metal. The stone itself
was really fine, a bright green stone like felspar capable of
taking a high polish; but it had cost the governor little, for it
was only the upper half of an old 'boundary-stone' which
had been cut down and re-used. The door, of course, had
disappeared, and it may have been as splendid as Sin-
balatsu-iqbi describes it; but every building of his that we
could identify was shoddily constructed in mud brick; undoubtedly he was doing his best, but his work was in sad
contrast to that of the earlier kings.

Dublal-makh was restored, but also enlarged, new
chambers being added on either side of the old two-roomed
shrine. The fact illustrates the condition of the long-
neglected monuments, for these new rooms extend beyond
the high pedestal on which Kuri-galzu's Dublal-makh stood.
In the course of the centuries that had elapsed the open

Plate 29

a. Kuri-galzu's shrine of Dublal-makh

b. The Courtyard of Dublal-makh

Plate 30

a. The Harbour Temple

b. Magic figures from sentry-boxes below the floors

courtyard in front of the Great Gate had been so filled with gradually accumulated rubbish that the five-foot pedestal was buried and the new ground-level was flush with the shrine's pavement, and it was on this flat ground that Sin-balatsu-iqbi built his new wings. He built, as I have said, in mud brick, but he copied faithfully the grooved walls of Kuri-galzu's shrine (which was still standing, apparently to its full height), gave a coat of mud plaster to new and old work alike and whitewashed it all over; the effect must have been excellent, even if obtained cheaply.

'I built the retaining-wall of the platform [of E-temen-ni-gur]' declares the governor, and here too our discoveries attest the truth of his claim. On the south-west side of the Great Court of Nannar, where it backs on the Ziggurat terrace, the Assyrian work is quite well preserved. He raised the level of the courtyard, which was deeply buried in rubbish, and laid down a mud floor; the wall was rebuilt in mud brick but again the elaborate half-column decoration first introduced by the Larsa king a thousand years before was reproduced. We found it standing four or five feet high with the whitewash still fairly fresh upon it, and a clay foundation-cone discovered under the floor of the northern gateway confirmed the authorship.

The terrace wall must have been rebuilt, as Sin-balatsu-iqbi says it was, all round the E-temen-ni-gur platform, but nothing of it remained. On the north-west side of the Zig-gurat, in the tangle of walls of every period which made the site so complicated, we did find patches of a brick pavement which he had laid down over the top of the ruined walls of the Larsa and Kassite kings, but the wall itself had been swept away by the builders of the Temenos wall of Nebu-chadnezzar and even its position was uncertain. The same was true of the south-west side of the Ziggurat; we found no trace of Assyrian work there. But on the terrace, in the area lying south-east of the Ziggurat, Sin-balatsu-iqbi was much in evidence. Here Kuri-galzu had built a special temple for Nin-gal, the Moon-goddess, but it was in ruins and appar-ently so deeply buried in rubbish that the governor, depart-ing from his usual practice of clinging to precedent, merely cleared the outer face of the containing-wall of Kuri-galzu, levelled the rubbish inside it so as to make a solid platform four or five feet high, and on the top of that proceeded to build an entirely new temple on up-to-date lines.

An entrance at the north-west end, now destroyed, led into a paved outer court with small shrines or service-chambers on either side and in the north corner a brick-lined well with a well-house above it. Facing the entrance was a lofty pylon gateway flanked by two smaller doors which gave access to side chambers; the pylon doorway opened on the fore-hall or Holy Place and corresponding to it in the back wall was the door of the sanctuary; the latter was at a higher level, approached by a flight of steps filling the door passage, and on this raised platform a rectangular screen of burnt brick-work formed the tabernacle in which stood the statue of the goddess (v. Fig. 19, p. 221).

The temple as we found it had been restored by Nab-onidus, but without any serious change of plan; only an inch or two below his floors we found the Assyrian pavement of bricks stamped with the name of Sin-balatsu-iqbi. These gave little more than his name, but a fuller text occurred on the clay foundation-cones; we found thirteen of these still in position, set upright, bedded in a little bitumen, in holes beneath the wfalls and floor of the sanctuary. 'For Nin-gal the Queen o E-gish-shir-gal, divine Lady of the crown, beloved of Ur, his Lady, Sin-balatsu-iqbi, governor of Ur, has built anew the temple of the beloved bride of Sin. A statue after the likeness of Nin-gal he made and into the temple of the "Wise God" he brought it. In E-nun, a dwelling built for her lordliness, she made her abode.' Again, how-ever, one must admit that the actual work did not come up to the governor's description. Not only were the walls of mud brick only, but the quality was so bad that the individual bricks could not be distinguished; they were so soft and crumbling that a stroke of the finger would produce a deep rut in the wall's surface, and in most cases the walls could be planned only by the edges of the (fortunately well-preserved) pavements laid against them; Sin-balatsu-iqbi's brickwork was, without exception, the worst that we encountered at Ur.

Even the hinge-socket stones of the doors were all old ones
re-used, bearing the names of kings of the Third Dynasty of
Ur, and though this may have been due to piety it was
certainly economical. Perhaps the most interesting part of
the building was the well. Only the upper part of it was the
work of the Assyrian governor—it had originally been made
by Ur-Nammu and repaired by later kings—but there the
bricks bearing his name instead of being all alike showed no
less than eight different texts, dedications of chapels or
statue-bases to eight different minor gods; we may conclude
that the side chambers of Nin-gal's temple housed these
subordinate deities who formed her court, but since the well
served them all the governor was at pains to insert in its
lining written witness to the presence of each. The little
collection of texts gave us a very distinct picture of the
catholicity of worship in a single temple.

The foundation-cones of Sin-balatsu-iqbi are the latest in
date that we found at Ur and represent the final development
of an ancient custom. From very early times such cones had
been employed, and always with a certain change of fashion.
Let into the sloping face of the mud-brick wall which held
up the terrace of Ur-Nammu's Ziggurat we had found
quantities of nail-like cones, the inscribed shaft buried in the
brickwork and only the rounded heads at regular intervals
making a sort of pattern on the wall-face—and even they
may have been hidden by a coat of mud plaster. Where one
of the Larsa kings had built out from the same terrace a fort
and postern-gate, we found his cones not in the wall-face but
buried in its core, arranged in neat rows behind the burnt-
brick skin of the gate tower; and these cones were much
larger than Ur-Nammu's, and instead of the small nail-like
head had a broad flat disc of clay on which the inscription
of the stem was repeated. The Assyrian cones had no base at
all and were placed under the floor instead of in the walls; in
the following age barrel-shaped cylinders take the place of
cones, and these are immured in the angles of the building.

In every case the inscription is hidden from sight, and it
would seem that the intention of the king is not to parade
his achievements before his fellow-men, but to keep the

record of his piety fresh in the mind of the god, who presumably can see through a brick wall; and probably there was, if not originally, at least as time went on, a second purpose. Everyone knew that the temple which the king built 'for his life' could not last for ever, but that its crumbling walls would one day have to be restored by another; if that later ruler discovered in the ruins the record of the first founder, he would in all likelihood respect it and even perpetuate it in his own inscriptions, and so his new building would acquire merit for the old king. This is what actually happened in a land where the continuity of tradition was so prized. In the very latest times, when Nabonidus repaired the Ziggurat he was careful to give full credit for its founding to Ur-Nammu and his son, and he has left on record the delight that he felt when deep in the foundations of an ancient temple which he was repairing he unearthed the foundation-tablet of Naram-Sin, son of Sargon of Akkad, and looked upon that 'which for three thousand years no human eye had seen'.

We cannot accept Nabonidus's date for his revered predecessor, for he is about a thousand years out in his reckoning, Sargon having reigned about 2380 B.C., but we can sympathize with his archæological enthusiasm. We had found plenty of Ur-Nammu cones scattered loose in the soil, but when for the first time we pulled one out from the mud-brick wall and saw on its stem the writing which had been deliberately hidden there more than four thousand years before, we experienced quite a different sensation, and though the cones of the Assyrian governor were set merely in the soil below the pavement, not bedded in brickwork, it was with a certain hesitation that we lifted them from the spot where the builders had placed them.

As we dug away the remains of Sin-balatsu-iqbi's temple we found evidence again of the piety which respects an ancient record. Lying together close to the foundations were four tablets, two of copper and two of stone, inscribed with the dedication of a building by Kuri-galzu. They must have been found in the course of some work of demolition, perhaps of a temple which was not to be rebuilt on the old model or on the old site. Useless now and of no intrinsic value, they had been given careful reburial in the temple precincts with the idea, so it seems to me, that they might still bear witness before the gods to the merits of the dead king of Babylon, enduring after his works had perished.

Possibly the same spirit of piety may account for our finding below the temple floors a stone foundation-tablet bearing an inscription of Gudea, who was governor of Lagash in the twenty-second century B.C., part of a stela with a dedication to Nin-gal by Ur-Nammu when he was still a vassal ruler and had not started his successful revolt against his overlord, and the head of a small statue of a priest finely carved in diorite which dates from about the same time. Such things had been consecrated as temple furnishings, and when they in the course of time were broken or simply out-moded and had to be discarded from the temple treasury there was still a natural reluctance to treat them merely as rubbish; it is not uncommon to find buried somewhere in the temple precincts a hoard of objects that had once adorned or been used in the building. A discovery like that is a stroke of luck for the archæologist, but it is apt to be misleading; one is tempted to assume that if the temple is accurately dated the objects, in that they belonged to it, should be of the same date. But this does not follow at all, rather, it is the reverse of the truth. Just as in a modern cathedral you may be shown treasures representing every period in the lifetime of the building, so the Babylonian temple was a storehouse of treasures handed down from a remote past and the offerings made by the faithful would not be lightly cast aside. The excavator who finds a temple hoard must make allowances for such piety and assume that the objects may be very much older than the temple.

Under one of the floors we found a small copper figure of a dog. This is something quite different; it is a contemporary object set here as a charm to protect the building. Another discovery that we made illustrated the custom. Sin-balatsu-iqbi, amongst his other works, rebuilt the ancient Gig-par-ku, or at least set up a building of his own on the site of the completely ruined Gig-par-ku of Kuri-galzu; as usual, he employed mud bricks of lamentable quality and the walls had for the most part vanished altogether, so that only by the edges of the burnt-brick pavements, where those survived, could we work out even bits of the groundplan; it was difficult to decide where any one room began and ended. But when we had done our best and started to pull up the floors we found further evidence which confirmed our rather theoretical sketch. Along every wall there was a row of brick boxes placed immediately below the pavement so that a pavement brick formed the lid of each box; the box was made of three bricks set on end, the fourth side, that facing inwards on the room, being left open, a sort of sentry-box; in each was a figure of unbaked clay which had been cast in a mould and then dipped in a bath of thick white lime on which such details as the features and the folds of garments were later painted in black with occasional touches of red. The work was extremely rough and the figures, impregnated with salts from the soil, were flaked and split in every direction, some of them in such bad condition that it was impossible to preserve them; but they were interesting none the less [*Plate* 30*b*]. There were snakes and dogs and gryphons, human figures and figures of men with the heads of lions or of bulls, with bulls' legs or fishes' bodies, every kind of well-disposed demon that might guard your house or keep off sickness and ill-luck; and with each there were a few calcined grains of barley and fragments of bones of small animals or birds. Cuneiform texts tell us about these figures and the ceremonies of their instalment with prayers and magic formulæ; now for the first time we had found them in position with concrete evidence of the little sacrifice that was solemnized when the guardians took their place in the sentry-boxes below the floor. And there was another point. The boxes were made of plano-convex bricks, the old bun-shaped bricks which had gone out of use more than a millennium and a half before. They must have been dug up from the older ruin-strata of the city and because of their antiquity were credited with some peculiar magic power that would increase the efficacy of the protecting demons. We shall see further examples of the archæological spirit that prevailed in the latter days of Babylon, but undoubtedly it was reinforced by a pathetic superstition that looked back across the uncounted ages to the fabulous beginnings of things when men and gods were scarcely to be distinguished and 'there were giants in the land in those days'.

IX

Nebuchadnezzar II and the Last Days of Ur

I<small>N THE</small> book of the prophet Daniel we read of Nebuchadnezzar that 'he walked in the palace of the kingdom of Babylon. The king spake and said "Is not this great Babylon, that I have built for the house of the kingdom by the might of my power and for the honour of my majesty?" ' and the prophet's description was fully justified. So was the king's boast. In 600 B.C. Babylon was by far the greatest walled city that the world has ever known, and Nebuchadnezzar had built it. He swept away all the works of his predecessors and set up in their place his enormous buildings; the modern excavators were hard put to it to find, under the deeply sunk foundations of the uppermost level, anything that was older than Nebuchadnezzar; over a space of more than ten square miles virtually every building was due to him. And his activities were not confined to the capital; at Ur also he embarked on an ambitious programme which seems to have aimed at the reconstruction of the entire city.

I think it probable that his work at Ur was begun only towards the end of his life. Naturally Babylon had to be considered first, and he would hardly have started operations in the provincial cities until good progress at least had been made in the capital—and for the rebuilding of Babylon many years of labour were required; most people would consider that his reign of forty-three years was none too long for the task. What is certain is this; that while of his three short-lived successors there is at Ur no record, when Nabonidus came to the throne only six years after Nebuchadnezzar's

death there was still a vast amount of building to be done
there, which would not have been the case had Nebuchadnezzar completed his programme; indeed, we know that
Nabonidus was sometimes finishing what Nebuchadnezzar
had begun. It was not always easy, or possible, to assign a
particular piece of building to the one king or the other, and
really it matters little; what is of interest is to know what Ur
was like in the sixth century after the two monarchs had
done their work. The question is even more complicated
because Nebuchadnezzar, as his complete rebuilding of
Babylon shows, was an individualist and an innovator and
even in matters of religion was quite ready to strike out a
line of his own, as will be made clear hereafter. Nabonidus,
on the other hand, was an antiquary and a traditionalist
who prided himself upon restoring an ancient building
exactly according to its original plan, 'not a finger's breadth
beyond or behind', as he says himself; and he might well
disapprove of and correct unorthodox changes made by his
predecessor. Thus, in the case of the Ziggurat, Nebuchadnezzar claims to have built 'E-gish-shir-gal, the temple of
Sin (=Nannar) in Ur', and that would necessarily include
the principal monument of the Sacred Area; we know that
he rebuilt the great courtyard, and built (perhaps for the
first time) two shrines occupying the angles between the
three great staircases that led to the top of the Ziggurat; it is
incredible that he should have done no work on the Ziggurat
itself, but actually not a brick of his has been found on it.
It is possible, though scarcely likely, that he left the restoration of the Ziggurat to the last and had not time to carry it
out; it is more probable that he did, or started to do, something that Nabonidus thought all wrong and so removed
bodily; the study of the remains makes it clear to my mind
that he did not simply attempt to reproduce the original
Ziggurat of Ur-Nammu (and that would have been out of
keeping with his character) but it yields no evidence at all of
what he did do. But of the Neo-Babylonian Ziggurat so
much is left that we can picture it in very fair detail.

Nabonidus found that the lowest stage of the ancient
tower was remarkably well preserved. To-day, when another

Isometric Projection.

SITE OF
NANNAR SHRINE

"SITE OF
BOAT SHRINE"

Fig. 18. Reconstruction of the Ziggurat of Nabonidus

two and a half millennia have passed, Ur-Nammu's walls of
burnt brick and bitumen still defy the effects of time; then,
all that the Babylonian king had to do was to relay the treads
of the triple staircase, repair the coping wall and rebuild the
domed archway at the head of the stairs. But above this
everything was in hopeless ruin; whether or not he had to
clear away a superstructure devised by Nebuchadnezzar as
well as any remains of work done by other late builders such
as Sin-balatsu-iqbi, he could not follow his favourite practice
of restoration 'to a finger's breadth' because there was nothing to guide him. It is true that we by careful digging were
able to recover the plan and character of the Third Dynasty
Ziggurat, but the methods of modern science were not those
of an ancient king in a hurry; he dug down in a corner of the
first platform and discovered in the brickwork there, (we
found the hole he made, neatly filled in with his own bricks),

as he tells us with great satisfaction, the foundation-tablet recording the original building of the tower, begun by Ur-Nammu and finished by his son Dungi, but there was nothing to show him what the tower had been like. All that Nabonidus could do was to preserve and use the lowest stage, treating it as a base for a Ziggurat of his own construction. In the course of centuries fashions, even for Ziggurats, had changed; Nabonidus followed the fashion and the Ziggurat which he set up was entirely different from that which he proposed to restore.

Instead of three stages the Neo-Babylonian Ziggurat had seven. Viewed from the front the effect was dramatic in the extreme. From ground level the three ancient stairways led up to the domed gate-tower at the top of the lowest stage; above that towered up six more stages, diminishing in size as they went up, with what looked like a spiral staircase encircling the building and leading from one stage to another and so to the topmost platform whereon stood the little shrine of Nannar, a small square building of bright blue-glazed bricks surmounted by a golden dome. So seen, the building corresponds very closely with the description given by the Greek historian Herodotus of the Ziggurat at Babylon, and it may be that, like that, our Ziggurat was painted throughout, each stage a different colour, answering to the colours of the planets; certainly the lowest stage was painted black, for some of the bitumenous coating is preserved, and the blue-glazed bricks of Nannar's shrine littered the site.

The visual appearance did not altogether correspond to constructional fact. Had the staircase really gone round the building in an uninterrupted spiral bricks and mortar would never have supported the weight of so stupendous a pile;[1] actually the steps were confined to the front of the building. Fortunately, terribly ruined as the Ziggurat was, there yet remained enough of Nabonidus's work to show us its nature. When you had mounted one of the three main staircases and had passed through the arched gate on to the first terrace there was on your right a little brick-built flight of steps

[1] The second stage alone would have been 162 feet high, with the other five in proportion!

leaned up against the wall of the second stage; the steps ran only as far as the corner of the tower and from that point a level gallery took you right round the tower to the centre of its façade where there was just such a shallow recess as Herodotus mentions in his description of the Babylonian Zig-gurat. Then you made a left-about turn to mount a second little flight of steps, this time leading up to the left, and so round the building on the flat to where, on the façade, a third flight running to the right took you up to the gallery forming the fourth stage; then round the building again to another 'sitting-out' recess, and so on. The total height of the 'Mountain of God' on which stood Nannar's Holy of Holies was just over a hundred and sixty feet. What we found was the brick pavement of the lowest stage, showing that Nabonidus made this uniform throughout, obliterating the stepped form of Ur-Nammu's first stage, so that at either end the Neo-Babylonian floor was nearly ten feet above the old, and on the whole conformed his second stage to that of the original; but here, on the façade, we found the first little flight of steps virtually intact and, on the left hand side, what at first seemed an anomalous feature, the front wall of the second stage (which, like the containing-wall of the little staircase, was relieved by the same sort of shallow buttresses as Ur-Nammu had used in the lower stage) stepped forward actually beyond the line of the staircase wall. Above this, everything had vanished. The problem of reconstruction bothered us for quite a while, but at length we realized that if we planned the third stage exactly on the lines of the second, but in reverse, and the fourth in the same way with its steps on the right hand side, as in the second stage, and so on for seven stages, we not only could explain all the features of ground-plan that survived but we had an abso-lutely symmetrical building, of a reasonable height, and one to which Herodotus's description of the contemporary Zig-gurat at Babylon would very aptly apply. This cannot be coincidence, and I think that we can fairly claim to have recovered the likeness of Nabonidus's 'Ziggurat of E-gish-shir-gal, which I have made anew and restored to its place'.

Nebuchadnezzar's main work at Ur was the building of

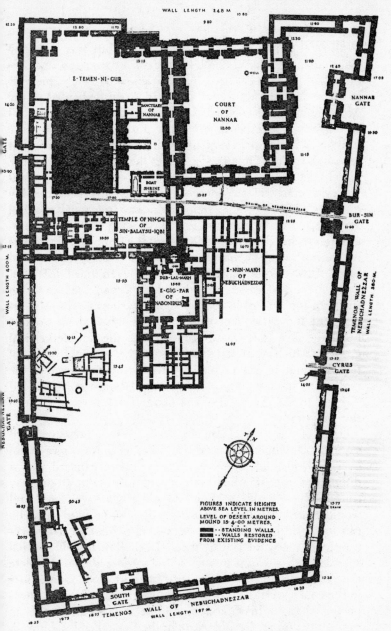

WALL LENGTH 248 M

E·TEMEN·NI·GUR

SANCTUARY OF NANNAR

COURT OF NANNAR

WELL

NANNAR GATE

GATE

BOAT SHRINE

DRAIN OF NEBUCHADNEZZAR

BUR·SIN GATE

TEMPLE OF NIN·GAL OR SIN·BALATSU·IQBI

WALL LENGTH 400 M.

TEMENOS WALL OF NEBUCHADNEZZAR WALL LENGTH 580 M.

DUB·LAL·MAKH
E·GIG·PAR OF NABONIDUS

E·NUN·MAKH OF NEBUCHADNEZZAR

CYRUS GATE

NEBUCHADNEZZAR GATE

FIGURES INDICATE HEIGHTS ABOVE SEA LEVEL IN METRES.
LEVEL OF DESERT AROUND MOUND 15·4·00 METRES.
▬ ·STANDING WALLS.
··· ·WALLS RESTORED FROM EXISTING EVIDENCE

DRAIN

SOUTH GATE

TEMENOS WALL OF NEBUCHADNEZZAR
WALL LENGTH 197 M.

Fig. 19. The Temenos of Nebuchadnezzar

221

the Temenos Wall (Fig. 19). There had been a Temenos
Wall in the time of the Third Dynasty, but this had long
since fallen into decay and nowhere did we find any evidence
of its having been restored by later kings. Nebuchadnezzar,
so far as we can tell, found a Sacred Area, dedicated to the
Moon-god, which consisted of religious foundations of all
sorts grouped together and in theory forming a unity, but the
unity was ill-defined; sometimes the outer walls of adjacent
temples were continuous, sometimes the buildings were more
loosely disposed, and it would seem that in fact the Sacred
Area in many places merged imperceptibly into the lay
quarters of the town. Nebuchadnezzar reformed all this.
A space 400 yards long and 200 yards wide was marked out,
a rough rectangle which enclosed all the important buildings
of Nannar's enclave, and round this was built a wall of mud
brick. It was a double wall with chambers in the middle of it,
the flat roofs of which would make a broad passage along
the wall-top available for the manœuvring of troops in its
defence; it was 33 feet wide and probably about 30 feet
high, the face of it was decorated with the double vertical
grooves which were traditional for the external walls of
temples, and it was pierced by six fortified gateways; the
main gate, having a high tower set back in a deep recess, led
directly to the entrance of the Great Courtyard in front of
the Ziggurat.

Parts of this great Temenos Wall are well preserved and
stand six feet high and more, and in other parts where it ran
over high ground and was therefore more exposed it was
difficult to trace it. We have not dug it right out all the way
round—that would teach us no more than we know and
would only mean the total destruction of the mud brick by
rain and wind—but having excavated carefully certain sections, we traced the rest by means of shallow trenches which
revealed only the upper courses, and so were able to complete
the entire circuit of the Temenos in eight days. Sometimes
in the course of tracing we were temporarily baffled by unexpected changes in direction, and it is indeed difficult to
explain the minor irregularities in the line taken by the wall.
In places, where the back of an old temple projected outside

the area pegged out, it has been ruthlessly cut away, and the wall of enclosure makes the new back wall of the building; elsewhere the line is deflected as if to enclose some monument which had to be respected, but as only too often the denudation of the surface has resulted in the complete disappearance of the monument we cannot accept the explanation as certain.

Possibly there was a simpler reason. Examination of the wall proves that it was built by various gangs of workmen each having his own section, and the collaboration between them was not very good in that the foundations of adjoining sections are laid at different levels and the projecting footings are not continuous; the irregularities of line may be due merely to faulty methods.

But the Temenos Wall was an imposing structure, and with its completion the Sacred Area took on a new character; it was much more a place set apart than it had been in the recent past. But the proper privacy of the Moon-god could have been secured by something much less extravagant than this enormous line of brickwork, and the wall must have been planned also as a work of military defence. Indeed, in the east corner of the Temenos there was an immensely solid square structure which cannot be regarded as anything other than a fortress-tower; it could hardly have served any religious purpose. In girdling Nannar's Sacred Area with a work of defence such as might be built round the palace of an earthly king the Babylonian monarch was certainly reviving a very ancient conception of the god as Ruler of the city and its leader in war whose house would be the final rallying-point for resistance against an enemy; his innovations were sometimes tied up with a curious respect for tradition.

I have said that he rebuilt the Great Courtyard of Nannar. He followed pretty faithfully the lines of Sin-balatsu-iqbi, the last worker on the site, but made one important change. The court had always been at a low level, so that in its south-west doorway a flight of steps led up to the Ziggurat terrace; Nebuchadnezzar raised the level so that the pavement of his court was flush with the terrace and the whole building became an extension of that terrace, E-temen-ni-gur, to which it had formerly been subordinate. When we dug down here we were astonished and at first very much puzzled to find, a little way below Nebuchadnezzar's paving tiles and above those of Sin-balatsu-iqbi, a thick layer of soil containing masses of broken sherds of the painted pottery of the al 'Ubaid period.

Usually when a builder raised the floor-level of a building it was because the old floor had been buried by rubbish accumulated in the course of years; he might throw down the upper part of the ruined walls and lay his floor tiles over the top of the levelled rubble. But the al 'Ubaid sherds could not have drifted in, nor could they have fallen from above; it was evident that Nebuchadnezzar was raising his floor level not as making the best of existing conditions but on a deliberately thought-out plan, and he had imported soil expressly for the purpose. But we knew from sad experience that to find soil rich in al 'Ubaid potsherds you have to dig very deeply, and Nebuchadnezzar could have got his filling-material much more easily. Then why did he go to such trouble? The answer seems to be that just as the 'sentry-boxes' which housed the guardian demons below the house floor were best made with prehistoric bricks, so the sentiment attaching to the painted pottery which stood for the oldest days of Ur's beginnings would sanctify the court of Nannar who from those oldest days had been the city's master and its god.

In one case then Nebuchadnezzar could be piously conservative, but in others he was very much of an innovator. A striking instance of this was given by his treatment of the ancient temple E-nun-makh.

This happened to be the first building excavated by us at Ur. A low hillock rising close to the Ziggurat mound seemed to promise good results, and a trench driven into its flank at once produced walls of burnt brick enclosing paved chambers. It was a small square five-roomed building (see Fig. 19); the door led into an antechamber against the back wall of which, facing the entrance, was a brick base for a statue, and four doors, two in the back wall and one at either end, gave access to the other rooms which ran back

Plate 31

a. The 'Museum label' from Belshalti-nannar's school

b. Ivory toilet-box

Plate 32

Persian coffins made of rivetted sheet copper

the depth of the building. The two inner rooms were an exact pair; each had a bench near the door and was divided into two parts by a screen; in the farther part there was a brick altar against the wall and in front of it a brick table; obviously each was a shrine for religious services. The two outer rooms were also a pair, but here there were no particular features to show their use. The duplicating of the arrangements in the temple was explained by the inscriptions on the bricks: it was the common shrine of Nannar and his consort Nin-gal, and in it each deity had his and her special sanctuary.

In front of the building stretched a brick pavement half enclosed by two projecting wings which had been added in mud brick to the original square of the shrine; immediately in front of the door stood an oblong brick altar for offerings, and to one side remains of a second and larger altar from which a covered drain led right across in front of the temple door. This could only mean that the altar was that for blood offerings—the victim would be sacrificed on the altar and its blood, passing in front of the shrine, would come directly before the god, just as would the other offerings placed on the central altar. On the line of the frontage of the mud-brick wings of the building there was a step down and the pavement, at a lower level, broadened out and ran on as that of a large open court.

The bricks of the pavement bore no stamp of authorship, but their size and character proved them to be Persian, belonging to the very latest date in the history of Ur, and as a gate in the Temenos Wall close by had been restored by Cyrus the Great, we can probably attribute to him the last reconstruction of the temple also. It was interesting to observe that the position of the building and the details of its arrangement agreed almost exactly with the description which Herodotus gives of the great temple at Babylon in Persian times, but subsequent discoveries were to prove more interesting still.

It was clear that though the floors were Persian the walls of the shrine were very much older; in the outer court there was an earlier pavement visible where the new had been broken through, and the same might be true of the chambers also. The order was given to test this by pulling up twelve bricks in one of the sanctuaries and digging down beneath them. Our Arabs, who were new to the work, and had always been told that on no account must they disturb any brick that was in place, could not understand this sudden sacrilege, and when they found the order was serious jumped to the conclusion that we were looking for buried gold, nor would they believe me when I said that what we wanted was a second brick pavement. I went off, leaving the men at work, but within a few minutes one of them came running to fetch me. 'We have found the gold!' he said, and sure enough just below the paving-slabs there was a whole treasure of gold beads and ear-rings and pendants and one gold pin topped with a little figure of a woman wearing a long dress. Somebody, probably in a moment of danger, had buried here part of the temple treasure, perhaps the ornaments worn by the statue of the goddess, and had never recovered his *cache*. The interesting thing about it (which in our inexperience we could not recognize at the time, but came to see it later) was that the little hoard contained objects of many dates; some of them were of Neo-Babylonian or Persian manufacture, but some of the beads were of types characteristic of times as remote as the reign of Sargon of Akkad; it illustrated well the fact that in temple treasuries things of value might be preserved not only for hundreds but for thousands of years. The discovery was as unexpected as it was interesting and, coming in the early days of our work at Ur, established our reputation. Nothing of the kind was found anywhere else in the room or in the other rooms of the temple, and nothing would convince the Arabs that we had chosen to lift those twelve bricks without knowing what lay beneath them.

Fortunately, the second pavement was there as well as the gold, and about one in every four of its bricks bore the long stamp of Nebuchadnezzar, and this lower floor reproduced in every particular that of the Persian period: there were the same benches, altars, and tables, and in the court outside the same altar in front of the door; only the second altar and the drain were missing, but the level between the wings of the building dropped as before to the wide outer court which reached to the temple walls.

The outer court was in bad condition, much of the pavement gone, and what remained curiously irregular, all in ridges and hollows. The reason for this was obvious from the outset and was proved as the work was carried down deeper: it had been laid over a series of chambers, and where the floor rested on the wall-tops it kept its level and where it had beneath it only the rubbish with which the old rooms were filled it had sunk or broken up altogether. These buried rooms were the store-chambers of the E-nun-makh of Kurigalzu's time, built by the Kassite king exactly on the lines laid down by his Larsa and Third Dynasty predecessors; all those early rulers (whose work has already been described in my former chapters) had preserved the original groundplan unchanged. According to that plan the small five-chambered sanctuary was a thing apart; it lay at the back of the building and was reached only by a passage which ran round three of its sides; on the other side of the passage there were store-rooms and priests' chambers occupying the whole of the rest of the temple area and completely masking the sanctuary—it was hidden away and made as difficult of access as might be. I have said that the sanctuary rooms were very small and would hold but few people at a time; taking this in conjunction with its inaccessibility, we are driven tlo conclude that E-nun-makh was designed for a secret ritua such as might be fitting in what was really a harem temple, the special quarters of the god as married: only the priests would enter here and in privacy wait upon the twin deities.

This ancient tradition was completely set at naught by Nebuchadnezzar, when he restored the temple; a comparison of the plans on Figs. 8 and 19 will make this evident.

The sanctuary itself, the small separate block with its five chambers, was preserved, but all the magazines in front of it were swept away. On either side of the sanctuary new wings were built, projecting so as to form three sides of a square, but the whole front of the original shrine was opened up; where the passage had been there was a raised pavement in the centre of which an altar rose, a statue-base was erected in the antechamber of the sanctuary facing its door, and where had been a maze of chambers the wide lower court afforded accommodation for a crowd of spectators. In the old temple everything had been secret; now a numerous public could watch the priest making his offerings on the open-air altar and behind him could see through the dim sanctuary's open door the image of the god.

There is no doubt that the remodelling of the building implies such a change of ritual, but how can this itself be explained? The answer is given by the Old Testament story of the Three Children in the Book of Daniel. However miraculous a tale may be, its setting must have a certain verisimilitude, must contain some element of truth. Now, the gist of the story is this, that Nebuchadnezzar made a great image and set it up in a public place and ordered that at a given signal everybody was to fall down and worship it; the Jews, who seem to have lived hitherto undisturbed in the land of their captivity, were by this order given the choice between idolatry and disobedience involving death. What was there new in the king's act? Not the setting up of a statue, because each king in turn had done the same; the novelty was the command for general worship by the public: for a ritual performed by priests the king is substituting a form of congregational worship which all his subjects are obliged to attend. So striking is the correspondence between the written story and the facts of the ruins and so completely do they explain each other that we must needs accept the background of the legend as historical. The alterations in E-nun-makh were designed deliberately with a view to the religious reform attributed to its builder by the Old Testament.

It seems fairly certain that some of the innovations made by Nebuchadnezzar were disapproved of by his more orthodox successor Nabonidus—possibly the unpopularity of the later king was in part due to his reversing a religious policy which had found favour with the priests but did not accord with the ancient traditions which Nabonidus so sincerely reverenced. This would account for the rebuilding by

Nabonidus of temples which had been 'restored' so recently that they could not have required any further work unless indeed it was to correct what had been in his opinion wrongly done; it also accounts for the difficulty which we sometimes experienced in attributing a building to one rather than to the other king when the names of both appeared on its bricks. The 'Harbour Temple' was a case in point.

To the east of the harbour basin at the north end of the city there was a low mound, much disturbed by modern seekers after treasure, on which were lying bricks stamped with the name of Nabonidus; many were loose, but some were still in position, patches of pavement belonging to a building of which no walls were visible. Obviously if the pavement lay at modern ground level there could not be much of the building left, but reckoning that the foundations of the walls must remain below-ground and would give us the plan of the structure we started to trench the area and the brickwork duly appeared. To our great surprise however it was the brickwork not of a few foundation-courses but of walls which went ever deeper down until at last we found their footings twenty-one feet below the modern surface. The excavation was the simplest job possible, for all that was required was to clear out the mass of perfectly pure sand that filled the building; when it was done we had what at first sight seemed to be a normal Babylonian temple so well preserved that we spread a matting roof over it, from wall to wall, (not merely for effect, but to protect it from drifting sand), and one could walk about in it forgetting the centuries (Fig. 20, and *Plate* 30a). It was a mud-brick building, but the external walls were faced with a three-foot skin of burnt brick. The entrance was from doors at either end of a passage on the south-west side and so into a forecourt at the south-east end in which stood a brick altar or 'table of offerings' and two more 'tables of offerings' flanked the great doorway leading to the inner court. Here again was a central altar of brick and a table of offerings; beyond was the sanctuary with two more tables and, set in a niche in the back wall, the massive brick base on which the statue of the god would stand. Behind this was the oracle-chamber. The

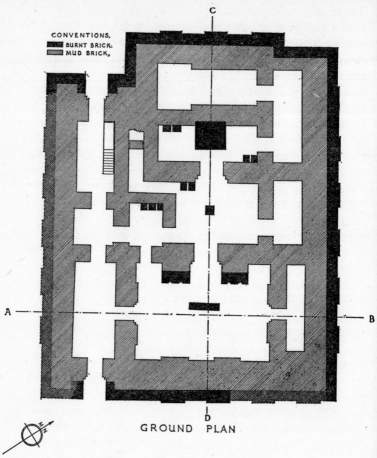

CONVENTIONS.
⬛ BURNT BRICK.
▨ MUD BRICK.

GROUND PLAN

Fig. 20. The Harbour Temple

burnt bricks of the outer walls and of tables and altars bore
the stamp of Nebuchadnezzar, so that the authorship seemed
to be undoubted; the plan was quite conventional, the walls,
smoothly mud-plastered and whitewashed (the whitewash
was wonderfully well preserved) presented no difficulty at
first except that one might perhaps have expected a somewhat more ambitious decoration for the temple sanctuary.
But there was a great deal that did call for explanation.

Those whitewashed walls had no foundations at all; they rested on the sand, and the whitewash went down to cover the bottom course. There was no pavement or floor, only the sand which we left on the level of the walls' base. The filling had shown no stratification, it was all uniform clean sand, right up to the pavement laid by Nabonidus twenty feet above our 'floor'. But the strangest thing concerned the furnishings; the altar, the tables and the statue-base were built up to the height usual for such (the tables 18 inches, the altar 3 feet) with bricks carefully and truly laid; but above this there was more brickwork very irregularly laid rising to the full height of the surrounding walls; thus the table in the outer court, which was of the normal long and narrow shape, took on the effect of a brick screen and the altar in the inner court became a brick column; no one could have placed offerings or done sacrifice on them. Clearly an explanation was called for.

In a very ancient text a governor of Lagash describes his building of a temple: 'The ground to a depth of (?) ells he dug out, the earth he . . . refined with fire. In accordance with its proportions he laid out a great building-area, therein he brought its earth back again, therein he laid the foundations and thereover built he a substructure ten ells high. Over the substructure the temple, thirty ells high, did he build.' The builder of our Harbour Temple began by digging a deep rectangular pit in the bottom of which he laid out the ground-plan of the temple, and accordingly he built walls to the height of just over twenty feet; these were neatly plastered and whitewashed. In the temple he built in burnt brick the proper tables of offering, altar and statue-base, fixed doors in the doorways and put on a temporary roof perhaps, like ours, of poles and matting—we found high up in the walls holes for brackets that would have supported the roof framework. Undoubtedly there was a service of consecration in the building, with the god's statue set on its base. After that, the roof was taken off and the whole building was filled with sand; the old earth that had been dug out could not be purified, considering the mixed nature of the soil here inside the city walls, but clean sand would be a perfectly good substitute. As the sand was poured in from above workmen laid bricks on the altar and tables, keeping pace with the rise of the sand (the fact that they were working from above would account for the irregular brick-laying) until, when the whole was filled, there could be seen only as it were a groundplan formed by the tops of the walls and of the temple furnishings, flush with the smooth sand surface. Then there began a new phase. The sand was topped with a pavement of burnt bricks, on the top of the walls, now become a foundation, new walls were built (to the height of sixty feet, if the ancient precedent was faithfully observed) and new tables and altar, built above-ground, rested on the bricks piled above the old. This was the temple in which man worshipped his god and did sacrifice; it derived its peculiar sanctity from the fact that it not only was a replica of but was based directly on the real house of god, inaccessible to man; the altar on which the priest made his sacrifice was holy because it was one with the altar of that hidden and inviolate shrine. The Lagash text which I quoted above reads like a dry and matter-of-fact architectural formula and of all the temples yet excavated in Mesopotamia only our Harbour Temple conforms to it; but the actual building gives us, as the text does not, the religious significance of the builders' ritual and illustrates an idea far more spiritual than is generally to be found in Babylon.

It was tempting to assume that Nabonidus, with his antiquarian tastes, was responsible for the whole building and had merely, for economy's sake, used old bricks of Nebuchadnezzar for the underground part, but even if Nebuchadnezzar was the original builder Nabonidus had chosen to set his personal seal on the work when he took it over, as he did, for purposes of his own; he may simply have laid a new pavement of bricks bearing his name in a temple already standing, but the temple was now to serve a new function.

From the entrance-door at the north-west end of the temple passage a brick causeway ran northwards to the wall of a huge building (its maximum measures were about three hundred and twenty-five feet by three hundred) founded by Nabonidus and called by him E-Gig-Par (Fig. 21). The

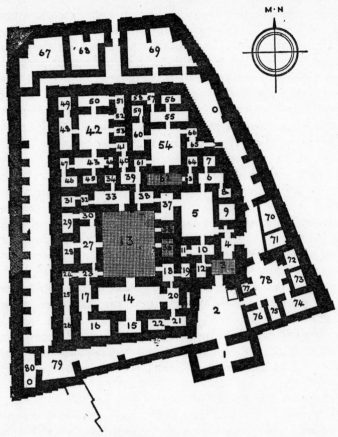

Fig. 21. The Palace of Nabonidus

construction throughout was in mud brick. The irregular
outline seems to have been due to the existence of other
buildings to the east which followed the orientation of the old
city wall, whereas the main axis of the new building was to
be directly north by south; the sides therefore are not
parallel. The enclosing wall is, on three sides, relieved by
the shallow rectangular buttresses traditional in Sumerian
architecture; but the east side (and a short section of the
south side also) present a feature which, so far as we know, is
purely Late Babylonian; the bricks are laid not parallel to

233

the general direction of the wall but at a slight angle with it and whenever the brick face projects sufficiently beyond the wall line (the projection is usually about a foot) the brickwork is stepped back to that line and thence is built out again to a fresh projection; the result is a series of stepped 'buttresses' like the teeth of a saw. This very curious form of decoration—for it must be decorative only, since it serves no practical purpose, whereas the vertical bands of light and shade do most effectively relieve the dullness of an otherwise blank wall—is commonly found in the houses of Nebuchadnezzar's Babylon and also in the Late Babylonian houses of Ur. Inside the enclosing wall but separated from it by a broad passage lies the building proper, this too having two of its walls buttressed in the normal way and two with the saw-tooth type of decoration. There were two entrances to the enclosure. At the north end there was a postern-gate flanked by large magazines; under its pavement we found eight brick 'sentry-boxes' containing the painted mud figures of the protective gods and five mud dog guardians. The main entrance was in the south wall, and this gave directly on the doorway of the inner building which lay back at the far side of a large open court and had against one of its jambs a big bitumen-lined tank for the domestic water supply. At first sight this inner building with its criss-cross of walls dividing it into sixty-four rooms looked like a meaningless labyrinth; but in reality it is a well-ordered residential complex. The rooms are ranged round light-wells (Nos. 5, 13, 42 and 54 on the plan); the principal residence is to the south, where room 13 is its light-well and opening on to it on the south is a reception-room (14) whose unusually solid walls suggest that it rose to a great height; the other blocks are evidently subordinate to this, but they are similarly arranged though on a smaller scale. Exactly similar arrangements are found in the secular buildings of Babylon.

Clearly this is a secular building, but none the less it is intimately associated with the Harbour Temple. Not only are the two close to one another, but south of the building there stretched a great square courtyard enclosed by walls and having a pylon gateway on its south side which included the Harbour Temple also; the latter therefore becomes an appendage of the great residence.

When Taylor dug at Ur, a century ago, he found an inscribed clay cylinder of Nabonidus which explains our building. 'On the thirteenth day of the month Elul,' he says, 'the moon grew dark and entered on his eclipse; "Nannar desires a priestess", such was (the meaning of) the portent.' Repeated sacrifices and consultations of the oracles made it clear at last that the priestess was to be none other than the king's daughter—the ancient custom which we have seen in force since the reign of Sargon of Akkad and even earlier than that was to be revived in these latter days. Nabonidus therefore dedicated his daughter as High Priestess of Nannar at Ur, giving her the name of Belshalti-Nannar, and he repaired for her, he states, the ancient building E-Gig-Par in which the priestesses of old had lived. There can be no doubt but that the great palace which we unearthed was that of the royal priestess, the sister of Belshazzar who in the book of Daniel figures as the giver of the feast at which the destruction of Babylon was foretold by the prophet; her father built for her a residence modelled on the palaces of the capital city, and he devoted to her use as a domestic chapel the Harbour Temple which he had either founded or taken over from his predecessor. The proof of this is of course the name of the building, E-Gig-Par, stamped on the bricks of its pavements, this being the name given in his cylinder inscription to the house built for the princess. But the palace is a new foundation whereas the inscription on the cylinder states that E-Gig-Par was an ancient building which he had to repair; there was here an apparent contradiction, but the difficulty was solved by the discovery that there were two E-Gig-Pars of Nabonidus, the second of which was on what the king might well suppose to have been the original site. It was not quite that, but it had a certain tradition behind it.

The great temple and priestly residence which was the Gig-par-ku of the Third Dynasty of Ur, which as such had been rebuilt by the Larsa and by the Kassite kings, had long since disappeared. When in Assyrian times Sin-balatsu-iqbi had restored the ancient shrines of Ur he had adapted to the use of the priesthood the Larsa and Kassite buildings on the adjoining site with an enlarged Dublal-makh as chapel and living-quarters at the south end of the Dublal-makh court-yard. This then was E-Gig-Par, and, as the brick-stamps prove, Nabonidus piously restored it.

But the quarters which an Assyrian governor had deemed adequate for the local priesthood would not satisfy a princess; they would house the junior ranks of the nunnery, but the royal Mother Superior required a palace, and since there was no room for such inside the Temenos it had to be built outside; but the traditional name was extended to cover the new building also.

The shrine of Dublal-makh was preserved very much as it had been in Assyrian times but the courtyard buildings were remodelled and enlarged; one part (see Fig. 19) was clearly residential, other rooms seemed to be offices for the conduct of temple business. Here we found quantities of clay tablets, receipts and vouchers for the issue of goods stored in the temple magazines, inventories, accounts, wage lists and so on. But another discovery threw yet more light on the character of the king's daughter. In a very much ruined room whose mud-brick walls rose scarcely above pavement level, one of the rooms fronting on the court which we had taken to be the business offices of the temple, we found a number of clay tablets of what are called the 'school exercise' type; they are flat discs of clay used for the teaching of writing. On one side the master inscribed his 'fair copy', some easy sentence often taken from a well-known text, and the tablet was then handed to the scholar, who, after studying it, turned it over and on the back tried to reproduce what he had read; some-times the copy is very faulty and sometimes the boy has made a second attempt on the same tablet. We found a number of these, and with them broken fragments of other 'school' texts, bits of syllabaries giving columns of words all beginning with the same syllable, much like an old-fashioned English spelling book, and one fragment of a dictionary on which was an en-dorsement 'the property of the boys' class'. Here was definite proof that the priestesses kept a school on their premises.

And a still more up-to-date touch was given by the contents of the next room. The pavement was very close to the modern surface, which was terribly denuded by weather, and not more than a foot of loose rubbish covered the brickwork; there seemed little hope of finding anything in such a spot. But suddenly the workmen brought to light a large oval-topped black stone whose top was covered with carvings in relief and its sides with inscriptions; it was a boundary-stone described above (p. 206) belonging to the Kassite period of about 1400 B.C. Almost touching it was a fragment of a diorite statue, a bit of the arm of a human figure on which was an inscription, and the fragment had been carefully trimmed so as to make it look neat and to preserve the writing; and the name on the statue was that of Dungi, who was king of Ur in 2058 B.C. Then came a clay foundation-cone of a Larsa king of about 1700 B.C., then a few clay tablets of about the same date, and a large votive stone mace-head which was uninscribed but may well have been more ancient by five hundred years.

What were we to think? Here were half a dozen diverse objects found lying on an unbroken brick pavement of the sixth century B.C., yet the newest of them was seven hundred years older than the pavement and the earliest perhaps sixteen hundred: the evidence was altogether against their having got there by accident, and the trimming of the statue-inscription had a curious air of purpose.

Then we found the key. A little way apart lay a small drum-shaped clay object [*Plate* 31a] on which were four columns of writing; the first three columns were in the old Sumerian language, and the contents of one at least were familiar to us, for we had found it on bricks of Bur-Sin, king of Ur in 2005 B.C., and the other two were fairly similar; the fourth column was in the late Semitic speech. 'These,' it said, 'are copies from bricks found in the ruins of Ur, the work of Bur-Sin king of Ur, which while searching for the ground-plan [of the temple] the Governor of Ur found, and I saw and wrote out for the marvel of beholders.' The scribe, alas! was not so learned as he wished to appear, for his copies are so full of blunders as to be almost unintelligible, but he had doubtless done his best, and he certainly had given us the explanation we wanted. The room was a museum of local antiquities maintained by the princess Belshalti-Nannar (who in this took after her father, a keen archæologist), and in the collection was this clay drum, the earliest museum label known, drawn up a hundred years before and kept, presumably together with the original bricks, as a record of the first scientific excavations at Ur.

Another antiquity belonged, apparently, not to the Museum but to the temple building. In front of one of the side doors of the antechamber of Dublal-makh there lay a round-topped limestone relief on which was represented the god Ea, patron deity of the ancient city of Eridu whose ruins break the line of the horizon some twelve miles to the south-west of Ur. According to the old Sumerian convention the god is shown holding a vase from which two streams of water are pouring to the ground, while fish are swimming up and down in the streams; as lord of the Waters of the Abyss Ea holds the source from which rise the twin rivers Tigris and Euphrates, givers of life to the land of Mesopotamia. The relief may have decorated the space above the door, but if so it was re-used, for it has nothing really to do with this Late Babylonian building but is a product of the sculptor's art of the Third Dynasty.

Another object, found this time by the door of the kitchen which Nabonidus added to the sanctuary, was certainly of contemporary date, but it again was a stranger to its surroundings. Crushed together under a fallen brick we found at least a hundred slithers of ivory, many of them minute in size and as thin as tissue-paper, the ivory having rotted and split into its natural laminations: so delicate were they that they had to be hardened with celluloid before they could be picked up from the ground. When put together, the fragments took shape as a circular toilet-box decorated with figures of dancing girls carved on it in relief; Egyptian rather than Oriental in style, the row of maidens hold hands and make a ring around the casket. This box was never made in Mesopotamia; it is the work of one of those Phœnician craftsmen of Sidon or of Tyre whose skill in ivory-carving had made them famous throughout the Mediterranean world; as an imported object it must have been a thing of price—indeed, that it was valued is clear, for it had been broken and riveted in antiquity—and possibly it belonged to the princess Belshalti-Nannar herself [*Plate* 31*b*].

In view of the immense amount of labour spent on the construction of the Temenos Wall one can assume that all the old buildings inside that Sacred Area were restored by Nebuchadnezzar and Nabonidus. But much of that area—at least half of it—has been so denuded by weather that scarcely a vestige of Late Babylonian work remains. But reconstruction was not confined to the Temenos. Our excavations on the line of the city wall brought to light here and there sections of late walling which were far too fragmentary to give an intelligible groundplan but did seem to show that Nebuchadnezzar had made some attempt to put in order the town defences. The ancient rampart, whose sharply-sloping face of mud brick had been patched often enough, was still serviceable, with a certain amount of repair, and it seems now to have been capped with a wall which incorporated the walls of various existing buildings but where there were none such was built *ad hoc*, linking them in a continuous line. One of the buildings utilized in this way was a temple at the south end of the city—the temple which in the time of the Third Dynasty of Ur had columns of mud brick (see above, p. 142); this was restored by Nebuchadnezzar. We found nothing that could tell us to what god the building was dedicated, nor was it of particular interest in itself, but it acquired interest from the method of its discovery, which was one of the lucky accidents of archæological work. We were clearing the top of the city rampart which at this point seemed surprisingly wide; all upstanding walls had been denuded away and when the men scraped off the few inches of surface sand there appeared only the smooth level of weather-worn mud brick. One workman, smarter than the rest, noticed that the bricks were not uniform in colour, some being reddish and some grey, and that the patch of grey bricks which he was working on began to take definite shape, and then that between the grey bricks and the red there was a line of white about as thick as stout paper. Actually this was Nebuchadnezzar's temple. The redder bricks were the foundation of the pavements, all the burnt bricks of which had gone; the grey bricks were those of the walls, and the white line was the whitewash which, applied to the upper part of the now vanished walls had trickled down between wall and floor. On such evidence we were able to work out the entire plan of the temple, and this we could verify later when we dug away the floors and exposed the wall foundations. In the following year precisely similar evidence enabled the German excavators at Erech to identify and plan the 'White Temple', one of the oldest buildings on the site; but the credit for first recognizing the importance of a mud-brick colour-scheme must go to our Ur workman.

The Neo-Babylonian period saw the temples and public monuments of Ur restored not indeed to their pristine splendour but at least to a condition better than had been known for many centuries; but the city which was thus adorned by the last kings of Babylon was a very different one from that which flourished in the times of the Third Dynasty of Ur and under the Larsa rulers.

I have described the crowded houses of the Larsa period (above, p. 175) with their evidence of prosperous trade and manufacture. All of them had gone. To what extent they had been preserved throughout the long Kassite period, or what had replaced them, there was virtually nothing to show; in the end the ruins of them, or of their successors, had been razed to the ground and on the higher level so formed a new town had sprung up. None of the houses went back to a time earlier than the Neo-Babylonian—they were all new foundations. It really looked as if Nebuchadnezzar's boast 'Is not this great Babylon which I have built,' applied equally to Ur. Of course we have to generalize from rather limited data because in few spots where we dug had buildings of so late a date escaped the effects of time and weather; but two sites did provide good evidence. In the low-lying ground north-west of the Temenos we found poor houses of the period in tolerably good condition—poor houses, because it was a bad site where nobody would live if he could avoid it, in good condition because instead of lying exposed to wind and rain their ruins had been buried by the debris washed down from the Ziggurat terrace. They were small and shoddy huts, one storey high, crowded together without plan or system, the typical slum of any oriental city. But another dig gave us much more illuminating results. Immediately south of the big group of Larsa houses excavated by us the modern ground-level rose to form a hillock, due, I suppose, to some vagary of wind currents, and excavation here laid bare the remains of houses which can probably be taken as typical of the main part of the late town (Fig. 22). It bore a striking resemblance to Babylon. The streets were wide and straight, with branch streets or sometimes rather narrow alleys at right angles to them separating the building-blocks. The houses were of mud brick only, lacking altogether the burnt-brick 'damp-courses' of earlier times, and very often their outer walls were built with the close-set 'saw-tooth' re-entrant angles which we found in the case of Belshalti-Nannar's palace. They were of one story only, the flat roof probably being used for 'sitting-out' purposes; the general plan was that of rooms ranged round a central court; on one side of the court, facing the entrance, was the reception-room with a retiring-room behind it and rooms of a more private nature on either side, with kitchen and other domestic chambers in the background. A curious thing was that in several cases the lay-out of the interior, while strictly regular in itself, was entirely askew with the containing-walls. It looks as if the direction of the streets, which of course determined the orientation of the house blocks, had been imposed on the builders by some arbitrary authority whereas everybody knew that a house must be sited in such a way that the reception-room faced the north and had the benefit of the cool breezes in hot weather; I cannot otherwise account for the very awkward clash between town planning and domestic architecture, and if my explanation is correct it would support the view that Ur was rebuilt on Nebuchadnezzar's order.

The most surprising thing was the size of the houses. Since

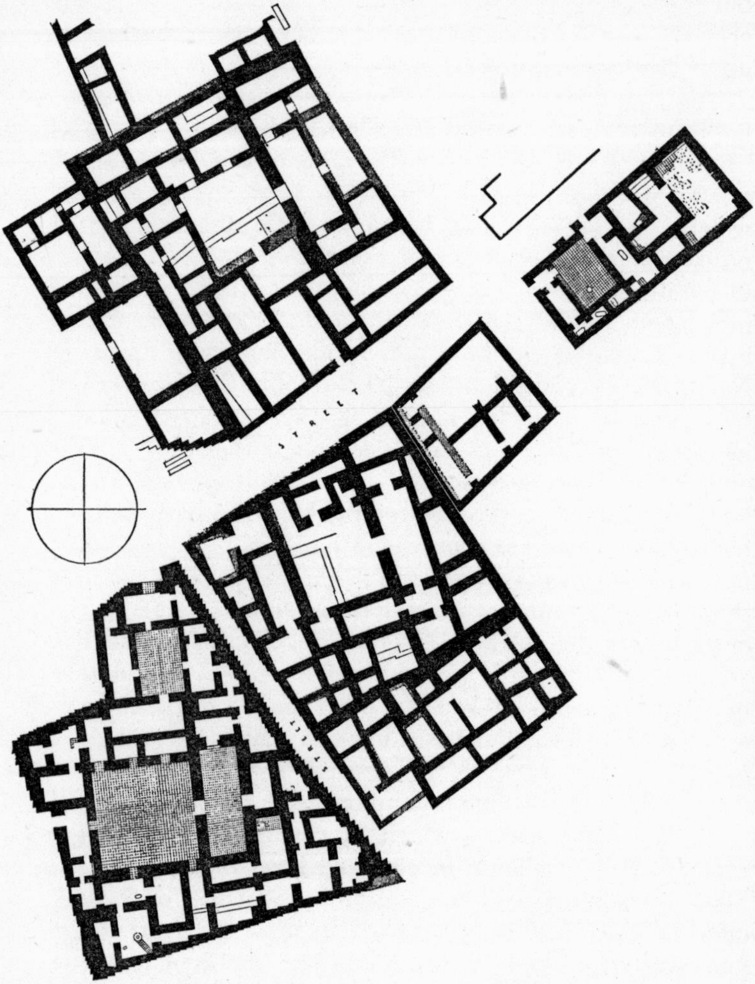

STREET

STREET

Fig. 50. Houses of the Late Babylonian period

242

all the accommodation had to be on one floor they would naturally be larger than the two-story houses of Larsa times; but these are great sprawling structures one of which may occupy an entire block measuring 150 feet by 130, and take up an area which in the Larsa town would have contained fourteen or fifteen houses. This must mean a tremendous fall in the value of building sites in the city, and that in its turn must imply that the population had been reduced to a fraction of what it had been in the old days. The people who were housed on such a scale were presumably wealthy, but no tablets bear witness to any great commercial prosperity. One family archive, covering several generations, was found in a large clay pot in one of the houses and does suggest at least what happened at Ur. In the reign of Nabopolassar, Nebuchadnezzar's father, the head of the family, Sin-uballit by name, lived at Babylon where he was in business—incidentally not too successfully, it would seem, seeing that of thirty-five documents bearing his name no less than seventeen record loans contracted by him. Later the family moved to Ur and occupied one of these great houses. If Nebuchadnezzar was trying to rehabilitate the decaying city his big programme of temple building (and perhaps his laying-out of the new town) is likely to have been accompanied by an attempt to recall to Ur families which had drifted away to more prosperous centres; one is tempted to think that a government housing subvention accounted for the spacious quarters in which the returned citizens established themselves.

An influx of people from 'foreign' parts would certainly explain a change in what is generally most conservative, the ritual of burial. We still find in the Neo-Babylonian Period, under the floors of the houses, the oval terra-cotta coffins, sometimes containing, sometimes inverted over the dead, which had been the mode for a thousand years; but side by side with those there are 'double pot burials' in which two big clay jars are laid on their sides, rim to rim, and the body is half in one and half in the other; it is a custom introduced from Babylon, and we do not find it at Ur until the reign of Nebuchadnezzar.

Nebuchadnezzar's motive in restoring Ur was doubtless political—to consolidate the South against any danger from a revived Assyria or from the Medes—also it satisfied his love of building. Nabonidus was actuated by religious zeal; he was a native of Harran where his father seems to have been High Priest of the Moon-god and Ur, as the main seat of that god's worship, could not fail to appeal to him. Neither considered the economics of the question, but the fact was that Ur had flourished as a trading and manufacturing city and now that trade had left it there was little reason for it to exist; the Neo-Babylonian reconstruction was wholly artificial and could hardly be expected to last. Then came the dramatic end of the dynasty as foretold by Daniel the prophet 'thy kingdom is divided and given to the Medes and Persians'; the governor of the Babylonian provinces east of the Tigris rebelled and marched against the capital; Belshazzar the king's son and co-regent fell in battle and Babylon was betrayed into the hands of the enemy and almost without striking a blow Cyrus King of Persia added the whole of Babylonia to his dominions. To the citizens of Ur it must have seemed that all was over, for the foe against whom its defences had been repaired now held it for his own, and the conqueror worshipped other gods than those honoured in its temples. How then should Ur go on?

But it was the unexpected that happened.

When we were tracing the course of the great Temenos Wall built by Nebuchadnezzar we found in one of the northeast gates the stone door-sockets in position in the brick boxes which kept the earth away from the hinge, and the bricks bore the inscription of Cyrus; the new ruler had repaired the circuit wall of Nannar's temple, and, as we have seen, it was almost certainly he who was responsible for the last restoration of E-nun-makh, the joint shrine of Nannar and Nin-gal. The inscription on the bricks has a familiar ring; 'the great gods have delivered all the lands into my hand', it begins, and we think of the proclamation of Cyrus in the Book of Ezra which also had to do with the restoration of a temple: 'The Lord God of Heaven hath given me all the kingdoms of the earth; and he hath charged me to build him an house at Jerusalem, which is in Judah.' That act of clemency, which to the captive Jews appeared miraculous, was an incident in a scheme applied to the whole kingdom: whether the god was Jehovah or Nannar mattered little to Cyrus; his purpose was to placate his people by subsidizing their particular forms of worship, and the temples of Ur gained a fresh lease of life from the catholic generosity of the Persian.

Unfortunately the denudation of the upper levels over the whole site of Ur has left us very little material to illustrate this last phase. The big Neo-Babylonian houses continued in use, handed down from father to son with little or no change. We found in them a fair number of tablets of a business sort, but it is always business on a small scale and of a local sort, the sale of a parcel of garden land, of a house or a slave, the lease of a property or the hire of labour, loans and debts—there are plenty of those—or questions of adoption and inheritance; they are the affairs not of a commercial city but of a country town. Not that people were so poor; in E-nun-makh we found on the Persian pavement a very beautiful bowl of veined agate and an ivory bowl with a handle in the form of two naked children carved in the round, both of them presumably offerings to the temple made by citizens. It was in a Persian house that we found the finest example of decorative stone carving that our excavations produced, a steatite bowl round which goes a procession of oxen carved in high relief [*Plate* 5*b*]; it is certainly not of Persian date—indeed it might go back to the Jamdat Nasr period, and how it came to be in a Persian's possession we cannot say but it must have been treasured as an antiquity. Even the domestic pottery suggests a comfortable pattern of life, for it is much better than was in use in older days and in particular we have now vessels of green-glazed earthenware some of which are highly decorative; that yet finer objects were in use was proved by the discovery in one house of a fluted silver bowl of exquisite workmanship. And another discovery told the same tale. Dug down into the buried ruins of the ancient Gig-par-ku temple from a Persian house of which every brick had disappeared we found two coffins each containing the body of a woman wrapped in linen and woollen cloths and adorned with beads of agate and gold and gold ear-rings; with them were glazed earthenware vases and one had also a bronze mirror and a godrooned bronze bowl, and there were too baskets and wooden vessels, these hopelessly decayed. The contents of the graves were moderately but not excessively rich; what was surprising was the coffins themselves, for they were of sheet copper elaborately riveted along the top and bottom and down the sides where there were upright stays; the coffins were of the usual Persian shape, oblong with one square and one rounded end, and at either end they had solid copper handles [*Plate* 32]. Innumerable Persian graves have been excavated but only one other such metal coffin has ever yet been found, and the presence of so rare a luxury must be set against the apparent poverty of buildings when we try to estimate conditions at Ur in Persian times.

Incidentally, our finding of the coffins had a curious sequel. One was in a very bad state, the metal badly decayed, the other relatively well preserved, but we did manage, with some difficulty, to lift them both and bring them back to London. There they remained many years, and at last the worse of the two, being a duplicate, was presented to the Birmingham City Museum. The authorities there were trying to mount for exhibition what seemed to be a sorry specimen when a piece of corroded metal flaked off one of the stays and brought to view an engraved pattern. Systematic cleaning produced on either stay a very lively engraved decoration of animals and flowers; the British Museum coffin was similarly treated and gave similar results. Almost at the same time there was published an object found in Persia and now in an American museum, a strip of copper which, as we can now see, is a coffin-stay, and it has the same engraved designs so exactly reproducing those from Ur that it must come from the same workshop as our coffins. But whether they were all made in Ur or in Persia there is no means of telling.

Another Persian coffin, found almost flush with the modern surface of the ground, yielded a no less surprising discovery. It had been plundered and there were left in it only a few fragments of broken bones and not even a clay pot; but, overlooked in the dust that covered the coffin's floor there was a collection of nearly two hundred seal-impressions in clay. 'Collection' is the right word, for the lumps of soft clay had been pressed against the gems (the finger-marks were plain on the back and there was no hole through which a string could have passed) and had then been baked to make them permanent; they were illustrations of the gems in a collector's cabinet. And the collector had been a man of catholic tastes; Greece, Egypt, Babylon, Assyria and Persia are all represented and witness to the varied artistic influences that were brought to bear on the Mesopotamian valley under the cosmopolitan rule of the Persians and the Macedonians.

The dated tablets in the Persian houses take our history down to the end of the fourth century B.C.—we have one of the reign of Alexander the Great and one of the seventh year of Philip Arrhidaeus of Macedon, 316 B.C. But though there may have still been rich men and artistic *dilettanti* at Ur, the city was dying none the less. The State religion of Persia had changed to Zoroastrian monotheism and the ancient gods were out of favour; even if there were no deliberate destruction of the old temples the neglect of them was almost as fatal. Inside the Sacred Area, against the south-west wall of the Ziggurat itself, a Persian potter set up his kilns and plied a sacrilegious trade; we found the 'wasters', the pots damaged in the firing, and the little clay tripods which kept apart the plates piled in the kiln and prevented the glaze from sticking them one to another, mixed in the rubbish with the blue-glazed bricks fallen from the walls of the temple which Nabonidus had built as the Ziggurat's crowning glory. In the west corner of the Temenos where Nannar's shrine had been we found above the rubbish that buried the Neo-Babylonian court scanty remains of the latest Persian period, walls crooked and irregularly aligned, without regard to the orientation of the Ziggurat hard by, ill built, sometimes of mud brick, sometimes of burnt bricks, whole or broken, bearing the names of divers kings, collected from the ruins of old buildings and now roughly relaid in mud mortar; the whole spoke eloquently of poverty and decay. Circular brick-lined pits sunk in the floors of rooms showed that they were used as stores and granaries. Under the floor of one room we found a pot containing unbaked tablets; most of them had reverted to their native mud, but one or two were legible in part at least, and they proved that these miserable chambers belonged to the priests of Nannar and that tithes were still being brought by the faithful to what must have been already a ruined shrine.

It was probably at the close of the fourth century that the event occurred which was to seal for ever the doom of Ur. In the old days the river Euphrates, or an important branch of the river, washed the walls of Ur on the west, and from it innumerable canals big and small led the water off into the fields which spread far across the plain, and up and down the main canals went the ships bringing trade from the Persian Gulf and from the other towns on the river-banks. To-day the Euphrates runs ten miles to the east of the ruins and the great plain is a barren desert. When the river changed its course we do not yet know, but the drying-up of the old bed meant the stoppage of water-borne traffic, the ruin of the whole elaborate system of irrigation, and the end of agriculture; there was not the energy or the capital for the installation of a new system, and the starving city had no longer any reason for existence. Gradually the inhabitants moved away to other homes, the houses crumbled, the winds sweeping across the now parched and desiccated levels brought clouds of sand which they dropped under the lee of the standing walls, and what had been a great city became a wilderness of brick-littered mounds rising from the waste.

APPENDIX

[Appendix]

The Sumerian King-list

SINCE the King-list is referred to several times in this book I print it here almost at full length, although the greater part of it does not really concern us. As a guide to the reader I have put an asterisk against the names that do occur in the text, and I have inserted various dates so as to give some sort of time scale. The dates are at best approximate but from the time of the Third Dynasty of Ur onwards the margin of error is not great; where authorities still differ I have based myself on the system of Professor Sidney Smith which in my opinion corresponds best to the facts.

A. THE KINGS BEFORE THE FLOOD

Name	City	Length of reign
A-lu-lim	NUN^{ki}	28,000 years
A-la(l)-gar	NUN^{ki}	36,000 years
En-me-en-lu-an-na	Bad-tabira	43,000 years
En-me-en-gal-an-na	Bad-tabira	28,800 years
Dumuzu 'the shepherd'	Bad-tabira	36,000 years
En-Sib-zi-an-na	Larak	28,800 years
En-me-en-dur-an-na	Suruppak	18,600 years

(Total), 8 kings, 5 cities, 241,200 years

The Flood came. After the Flood came, kingship again
was sent down from on high.

251

B. THE KINGS AFTER THE FLOOD.

The First Dynasty of Kish

1. GA-UR	1,200 years	14. Ba-li-ih	400 years
2. GUL-la-		15. En-me-	
Nidaba-an-na	960 years	nun-na	660 years
3. (?)		16. Me-lam-kish	900 years
4. (?)		17. Bar-rak-	
5. Ba-.		nun-na	1,200 years
6. (?)		18. Mes-za-. . .	140 years
7. Ga-li-bu-um	360 years	19. Ti-iz-gar	306 years
8. Ka-lu-mu-mu	840 years	20. Il-ku-u	900 years
9. Ka-ga-gi-ib	900 years	21. Il-ta-sa-	
10. A-tab	600 years	du-um	1,200 years
11. A-tab-ba	840 years	22. En-me-en-	
12. Ar-pi-um	720 years	bara-gi-si	900 years
13. Etana	1,500 years	23. Ag-ga	625 years

(Total) 23 kings, 24,510 years

The First Dynasty of Erech

1. Mes-ki-ag-ga-se-ir	325 years	7. Utul-kalamma	15 years
2. En-me-kar	420 years	8. Labasher	9 years
3. Lugalbanda	1,200 years	9. Ennunadanna	8 years
4. Dumuzu	100 years	10. . . . he-de	56 years
5. Gilgamish	126 years	11. Me-lam-an-na	6 years
6. Ur-Nungal	30 years	12. Lugal-ki-aga	36 years

(Total) 12 kings, 2,310 years

The First Dynasty of Ur

*1. Mes-an-ni-pad-da	80 years	3. Elulu	25 years
(c. 2700 B.C.)		4. Balulu	36 years
*(1A. A-an-ni-pad-da)			
2. Mes-ki-ag-Nannar	36 years		

(Total) 4 kings (*should be five*), 177 years

The Dynasty of Awan

(Total) 3 kings, 356 years

The Second Dynasty of Kish

1. (?)	201 years	5. KU-E	300 years
2. Da-da-sig	(?)	6. . . . nun-na	180 years
3. Ma-ma-gal-la	360 years	7. I-bi-ni- . . .	290 years
4. Ka-al-bu- . . .	195 years	8. Lugal-mu	360 years

(Total) 8 kings, 3,195 years

The Dynasty of Hamasi
Hadanish 360 years
(Total) one king, 360 years

The Second Dynasty of Erech
En-uk-du-an-na 60 years
(Total) Kingship lasted 120 years. They ruled 480 years

*The Second Dynasty of Ur
(Total) 4 kings, 108 years

The Dynasty of Adab
Lugal-an-ni-mu-un-du 90 years
(Total) 1 king, 90 years

The Dynasty of Mari
(Total) 6 kings, 136 years

The Third Dynasty of Kish
KU-BAU (a woman wine-seller) 100 years

(*Note.* Many of the above dynasties must have been more or less contemporary, but we know nothing decisive about them. From this point onwards the amount of overlap can be better checked and the dynasties are therefore put in parallel columns.)

The Dynasty of Akshak (c. 2600 B.C.?)		Governors of Lagash (c. 2600 B.C. ?)	
Unzi	30 years	*Ur-Nina	30 years
Undalulu	6 years	Akurgal	
Urur	6 years	Eannatum I	
Puzur-Sahan	20 years	*Enannatum I	
Ishu-il	24 years	*Entemena (c. 2500)	
Gimil-Sin	7 years	Enannatum II	
		Enetarzi	
		Enliarri	
		Lugal-anda	
		Urukagina (c. 2380)	

The Dynasty of Agade (Akkad)		The Fourth Dynasty of Kish	
*Sargon (c. 2380)	55 years	Puzur-Sin	25 years
*Rimush	9 years	Ur-Ilbaba	6 years
Manishtusu	15 years	Zimudar	30 years
*Naram-Sin	55 years	Usi-watar	6 years
Shargalisharri	24 years	Ishtar-muti	11 years
'Who was King, who was		Ishme-Shamash	11 years
not King?'		Nannia	3 years

The Third Dynasty of Erech
Lugal-zaggisi 25 years

Governors of Lagash	The Dynasty of Gutium (c. 2228 B.C.)		The Fourth Dynasty of Erech	
Ur-Bau	Imta	3 years	Urinigin	7 years
Nam-makhni	Inkishu	6 years	Ur-gigir	6 years
Ur-gar	Nikillagab	6 years	Kudda	6 years
Dar-azag	Shulme	6 years	Puzur-ili	5 years
Lu-Bau	Elulumesh	6 years	Ur-Babba	6 years
Lu-Gula	Inimabakesh	5 years		
*Gudea	Igeshaush	6 years		
Ur-Ningirshu	Iarlagab	15 years		
Ur-lama	Ibate	3 years		
	Iarlagash	3 years		
	Kurum	1 year		
	. . .	3 years		
	. . .	2 years		
	Irarum	2 years		
	Ibranum	1 year		
	Hablum	2 years		
	Puzur-Sin	7 years		
	Iarlaganda	7 years		
	. . .	7 years		
	Tirigan	40 days		

The Third Dynasty of Ur		The Fifth Dynasty of Erech	
*Ur-Nammu		*Utu-khegal	
(c. 2112)	18 years	(c. 2120)	7 years
*Dungi	47 years		
*Bur-Sin	9 years		
*Gimil-Sin	9 years		
*Ibi-Sin	25 years		

The Dynasty of Isin

Ishbi-Irra (c. 2021)	32 years
*Gimil-Ilishu	10 years
*Idin-dagan	21 years
*Ishme-dagan	20 years
*Libit-Ishtar	11 years

The Dynasty of Larsa

*Gungunum	27 years
Abi-sare	11 years
Sumu-ilu	29 years
*Nur-Adad	16 years
*Sin-idinnam	6 years
Sin-eribam	2 years
Sin-iquisham	5 years
Silli-Adad	1 year

The First Dynasty of Babylon

Sin-muballit	29 years
*Hammurabi (c. 1783)	43 years

The Elamite kings of Larsa

*Warad-Sin	12 years
*Rim-Sin	61 years

INDEX

Index

259

*Printed in Great Britain
by Ebenezer Baylis and Son Ltd
The Trinity Press Worcester.*